Dying to Live

A Memoir

By Karol Donnelly

ISBN Number: 9781700470232

Please Note

This is a work of nonfiction; the people and events described are based on reality. In certain instances, however, some names have been changed by request.

Regarding the organ donation process in Ireland and the UK, the identities of donors remain undisclosed to recipients to protect the privacy of the very special donors and their grieving families. The name I gave to my donor, James, is therefore not an actual identity but a name that, to me, represents a strong and kind man. Any perceived connection to a real individual is purely coincidental.

Acknowledgements

I wish to thank a number of people, without whose care, support, patience, love, expertise and inspiration this manuscript would have remained a dusty forgotten collection of diaries.

To Professor John Hegarty, who initially suggested that I put my frustrations and emotional turmoil to paper. As well as a superb hepatologist, he remains a wonderful, caring and well-loved gentleman.

To each and every member of staff at St. Vincent's University Hospital, Elm Park; your expertise, skill, dedication, support, care and friendship will never ever be forgotten. Words just can't express my gratitude to you all – I just wish I could name each of you.

To the staff of both the Mater Private and Mater Misericordiae Hospitals, thank you for saving me from the very edge of life and for putting me back together; your intervention at such a critical stage of my illness will always be extremely appreciated.

To my fabulous circle of wonderful friends, new and old; on so many occasions you brought light to my darkness. As quoted by L.M. Montgomery 'true friends are always together in spirit'. Noel – I wrote my book, as promised! My next goal, please?

To neighbours, acquaintances, well-wishers and strangers – a huge thank you for your prayers, candle-lighting, gifts, good wishes and genuine concern.

Grateful appreciation to Alex for your valued advice and continuing support in my self-publication endeavours.

And finally, but most importantly - to my long-suffering and constantly endurant family, whose completely unwavering support, patient dedication and endless love saved me from the sometimes-almost-consuming swamp of despair, willing me to wade through the muddy waters of illness again and again – and again.

I love you all so very much.

To My Mum and Dad, Gabrielle and Barry –
thank you both ever so much for your unwavering
support and love.

Prologue

I am a scientist.

I am on the cold, dark pier, awaiting my turn. I feel apprehensive; afraid maybe, but also very excited. I've worked so hard and now I'm here; chosen a part of a highly-trained team of experts to explore the cold murky waters for the so-called 'monster of the deep'. Monster, creature, strange beast, mutant reptile – all dramatic names given to raise the profile of my small West of Ireland town. My colleagues and I are certain of its identity but cannot disclose it. Capturing the animal is now our only goal.

The water laps and trickles; easing the atmosphere and relaxing me. Hushed whispers and murmurs play in my head, no doubt some of the spectators here to watch. The monitors too, make their presence known, with rhythmic beeping, interrupted by other instruments with varying tones. "Recording dissolved oxygen and temperature" I muse, "depth too; we'll need to know what depth to dive to."

My oxygen tank is close at hand, my life-giving tank of air to keep me alive.

A girl approaches me. "It's late" she smiles, "Why don't you rest a while, try and get some sleep?"

I don't recognise her as one of my colleagues; she must be a visiting scientist from another country. Ecuador, maybe, or India.

"Karol, sleep now" she urges.

"Sleep? How can I possibly sleep on this so-so important night?" I think. "The expedition needs me, needs my expertise, my knowledge. I cannot rest – it's almost my time to dive."

As though she reads my mind, she whispers,

"I will let you know when it's time".

Reluctant yet admittedly exhausted, I realise that I'll benefit from rest before plunging into the black, icy water. I close my eyes, lulled into a deep sleep by the beep, beep, beep of instruments and the lapping water.

Minutes or hours later, my heavy eyes open. I'm in a room, a dark, dimly-lit room. A large tank stands in front of me, filled with water. Inside the creature lurks, its grey form huge and unmoving. Beside the tank stand a man and a small boy. They look into the tank and then to me. The man's teeth glisten against his dark skin. He has a serious expression, cross maybe, or thoughtful. He holds a pen in his left hand. I try to focus on the boy, but it's difficult to see him.

"They dived while I slept" I cry to myself.

While I feel so disappointed, I also feel a sense of relief. The water was probably so cold and it's so dark, a little daunting maybe. I am suddenly overcome by a feeling of immense fatigue that the pier feels like a big, comfortable bed. My heavy eyelids close once more.

When I awake, the tank is gone. I am alone with just the monitors and their constant voices. It's bright – and warm. The dark gloomy pier has been replaced by a whiteness – a soft white bed, white walls and flowing pastel-coloured curtains. I lie on my back, barely moving, tiny arms by my sides.

I am a scientist. But right now, I am the country's newest liver transplant recipient.

Begin the Begin

18th April 2011

Dear James,

Right, how are we to do this? Ultimately we are mere strangers, yet I feel it is important that we become more familiar, closer to each other, more 'together'. It makes sense; we've been thrown together (flung mercilessly even) on this journey and yet I know little about you. You know nothing about me. But we have a link; we share something that makes our relationship quite special. There's a palpable intimacy between us that reaches far beyond familiarity yet we seem to have skipped the basic parts of our relationship. Like a one-night-stand scenario; an uneasy couple who've shared something intimate (blissfully wonderful or otherwise!) and who can't share one moment of eye contact hours after the event. I refuse to let us become awkward. To me, it's important (vital even) that we bond, know each other, share more of ourselves (even more, I should add). I figure that since meeting on a regular basis isn't a feasible option, we can maintain contact and build on our relationship through the medium of writing.

So, you'll be the recipient of my meanderings through my writing. I intend to start right at the beginning and introduce you to me. You, perhaps, know me as a liver transplant recipient. I am, was, and will be more than that. These days, I feel generally labelled by my liver status; even by myself I regard my life as 'before and after 2006'; it's become my reference point. You need to know more about who I am. I deserve to know more about who I am! (Most people find out new things about themselves regularly – it's natural to evolve and re-discover oneself every now and then). This script, though, definitely doesn't have the potential to be a narcissistic account of the life of Karol. These musings describe my own experiences; I'm not a writer, nor have I any inclinations to be. I'm not a psychologist or a physician so please excuse my poor script, my ignorance about medicine and brain physiology. I've read and

1

familiarised myself with basic psychology, altruism and human 'goodness' but it doesn't qualify me to form a definitive opinion on it all. My opinions expressed are my own, my thoughts formed over years of nature and nurture. This is my life.

To keep it real I'm going to write to you as often as I can; good days and bad, through the ups and downs. Yes, James, I have bad days, days so dark and lonely that only the passing of time is mending (it's work in progress). I get through, mainly because I owe you that much, you and a small band of family and friends.

I'm not a hero, a champion or an idol of some sort – so maybe talking and writing about myself gives the impression that I'm a pretentious, egotistical person warranting the attention of some such person. That couldn't be further from the truth. For as long as I remember I've wavered around the line of self-confidence – freckles, red (auburn) hair, shy parents and Catholic upbringing. . . need I say more? In school I was probably something of an introvert. I always found socialising one of my biggest challenges. Yes, I had friends, a few good friends but can I possibly say that I was at my most content when my head was stuck in a book or when I was saving frogspawn or counting new swallows. I loved, and still find the greatest joy in learning. I felt tortured as a child when I was a teacher's joy; the child who was used to teach the slower classmates and always the one who sailed through spelling tests and maths problems. I struggled only with my social life. Being a teacher's pet or 'a lick' made me want to be less clever; I wanted to belong. But now, most of the time, I try to accept me for who I am. I am smart and this should not be perceived as a handicap or a curse. I can admit now having fewer friends than the cool kids but being true to myself, shyness and all, was and still is who I prefer to be. On the advice of my hepatologist, henceforth labelled as Prof., I should find someone with whom to share my emotions, express my anger and fear, explore my inner feelings and test the null hypothesis of 'I am insane'. (For the record, I am perfectly 'normal' – whatever that is!).

So, aside from wanting you to know more of me, to share myself with you, there's another reason why I write. Simply put, it's good for me, therapeutic even. I need a 'person', an impartial adult who won't judge me for my moods, my seemingly ungrateful days (I'm never ungrateful, never), won't feel awkward by my pain and fears. I have friends, fewer as I've gotten older and as I have become 'less fun', who I know are there for me and try to be as understanding as they can be. But they just don't 'get it' and I don't want to waste precious time explaining how it feels to live in my shoes. My family, too, have been, in general, so supportive and strong in helping me on this journey. I've burdened them enough. My family life has changed significantly since 2006. Subconsciously I feel as though I've fractured it – put it under such immense pressure that five people withstood for such a long period. They've been bashed and thumped to such an extent that in some ways, they've become unrecognisable. Family structure too has changed. I was the brave daughter, the strong one, the sister with lots going on, always busy, studying, working very hard in a difficult field or the daughter who had holidays at least three times a year. Suddenly I became the sister and daughter who needed her family almost as much as a baby does. I can't expect to depend on them indefinitely. I now feel that you're someone I can trust to tell my innermost thoughts, my dreams, hopes, fears and wishes. You can appreciate the journey I've travelled and more than anyone, you know of the fragility, the delicate strands, the uncertainty, the cruelty of life. I can only talk to myself so much without fearing for my sanity – I think you're the best candidate for the ruminations of a reluctant transplantee.

I'm not entirely sure where to begin the story about my journey to you. It was, as anyone would imagine, quite dramatic. It was also very fast. The rate at which events occurred almost out-competes for drama the actual proceedings. I'm going to take my time though; hold a steady pace with my story which, when I am forced to explain, generally comes tumbling out in a random, convoluted chain of events that ends with 'emergency transplant'. For most people who care to ask (but may not necessarily 'care'), that is the concluding part of Karol's story; the end, the 'happily-ever-after' bit. For me, the principal character, the liver transplant is almost like the beginning of my story. Next comes months in hospital, years of recovery, learning how to live again, in addition to a multitude of crises, minor dramas and furious balancing.

People say that everyone has a story in them. I do. One could answer that's where many stories should stay - but in my case, and now yours, I'm going to let mine out, release my story bit by bit to you, if you'll care to listen.

How do I begin? How about with the present day? Today, I am five years and one month post-transplant and I had a good day. Nothing unusual happened; I just feel happy. To say those four words still makes a subconscious voice say 'don't say that, it will jinx things'.

That's how I feel. I feel as though I live on the edge of my life, in a place between pure joy and horrendous hell. By admitting that I'm in a place of joy and near-perfection I anticipate that fate or a karma-fuelled event will once again hurtle my life from its straight path onto a helix of unfathomable and scarily random events. Vulnerable, that's how I feel. I constantly feel vulnerable, susceptible and 'on the edge'. For 31 years of my life I was healthy, strong and active and in ways I felt invincible. Okay, invincible is a slight exaggeration so I'll just go with 'ordinary'. I got head colds, stomach bugs, had bicycle accidents and one or two minor car crashes. Those 'ordinary events aside', I imagined that I would live to be at least 60, avoiding heart disease and other 'preventables' by taking good care of myself. The cancer threat was always at the back of my mind; inconceivably I assumed that an oncology-related illness would be my downfall. Then, that security, the cheeky assumption of a thirty-something evaporated and became just a presumptuous postulation.

For today, the 'I just feel happy' statement is undeniably, irrevocably and almost-completely because of you. I've never told a man before that my joyful day was entirely because of him. Between you and me, I have an issue or two with relationships but, that notwithstanding, I generally have the upper hand in my own happiness and firmly believe it's of my own making.

But back to today – it is a rare sunny day and I woke early for work. See, nothing exciting so far. I enjoyed a leisurely breakfast of cereal (a mix of two types), pancakes and juice, while listening to the radio. As usual, I spent too long in the shower but instead of rushing and getting flustered by my lateness, I put on my favourite trousers with coloured top, completed my outfit with open-toe wedges and calmly drove my VW Golf the seven-minute journey to work. Work was busy – I'm coordinating an environmental assessment of a development plan so meeting with my team was a priority. Today, I felt focussed and productive, happy with my report; some days my brain is a little dull and I find it difficult to concentrate.

Work day aside, I met a friend for lunch, shared a laugh or two and planned a kayaking outing over the weekend. I also decided to enrol in a hiking club and completed my membership form. Am I boring you yet?

After practising some pieces for my grade 4 clarinet exam, I took a much-too-short walk by the lake near my house.

That was my day – a pretty much uneventful, perfectly ordinary, run-of-the-mill, take-for-granted kind of day but, for me, that's the kind of day it wasn't. It was a day that I laughed, walked, worked, enjoyed and lived. I breathed on my own. I walked on my own and, in my upper right quadrant, my . . . our liver silently functioned perfectly on its own. I find that far from ordinary. Tears still well up at that thought, at the reality that you gave me the shot at life that was so cruelly robbed from you.

You know, I was and still am pretty angry to have met death in a face-to-face battle at 31. (For the record, I should point out that my use of adjectives is admittedly understated. My 'pretty angry' essentially means incensed, outraged or furious. I'll work on expressing my true feelings a little better). Where was I? Yes, my battle.... Apparently the battle opponents were very closely matched. My combat tactics weren't always on target and I made a few slips along the way. I stumbled, lost my footing and even fell during and post-transplant and that was all while lying on an operating table and in an Intensive Care Unit bed.

I've just read the last few lines. What am I doing with my ridiculous euphemisms? For the record, James, my stay in hospital was a rollercoaster journey fraught with the drama of a complicated surgery (once your very welcome liver was found to match my needs), life-threatening infections and a horrendous prognosis that if I lived, my mobility would probably be limited. Also, my brain activity was beyond active, with new immunosuppressive medication, morphine and accumulating toxins ensuring that seizures were a regular occurrence. When I was described as 'critically ill', my family treated this as very welcome news – the previously 'dangerously ill' description somehow seemed that little bit closer to, well, the other side of life's coin. Funny (not humorous, funny in the peculiar kind of way) how one day in March 2006, I was a scientist, a careerist with a mission and within days my only role was to fight death for my life.

I suppose I could introduce my drama by setting the scene.

oOo

It was mid-March 2006 and I was undertaking fieldwork in the uplands of south Mayo. Honestly, Mayo is probably one of the most beautiful places in Ireland but does it rain! Big drops of rain plopped onto the windscreen of my car and though I was suitably dressed I felt miserable. I had an ache in my right shoulder and was a little nauseous. I was quite tired but decided that was because I had been to a concert with my sister two nights previously. It wasn't a late night, but my energy levels seemed to have dipped recently and it was my first night out in months. My GP had recommended multi vitamins when I mentioned my tiredness to him. Steeling myself for a soaking, I pulled myself out of the car and proceeded to pull on my studded waders. Getting my bearings, I realised that my sampling site was approximately a ten-minute walk from my car. I collected my gear – pond-net, plastic tray, sieve bottles and funnel and began my hike.

"Not so bad", I thought, when the sun peeped through the thick clouds, "it might clear up yet".

I reached the river and assessed the bank. While it was steep, there were lots of trees and shrubs to cling to as I made my way into the water, using the handle of my net as a prop. I looked at my watch and began kicking the river substrate with the toe and heel of my boot. I should explain that I was collecting freshwater animals – macroinvertebrates – including insects, snails, leeches and bugs. Why – you ask? Simply, without me going into boring, unnecessary details about pH, oxygen and nutrient concentrations, the quality of surface water can be assessed by the abundance and diversity of freshwater animals – the ones without backbones!

After two minutes I scooped up the net and, with the mouth above the water level, began to shake it steadily to dislodge the excess sand and gravel. I paused, looked at the contents of the net and shook it again. Satisfied with my sample I threw the net over my left shoulder and climbed up the river bank, using my right hand for support. The sample tray already contained some river water and I carefully closed the mouth of the net while I turned the contents out onto the white tray. Insects, worms, mites and crustaceans tumbled out, as well as leaves, pebbles, an acorn and other items from the water. As always, I knelt on the inside of my pulled-up waders and leaned into the tray, arms folded. It generally took at least two to three minutes until the specimens teamed all over the tray – I imagined that the insects were all in deep shock and it took them a few minutes to get their bearings! I identified, counted and recorded the invertebrates and their numbers. I knew it was a good river – the good water quality indicators were there, as well as the usual ubiquitous crustaceans, beetles and more common mayflies. I poured the contents through my sieve, examined the tray for leeches and flatworms and tipped the sieved material into a wide-mouthed container. Then, the cruel but crucial part – I poured methylated spirits on top of the little guys. I watched them squirm and imagined their pain. To me, this was all second nature – I had done this hundreds of times during my student life and career.

Following the brief physical examination of the river, I gathered up the equipment and headed for my car. The day had become quite mild and the rained had lightened considerably. I looked up at the sky and then it happened. I suddenly felt very light-headed and unwell. In an instant I knew I had to be sick and there were just a few seconds to comply. I dropped everything and got sick at the foot of a tree, while I tried to steady myself against its trunk. As I stood there looking into the vomit-spattered grass, I felt slightly relieved, slightly better and even slightly bemused.

I knew I should go home for a lie-down. Dropping the equipment back at the laboratory, I drove home. My reflection in the rear-view car mirror was one of a very pale, slickly woman. Again, I noticed my eyes, with black rings underneath, had that slight yellow tinge that my Mum regularly commented on.

That was my last day on the rivers project. For months that exciting project that I had been given charge of continued, but without me.

It's strange now how my memory of that day is still so clear, so vivid; like it was just yesterday. It was a Friday and I remember the weather, the river conditions, the walk to my car and my mood. I remember feeling calm and unafraid as I got into bed and settled into a deep, sound sleep.

19th April 2011

Dear James,

Last night it occurred to me that I told you I was a previously fit and healthy person – before 2006, that is. Now, I feel that I must enlighten you a little and give you a more insightful description of my health status before our eventual 'encounter'. While I was fit and well, there was an underlying challenge that I was aware of. One time I would have said that this was nothing to be alarmed or concerned about, would have even called it harmless, and consultants would have agreed, but as my life story unravelled I realised and you too will understand that that could not have been further from the truth.

I am the carrier of a silent killer, a nasty and evil disorder that in its rotten silence crawled through my body and wreaked havoc. As I re-read that line, I think I'm being a tad melodramatic. The bits about the silent killer, wreaking havoc and horrible disorder are all true but crawling through my body has an air of a horror movie to it! I'll lose the drama and just explain clearly as, between you and me, I'm quite tired today and now a little cranky.

Back when I was a degree student, I experienced episodes of loss of my consciousness. I didn't pass out, faint or fall over. On the contrary, when this happened in company, nobody noticed anything different in my appearance, behaviour or demeanour. It usually happened periodically, maybe every few months, and there was no pattern of where or when it would happen to me – I could be in class, watching TV or having a conversation with someone. Basically, and this is a tough one to explain, it felt like my awareness of my environment was lost for a few seconds. While not unconscious, I wasn't capable of having a conversation during an 'episode', as my brain seemed to freeze and stall. (If I were a PC, I'd have to re-boot!). If, during one of my episodes, a simple question was asked of me, even one as blatantly simple as one plus two, I wouldn't be able to engage my brain to get or give the answer. It sounds strange and initially it frightened me. Frightened and angered me – it sometimes happened at very inappropriate times. When I visited a doctor about it, he honestly admitted he was uncertain about what I was describing. Today I wonder if he just assumed I was smoking pot or drinking too much. It was neither, for the record!

When I, a few months after the initial episodes, began work (real work, not summer job stacking shelves and checking out groceries) I decided to see a neurologist.

So long ago now that I only vaguely remember, I know that I underwent an electroencephalogram or EEG. Although it was normal and my electrical impulses were doing whatever it is electrical impulses are supposed to do, I was diagnosed as having temporal lobe epilepsy. Then it made sense, the loss of awareness, sometimes accompanied by a strong sense of smell, the feelings of déjà-vu and the tiredness, unbelievable tiredness afterwards – all symptoms of epilepsy. James, I can't believe this now after everything that has happened, but at that time I felt that my twenty-something life was turned upside-down. I was gutted to hear that I would have to be on medication for a long time, maybe for life. I was so distraught that I burst into tears when I left his consulting room. Then, I began to read the side-effects of the medication, as if to torture and upset myself further. There were some body changes that no young woman should ever have to consider; increased body hair, weight gain and hair loss spring to mind (I imagined increased hair on my female face and my long auburn hair falling in clumps from my head). Thankfully, none of these abhorrent things (in a young woman's eyes) happened but the concern of my GP was another side-effect of the meds – thrombocytopenia or a decreased platelet count. (For what it's worth, that medication has very recently been described as this generation's thalidomide so goody for me that I switched to new meds after a year or so of sodium valproate).

His investigation into the impact of the new medication on my blood count serendipitously turned up something very unexpected, two things actually, and only six years later did the mystery, speculation and uncertainty of these findings become so significant…but I'm jumping ahead of myself.

Firstly, for the first time in my life, I had blood taken before embarking on the course of my new medication. The results showed two things – I had an elevated platelet count and my liver function tests were slightly abnormal. I still took the anti-epilepsy medication with the assurance that blood tests would be repeated and would undoubtedly be normal.

And so began the regular cycle of blood tests and, invariably, my liver function tests, the concentration of specific enzymes in my blood, were above the normal recommended limit and my thrombocytes or platelets also were higher than expected.

With the realisation that, a little over a year and quite a few blood tests later, my platelet count hadn't reduced but was actually gradually showing an upwards trend, I was referred to a haematologist. She, after repeating blood tests yet again, decided to perform a bone marrow biopsy to investigate further. I have no intention of torturing you with the details of a small woman drilling a hole in my hip to get a bone marrow sample – so I'll just say that it was as painful as one would imagine! She confirmed I had a blood disorder which meant that my bone marrow was producing waaaaaay too many platelets. Platelets are those tiny blood cells responsible for blood clotting – vital but in higher concentrations than normal, the body's clotting mechanism can be disrupted. My haematologist explained, all those years ago, that there was really nothing for me to worry about, or little that would be done. The tendency for my blood to clot was more likely than other non-blood-disorder people but, since I was in my mid-twenties, I was considered a low risk case. I began a course of aspirin on alternate days and moved on with my life, safe in the knowledge that this blood disorder might only potentially affect me when I reached my fifties, or even sixties. Maybe you're beginning to see where this is going.

So now that I've described my 'baseline data', I'm going to continue with my story, taking up on Monday morning after my sampling-and-sick adventure.

I don't remember the weekend following that Friday afternoon. I have a vague recollection of staying in bed and drinking cold drinks to keep hydrated but I remember little else. It's bizarre that my memory of the entire weekend isn't anywhere to be found. I have written a diary every day since I was fifteen years old and that Friday was the beginning of a huge abyss in the record of the life of me. (For your information, I only began writing again in January this year – for some unfathomable reason I wasn't able to put my feelings or thoughts to paper until then.)

Sorry, I got distracted. . . on Monday morning, I knew I had to stay in bed; my energy levels had dipped again and all I wanted to do was sleep. On Tuesday, at my parents' house (Mum has come to collect me from mine the previous evening, as she thought I could do with some fussing – something she does very well!) I continued my sleeping pattern. On Wednesday, my right shoulder ached but there was also another problem; a new pain in my lower back was agonising and there was a strange dragging sensation in my abdomen – as though someone had replaced my internal organs with cobbles.

At the weekend my Mum persuaded me to see her doctor. Ridiculous though it sounds, I felt I was getting better and didn't want to cause any fuss. I felt I just needed rest and soon I'd feel fine. Mum admitted to me recently that she woke me up one night to ensure I was asleep – my sleeping was becoming deeper and she was worried that I'd slipped into unconsciousness.

Her doctor listened to my symptoms – a very distended abdomen now completed the list – and he promptly sent me to my local hospital. No spare clothes, no bag, toothbrush or book - Do Not Pass Go, Do Not Collect £200. I had never been admitted to hospital before. Sure, I've had some tests – on my brain and my bone marrow – but this was new to me. Once admitted, following donating more of my blood, I underwent some other tests. I have no idea what tests as I remember nothing much from the few days I spent at that hospital but I imagine I had an ultrasound and maybe a CT scan. My outstanding memory is this one. . . I'm lying in bed and a tall doctor comes into my room and stands at the foot of the bed. He pulls the curtain for privacy – though the privacy a flimsy short curtain provides is undoubtedly pretty poor – and we talk. Sorry, he talks, I listen. I have nothing to say – I have begun to get physically sick more often and feel quite groggy. Sleeping is my source of relief and for some strange reason I don't think it's strange that all I want to do, all day, every day, is sleep. He tells me that the tests have shown that I have a blood clot in my hepatic system. Because I'm in a general hospital, he explains that there's nothing that they can do for me; I need specialist treatment. He has been in touch with the National Liver Unit and I will be transferred there without delay.

Do you know what went through my head? It wasn't fear, worry, terror, horror, panic or any of those obvious feelings that one would expect. I actually thought,

"Flip, what an awful inconvenience – I have to get dressed and move from here". I don't like fuss. I didn't want a trip to a Dublin hospital when I had become familiar with my local one. There was no option.

5th June 2011

Dear James,

I haven't written in a few weeks. I've been extremely busy and have also been on holidays to a beautiful part of Italy. I enjoyed a complete break from life-as-I-know-it, escaped the routine and generally took some time out. I need to do that every once in a while.

I holidayed alone, a solo traveller, on my ownio. It's not the first time I've done so. Whenever I do I feel exhilarated, confident, at ease with myself and strangers. There's something curiously refreshing, exciting and even a little daunting about being in a strange country surrounded by complete strangers, and striking up conversations with new people. I feel proud of myself, invigorated and less shy; I feel like me, the real me. I travelled with a group of (in general) middle-aged people. They were all so nice – and fun. I participated in all of the tours – the Amalfi Coast, Ravello and Positano. My room overlooked the Bay of Naples and a balcony allowed me to sit and stare in awe at Mount Vesuvius which I climbed during that great week.

But I also feel dreadfully single!

Yes, James, I feel alone and more than a little lonely. Like a single shoe or one earring. A lone ranger in a holiday of couples, pairs and un-singletons. I met one couple who had just gotten engaged – in a gondola…sad and naff but true.

13

Don't get me wrong. I'm not a naïve silly creature who yearns for an engagement ring in Venice, rose petals and chocolate strawberries (well, not every day). Laughing aside I think, I know, I have a grasp on what love is about. For me it's summed up in this quote,

'Love itself is what is left over when being in love has burned away'.

Some might call me an unromantic, stone-hearted spoilsport, but I've watched and analysed enough couples to pick out the true love from the together-for-dependence, married-because-I'm-almost-30, settled-for-less, biological-clock-watching types.

I know what I'm looking for in a man – there's just the problem that he's usually married or not interested in introverted redheads! The ideal man for me would have to be clever and funny, making me laugh and seeking out the simple pleasures in life. Not a money-lover or someone who takes life too seriously. I love ambition but not if it interferes with 'us'. I've met a man I would have married but I let him get away (I kid myself – maybe he wanted to get away?!). He was clever, handsome, funny and had an optimistic attitude to life – fiercely independent and strong. . .so, even though I might not have been 'particularly in love' with a lot of men, I've met quite a few special ones who came close so really I've been quite lucky in love. Just not at the moment!

Am I asking a lot to hope I'll meet 'the one'? Am I now just being greedy? I am lucky and blessed to be alive and I still want more, feel I deserve more. Have I already cashed in my lucky chip? Did I not already get my genie-in-a-bottle wish on the day that you and I were thrown together? I hope not.

But, back to more serious and pressing matters – the reason I sat down to write to you – before I became so distracted with my love life, or lack thereof.

When I last wrote, I described my transfer to the National Liver Unit. My journey there is a complete blur; a hurried ambulance ride with my Mum, who insisted I drink sugary tea. I don't drink tea, sugary or otherwise. On the journey I drank two cups of the stuff – without question. Something was seriously amiss.

My arrival to the hospital is vivid – I have some recollections of that. Mostly I remember getting into a new big hospital bed and meeting Diarmaid, the tall youthful registrar. He asked me numerous questions and introduced me to the sinister *Budd Chiari* syndrome he believed I had. My scans had shown a large thrombus in my hepatic vein, which was blocking, almost completely, the flow of blood from my liver. This sounded serious, but what was my knowledge of liver function (in contrast to what it is now)? *Budd Chiari* syndrome is named for the two people who described liver dysfunction as a result of a blockage in the hepatic veins. Pressure was building up in my portal vein, the vein carrying nice fresh oxygenated blood to my liver (or trying to, in my case) and this portal hypertension had to be relieved. My now hugely-swollen abdomen was filled with fluid, leaked into my peritoneal cavity – ascites was my new word of the day. Ascites was what was causing my back pain and also the reason for what felt like huge pressure on my internal organs. I was literally carrying around a bellyful of leaked fluid – kilos of the stuff. I was quite ill. Though it was almost certain the thrombus was the cause of my liver dysfunction, it wasn't confirmed that my blood disorder was the cause – not yet. To investigate my medical history more thoroughly, Diarmaid asked if I had gotten a tattoo recently, visited a developing country or encountered any water-borne diseases or parasites. I froze in shock – my work! Had I developed problems through my work? I had been vaccinated and surely I had taken precautions against leptospirosis and protozoans, water-borne bacteria and viruses? I used gloves, hand sanitizers and was meticulous in the lab and on field work. Jeez, my sister calls me Monica after the hygiene-obsessed character in *Friends*. I work with water, sometimes encountering raw and treated sewage, I told Diarmaid, apprehensively. I also admitted that in my college days and in my twenties, I enjoyed partying, and though I never took illegal drugs, I regularly 'binge-drank' with friends. In college, that was the norm. I shared with seven other girls and our house was regularly the one where my other classmates would gather before we went to pubs and nightclubs. We drank spirits, shots and, as most students did, impressed each other with how fun we were while over the limit. He shook his head at my confession, saying that it seemed likely my problem wasn't alcohol, drugs, water-borne infections or hepatitis. While he had to rule out other causes of liver disease, the evidence pointed to oxygen deprivation and the resultant necrosis of my liver. I understood then that my liver was the reason I felt so ill, so tired, exhausted and listless. I just didn't believe it or accept it. Hadn't my liver function tests shown irregularities for almost six years and I had felt fine? My GP had described my liver function tests as incidental. Christ, I thought I had gastroenteritis just days ago. And now, this young registrar was speaking of a serious liver disease. Me – with a liver problem? Liver disease was only for old people and alcoholics, right? I looked after myself, ate well and exercised very regularly. In fact, I had never been so fit in my life; swimming three times a week, hiking and jogging. Liver disease was one of the few problems I truly never expected to encounter. I snapped back to the present and my next reaction was – ok, what's next? How do we fix this? What do I do to clear the blockage? TIPS – that was Diarmaid's response (more new lingo for me!). TIPS – transjugular intrahepatic portosystemic shunt – passing a narrow tube into my jugular vein in my neck where it would follow the vein to my liver. There, a shunt would be inflated within the clot and (hopefully) the blood would flow once more.

TIPS was pretty routine, he continued. I would be unconscious but it really wasn't called a surgery, just a procedure which was undertaken periodically.

I was stunned. It was all a huge volume of news to take in . . . *Budd Chiari* syndrome, ascites, TIPS, liver disease . . . my head swam. Diarmaid never faltered and his confidence and reassurance made me feel, unwillingly, confident. I liked the word 'routine' and 'non-surgical' though I felt that passing tubes into my neck to improve my liver was a little like operating on someone's heart through their anus.

Diarmaid gave me some reading material on TIPS, winked and left me. I felt calm – relaxed even. Maybe it was the drugs or my exhaustion and confusion but once I processed this new information, I felt ok. I've always had a huge interest in medicine – if circumstances allowed and my self-confidence had been better I would have studied it – and my Mum and I enjoyed and still enjoy conversations about anatomy and physiology, new surgeries and medicines. There were always lots of medical dictionaries and reference books in our library at home and my fascination with all things health was nurtured from an early age. Maybe this was the reason why I felt calm and bizarrely excited. I understood the problem, the simple-yet-tricky way to solve it, and I felt that once this procedure was undertaken I could somehow embrace the strange yet necessary toying with my body. I could hand myself over to an unknown surgeon for just a small while. Does that sound too weird? Too relaxed and calm? I think it makes me sound like a scientist, only with a radical 'cool' experiment being conducted on me. It was a challenge I faced and I like to challenge myself.

Then I met Prof. I was, as usual, lying in bed mentally preparing myself for my TIPS when a tall, elegant man appeared at the foot of my bed with a,

"Hello, young lady".

He was surrounded by a group of very young people – junior doctors, I later realised. He didn't introduce himself, I think, but he had a presence that demonstrated his senior status – and utter competence. He asked me to discuss my symptoms; by then I was experiencing severe diarrhoea and my distended abdomen was, it seemed, becoming bigger. Also my back and right shoulder were immensely painful.

He examined my abdomen, doing that now-so-familiar liver percussion by placing his hand in various locations on my left and right side and listening for dullness or resonance (ascites or a build-up of abdominal fluid from an unhealthy liver will produce a dull sound at the touch of an examiner's hands).

He asked me what the plan for me was to which I answered that TIPS was proposed for the following day.

He looked at his little people and asked them to define TIPS. Silence, no answer, no response... I felt so sorry for those doctors having this daunting man as a mentor. He seemed very cross and gruff. I was so wrong. Prof. Hegarty turned out to be a man whose presence would fill me with confidence and hope, reassurance and trust. He is a genius and a very likeable and kind, caring man, whom I'm so happy to have in my life. I am also certain that those young doctors learned – and never forgot – what TIPS was.

Later I spoke with one of my room-mates who had had a TIPS procedure just days before. To me, the girl looked horrifically thin and sickly but she explained that before TIPS she had been very ill indeed.

In hindsight I looked at the girl and the others around me as though they were genuine bona fide people with liver disease. The little old woman in the bed opposite was the colour of greenish-yellow with jaundice and her snow-white hair dazzled. She slept all the time. The lady in the bed next to mine had recently undergone a liver transplant. She walked the floor and corridor a lot, head in the air with a straight back. (It was months later before I realised the importance of walking with a straight back – with a huge abdominal tear, it's so much easier and less painful to hunch one's shoulders, hence using fewer muscles and lessening stretching of the wound). She explained that her transplant had occurred two weeks before and already she felt well and less tired. She was happy, beaming almost, and her determination to leave hospital was proven by her constant walking. She was the first liver transplant recipient I ever met. While she was happy and looked healthy and well, I pitied her. In my mind, she had crossed a line, stepped into a new world of medication and consultations, scars and fear. To me she was a step closer to death and there was no turning back to normal for her.

As I said, these people were real victims of liver disease – one or two had already suffered liver failure. I wasn't like them. My liver was impaired by a blood clot, but my trip to the operating theatre would resolve that. I didn't belong to their club. What's that Groucho Marx line? "I don't want to belong to any club that will accept people like me as a member".

My plan was to have the procedure, feel fine and leave. I planned some time off work and maybe a holiday? I made lots of post-procedure plans. As we now know, my plans backfired.

9th July 2011

Dear James,

I am aware that I'm approaching the point in my story where both our worlds came crashing down, the point where our worlds collided. Me, in my early thirties, with lots to live for and enjoy, and you – precisely the same. So much to live for, to experience and love; but for both of us, so little time.

Me, I was oblivious. I was preparing for my TIPS procedure. My Mum, staying with relatives close to the hospital, spent all of her days with me. My Dad and sisters were working, but we spoke by phone most days. I assured them that I was feeling much better and would see them soon. My TIPS procedure was scheduled for a Tuesday and they would visit me after that. Mum and I generally chatted – I didn't have energy for moving about the hospital and I certainly wasn't in any state to go outside the hospital. From the day I arrived by ambulance until two months later, I really didn't know where my hospital was located. That's almost an amusing realisation now, years later, when it's become a place I grew to know so well, and a trip there now is second nature.

I had become resolute and somewhat relaxed about my procedure, but anxiety was etched on my mother's face. She hid it well, though, with jokes and smiles, making easy banal conversations about local news, hospital food and new people she had met. She was keeping her worry and fear from me while I, in turn, made attempts to reassure her with my limited knowledge of liver function.

I'm now perplexed at how relaxed I actually was; my abdomen was now so large that my walk was very awkward and slow. I have a memory of my Mum washing my hair as I was just too weak and heavy to manage it myself. My back pain was a constant dull ache. I was vomiting routinely and eating was a daily battle as my appetite was no more. Apparently there were expectations that I might vomit blood, so I kept a close eye for that. In a way, it was a good introduction to my now-constant vigilance and health-assessment routine.

I constantly wonder how you spent your week. Were you working? Were you spending time with friends and family? Did you enjoy your time? Or were you, too, in hospital? Were you, too, oblivious to your cruel fate?

When I think of us, both ignorant of the outcome of my story, I am so sad, petrified, terrorised - and guilty. I was dying, though I didn't know it, but you were too. Only, for some reason I cannot fathom, for some purpose I still haven't figured out, and surely never will, I got saved and you didn't. On tough days, I cry for you and on happy days, I grab life with both hands, smile and live it – with you in my mind. Today is a bad one, I'm afraid, and tears are rolling down my face as I write this. How does one handle this? How can I bear that I am only here, sitting writing to you because you were the unlucky one? You were the one who didn't get saved. People spend years pondering on the mystery that is life and death. For religious people, the journey is life with the final destination being the reward of death – and the wondrous afterlife. Though few really want to arrive at the final destination, do they? Of course, our basic instinct is self-preservation, to protect ourselves from harm, from pain, from death; when the eventual time beckons, everyone from the deeply religious to stoic atheists wants more. They'll bargain just about anything for time, will exchange or promise everything they have for just one year, one month, even one day. I know now what that's like – I just don't know how to manage these feelings. But I should continue where I left off – reaching TIPS day.

On the evening before my procedure, I read through the patients' information on TIPS. There were 'terms and conditions' and risks associated but I signed my consent, hoping that the risk of brain injury would not visit me. I couldn't face somehow morphing into an unrecognisable version of me, waking up with a new personality or, worse still, with a limited memory of 'me'…

Diarmaid told me that I would be brought to theatre the following morning. I felt nervous and apprehensive of course, but pretty ok. There was a confidence and coolness about him that soothed and calmed me. Mum prepared herself to leave on Monday evening and we said our goodbyes. She promised to call in to see me in the next day before I left for the theatre.

Then one of the nice nurses came over to chat with us both. I'll never forget her parting words,

"Don't worry, Karol's name is on the liver transplant list since today".

My reaction was immediate.

"No" I thought, "no".

I felt cold and hot all at once and my heart raced. With tears welling in my eyes, I looked at my mother. Her paleness, her wide eyes and silence betrayed her shock.

I shook my head as the nurse tended to another patient.

"No" I said, "I don't want that. I won't have another person's liver. I'll do this, I'll have this procedure and that's it. I won't do anything else. I don't want that, Mum".

She wasn't in any position to calm me down.

We sat in silence until I said,

"It's obviously a just-in-case plan. Maybe they put everyone's name on a list and remove it when there's no need for it to be there; leave space for people who really do need transplants".

Some might say I was in denial, that deep down I knew this was my ultimate fate; that it was just a question of when. That's not the case. Maybe I was stupid or ignorant, but I didn't see it coming. I can honestly say that I was one hundred per cent certain that I would not end up a transplant recipient. My liver didn't need replacing, just treating.

Mum nodded in agreement.

She advised me to get some sleep and not to listen to anyone else but Diarmaid. He hadn't spoken of a transplant.

I am sorry, James. Admitting this makes me feel so guilty. I definitely didn't want your liver. Does that sound just ungrateful? I didn't want it, yet it was there for me. If I had any choice I wouldn't have taken it; I just wanted my own. To me, a liver, a second-hand liver is like clothes worn by someone else and cast aside. It's such an abnormal procedure – popping in the organ of a dead person into someone living; it's barbaric and unnatural. I'm sure I'm supposed to happily say that I bonded with my new liver straightaway and that I was delighted and happy to have it. I'm sure I'm supposed to speak happily about 'the gift of life' as many transplant recipients do. That I woke up from my surgery with a new lease of life, feeling stronger, healthier and happier. That seems to be what most transplant recipients say. But I must be true to myself and say that I'm not Mary Fucking Poppins or a shiny happy person grinning delightedly with a new organ as though it's a new accessory or piece of wonderful jewellery. I am me and call me crazy, delusional or just a horrible ungrateful bitch but at that time I wanted to keep my own liver, necrotic and useless as it was. On that night, I decided to take things one step at a time. When, no, if, in the future, the time came for me to need a liver transplant and receive some donor's cast-off organ, it would be my choice, I would be in control and I would be the person to decide what I wanted done to my body.

Isn't life a bitch?

Dear James,

Nothingness, no pain, no dreams, no moving toward the light, no sensation of floating. No voices or bright tunnel or faceless friends beckoning me to a happy place of joy and fresh fragrant gardens. Nothing. Anaesthesia – a place of absolute emptiness and pure nothingness; the place between life and death – a grey world of in-between, where fate would determine which way I would fall – to the light brightness which is life or to an eternal darkness of black sleep.

Fate – and the hands, minds and hearts of transplant surgeons armed with my new liver.

The chapter of my life which begins my, admittedly, most trying and challenging time, is incredibly difficult to describe. Yes, because it's sad and tragic and scary and recalls some horrible, horrible memories, but also difficult because I wasn't really 'there' for the introduction; I don't really know what happened. I cannot describe the rushed scramble for a suitable liver or give my own account of when the haemorrhaging began and my heart stopped. I can't describe my feelings of fear and worry as my own liver essentially gave up and my jaundiced, dying body was placed in a medically-induced coma. I can't speak of the waiting, the bargaining, the speculating as my life was gradually slipping away from me.

So you, like me, will just have to settle for the collaged and patched-together version of events from my medical records and accounts form my family and medical friends.

At 1.30 pm, on 28th March, a Tuesday, my TIPS procedure was undertaken. An 8 cm/2 cm Viatorr stent was passed into my jugular vein to access my hepatic system. As I explained before, the purpose of this stent was to take some pressure off my portal system. What the surgeon discovered during the TIPS procedure was quite dramatic.

The thrombosis was very extensive, much more extensive than the CT and other scans had shown. Not only was it blocking my hepatic vein but a dark, hard mass of coagulated blood extended into my splenic vein and superior mesenteric vein. My spleen was quite enlarged and the caudal lobe of my liver (the narrow piece of its wedge) was very large and swollen. This was far from good news. Essentially it meant that though the stent had been positioned successfully at the hands of a consultant hepatologist, the thrombosis was too large to manage by TIPS alone. Even if the blood flowed through the stent, there was little flow of blood elsewhere in my hepatic system.

Without further treatment, my condition would just deteriorate further. The movement of blood, already struggling to flow, would soon be completely stopped. There was little that could be done except to try and dissolve the huge thrombosis.

Briefly, because I don't want to be boring or too technical, I was begun on a TPA (tissue plasminogen activator) infusion – basically a treatment to break down the clot – and rid my body of some or the entire blockage. The main risk associated with thrombolysis was the possibility of a haemorrhagic stroke and head trauma – but neither option, large blood clot nor a haemorrhage, was a good one.

Meanwhile, Mum was advised by Diarmaid that though the TIPS procedure was successful, there were other issues. He asked if my other family members were nearby to which Mum explained that my Dad and sisters had plans to visit me from Mayo the following day, Wednesday. Diarmaid's reaction was palpable and his split-second pause before a nod spoke volumes to my Mum. It was urgent that Dad and my sisters spend time with me. Mum didn't question his blatant reaction – deep down she knew.

My Dad and sisters arrived on Wednesday. By then, I was apparently in my new home, the High Dependency Unit. Hooked up to a number of machines which beeped endlessly, I received IV medication and the all-important thrombolytic treatment. I have no recollection of that day. Many of my memories of that time of my life are so messed up and confused. The sequence of events isn't right, I can't differentiate night from day and though I apparently chatted to my family and signed a Mother's Day card that Wednesday, it's all completely erased from my memory.

The events of that Wednesday evening may explain why.

Mum was with me – had Dad and my sisters left? I don't know. But this version of events comes directly from Mum.

She sat with me while I slept. Suddenly, my blood pressure monitor began to alarm. I became tachycardic; my heart rate was beating way too fast, and the quiet room was thrown into a frenzy as two nurses called for help. Mum caught the words 'cardiac arrest' and 'haemorrhage' before being asked to leave.

I've never demanded the exact version of events, afraid, even now, of hearing that I was shocked into life, or that I was bleeding out, receiving transfused blood while my own blood left my body in a torrent of red water. I imagine scenes similar to those of ER; someone demanding '10cc of epi!' while the heroic young doctor yells 'clear' and shocks my heart back into action. . . the looks of panic replaced by looks of relief as my heart begins and my blood pressure returns to normal or near-normal. Maybe I watch too many gory medical dramas or maybe now some years later, I can feel safe and secure in the knowledge that it is in the past, that since I survived I can almost 'enjoy' the drama and theatrics. I did hear it in all of its dramatic glory from one of my favourite nurses, months later while still in the High Dependency Unit. She was proud of me and described me as a 'miracle'. She mentioned my heart stopping, acute haemorrhaging and the frantic efforts to save me. After our conversation, tears just engulfed me and I cried hysterically. I didn't want to visit the scene, I wasn't ready to accept how close I came to . . . it. That's just one example of the conflicting emotions that I have, even now. Intense paralytic fear, pride, bravery, excitement, relief, joy and sheer wonder – all in one snippet of a story. Also, another recurring emotion is the rejection of the story as my own; the refusal to accept that this happened to me. It was too much to take in – and again and again this is what is the most difficult part of all of this, all of this story. The enormity of what happened makes me feel detached, as though the story belongs to someone else. Dramatic, exciting TV-type stuff never happened to me – it happened to others. It happened to people outside my family circle, people who were very ill or lived lives that attracted drama. How could all this terror and scariness visit my 'boring and normal' life?

But I'll continue with the facts without interrupting with my feelings – there's more time for that again. The thrombolytic treatment, as not so much expected but deemed possible, had caused severe acute bleeding in my GI tract. Identifying the source of bleeding was difficult as bright, fresh blood obscured all views by scope. Eventually it was traced to my large intestine when my stomach, oesophagus and duodenum were deemed clear. As I continued to bleed, my heart (mechanical pump that it is) initially beat rapidly but then refused to continue. Who could blame it? It was pumping blood all around my body, but much of this was not enclosed in arteries or veins. My heart refused to pump free blood, refused to push more and more escaped blood into broken, leaking blood vessels. The transfused blood I was receiving was being lost as fast as gained so my sensible heart wisely stopped.

After the bleeding finally stopped (I've no idea how or for how long I bled and I've never asked) the 'real' Karol was gone. Following the drama and terrifying scariness, there was a dramatic change to me, personally. Medically, I was described as 'agitated', 'confused' and 'unresponsive' and there was 'neurological deterioration'. Personally or, to me, the human being with feelings, thoughts and an identity, the 'me' that I know was gone. Now, years later, I could describe the preceding days as the final scenes of a life that I took for granted, a life that I never questioned and always expected to just 'be there'. Like you, though, a door was closed on my life. I just wasn't myself anymore. I know that a psychiatrist or psychologist would offer deep profound definitions of 'self' and question my meaning of this statement. The only explanation I can offer is that the person in control of my life was no longer in control; she was a helpless shell of a person. She was a flailing, confused wreck.

Following the severe bleeding I, unwillingly, unknowingly handed over complete control of my life to a group of hepatologists, haematologists, surgeons, neurologists and transplant coordinators. I was listed as fulminant; in liver disease terms I was at Grade III or IV encephalopathy. My liver had given up. After all the years of struggling with limited blood flow and fighting to do its duty as it became sick, swollen and weak, it finally succumbed.

I was therefore heavily sedated and the next steps were devastating. After a brain CT to rule out an intracerebral bleed or oedema, I was listed for super-urgent orthotopic liver transplant.

At 6.30 am on Thursday morning, following persistent neurological confusion, I was intubated and placed on a ventilator. Though I was 'haemodynamically stable' I didn't have much time. I was listed in first place on the super urgent transplant list of Ireland and the UK and my waiting time began.

Wow, that was a very heavy piece of correspondence. All about me! But, this is what I promised, difficult as it is (more than I thought it would be).

It's a cold, dark, stormy night outside and I love this time of year. Autumn – in all its vibrant glory, the golds, browns and reds of the decaying leaves. Maybe this will sound a little corny or pseudo-poetic (I'm not a poet nor do I aspire to be one) but the waiting time in the HDU was like my autumn. Not quite winter with its raggedy finality, but damn-near almost. I was clinging on like a shrivelling leaf on a tree, not aware that just one gust or one rapid movement could dislodge me forever. I clung on.

Now I can say it was really in my spring – my favourite time of year when nature is fresh and new, young and ripening. While my old decaying life was in autumn and withering to winter, it was to spring and to a fresh newness I eventually moved, turning my back on winter, for now.

21ˢᵗ November 2011

Dear James,

I'm feeling a little unwell today – lung infection with a blocked-up nose, slight fever and a headache as though my two ears are caught in a vice-grip. I've been to my doctor and now I'm happily tucked up in bed. I'm happy enough, enjoying a little timeout from it all. To be honest, I've been quite anxious with my work recently; it's been hectic and I tend to take it seriously. So, as I'm lying here in my big double bed, snuggled under a warm duvet, I'm scolding myself for, once again, falling into the habit of letting work and other life issues dictate my mood and health. When I was on sick leave some five years ago, it seems that my employers didn't have much hope for seeing me return to work – they hired a young guy to carry on my work. Is that not enough of a kick in the arse to bring home the obvious realisation that, in the workplace, I am replaceable? Everyone is replaceable! It wasn't nice to feel that at the time, but with that came the resounding 'now for you!' and the blatant truth that the world didn't grind to a halt because my expertise wasn't available. It also taught me that if Karol the scientist wasn't the important part of me, then Karol the friend, Karol the daughter, sister and person were the essential elements to protect and love. Does that sound like I've picked up an Eckhart Tolle book and 'become enlightened by love'? Maybe it does a bit…

Anyway, I'm lying here in my small buttermilk-painted and slightly cluttered bedroom, two small windows to my right. I can see it's a sunny day from the blue sky, barley flecked with fluffy clouds and the insects buzzing at my window. The two windows and blue sky are a throwback to my room in hospital; my High Dependency Unit room. It was summer and almost every day, an azure blue coated the sky. I couldn't move much, barely at all, so my view never changed. A blue, generally cloudless sky and the green bronze roof of a church. Visitors (strictly family only) would look out and describe large ferries travelling to Wales and of little sailing boats; I wondered if they were just making it up. Was the view really of numerous hospital buildings, boring carparks and dirty streets, and they invented an exciting happy world with its foamy sea, holiday-makers waving from ferries and sandy beaches with screeching sea-birds and carefree walkers?

I later got to see more of the real view when we took a trip to Wales on one of those ferries – it was a promise I made to myself as time went on and my condition began to improve. It was beautiful and a huge day for me to be on the blue sea with the sky above instead of just imagining it from a sick bed.

Now, I'm taking up my story from before as I lie, surrounded by machines, in a hospital bed. My family, aware that there was only one chance of my survival, were advised to get some rest and were staying near the hospital.

I was, as I mentioned before, stable but on a ventilator and seriously ill. The liver is a vital organ so, once it's compromised or in my case, pretty useless, toxins begin to build up in the brain, in the gall bladder and basically the body begins to become poisoned by its failing to rid itself of ammonia and other metabolic by-products. I'm not certain how useless my liver was that night but something apparently deteriorated further as my Mum got a call from a doctor, whose name she didn't recognise, advising her that I was being transferred to the Intensive Care Unit. As she had been sleeping, she thought it was a dream, or a ridiculous mix-up, some sort of sick joke. He advised her to stay where she was until he phoned again later in the morning, once I had been stabilised. He phoned again within a few minutes. It was time for the family to come in and be with me.

I still can't use words other than 'come in and see her' to express what he really requested her, my Dad and sisters to do. He summoned them to my bedside to spend time with me, to talk with my unconscious wasted body, to say whatever they felt was necessary or appropriate. Maybe goodbye was the most appropriate word? Maybe the ticking clock and absence of a liver to replace my broken one were evidence enough for this doctor to admit defeat. I'd be a fool to think that all of his hospital stories were successful and happy. For him, my story might just have had a 'hard luck' ending.

Maybe my family too, thought the same. How do I ask them if they had given up or if they somehow stayed hopeful, in an almost-useless situation? I would consider my Mum and Dad quite religious, with a strong faith in prayer, God and the saints. That said, they also have a deep, unwavering belief in the afterlife, something I don't or maybe just can't quite share. I imagine that a number of scenarios forced themselves into their thoughts. Now, I place myself in the situation if it were one of my sisters' lives ebbing away in a hospital bed while I sat by. I cannot imagine the scenario for long. I feel pain; also helpless and powerless, wanting to do something heroic or important, but knowing that there is absolutely nothing I can do to make things better, to make thing right or normal.

And so, the players played their roles. For minutes or hours, I'm not sure. Maybe hope was beginning to fade and the resignation to a dim reality was dawning. (You know, I feel very uncomfortable speaking about myself like this! Maybe they were just wishing I'd get on with it and die so they could all get a night's sleep?).

Hope was fading and really I was too. Then they saw it. As Mum and my older sister, Noranne, sat by my bedside, they were both drawn to the window. It was a cloudy starless night and neither, to this day, knows what drew them stare at the sky. For a few seconds, the sky cleared and they saw a bright twinkling star, so visible to both of them and so eerily vivid and clear in an otherwise obscured dull night. They looked at it and then at each other. I'm not even sure why I'm telling you this. It was a planet or a star, right; just visible after some thick cloud was displaced, simple as that. There was no mystery, no miracle or no deep meaningful reason why it appeared and burned bright and then left. I'm a cynic, a natural-born cynic, and the story of this star, while it sent a shiver through me when I first heard of it, soon became a no-nonsense sighting of a common star, during a bad time when a 'sign' or some 'ethereal signal' was needed. (A very welcome healthy liver would have been pretty nice too.) On seeing the star, though, my sister and Mum knew everything would be okay.

Within minutes, Jennifer, the transplant coordinator came with news to my family. While she warned them not to become too hopeful, she announced that there was a liver on its way to the hospital which was possibly a suitable match for me. It was slightly bigger than my own but it was healthy and young. She continued that there would be a number of analytical tests undertaken by the liver surgeons to ensure it was suitable for me. She also reminded them all that false alarms were common; while the organ seems a perfect match, for one reason or another, a transplant is not undertaken.

My sister asked if they would surely go ahead with transplanting this liver, even as a temporary measure until the more suitable one would be located; Jennifer explained that a transplant would only proceed with the ideal liver for me. She left us alone.

The slowly ticking clock began to beat with an urgency and breathlessness that proved there was no time to waste. After some time - who knows how long - Jennifer returned with the team of people I can only assume consisted of surgeons, hepatologists, nurses and registrars. A brief smile from Jennifer assured my Mum that the liver, your liver, was suitable. After being assessed the consensus was that my transplant could and should begin as soon as possible. As my family finished their goodbyes and wished me well, I was wheeled back to the theatre that I had walked into just a few days before.

Following the routine preparatory phase of attaching me to heart rate and blood pressure monitors and a breathing tube, placing several drips and cannulas in my neck, wrists and groin, and a catheter in my bladder, my liver was removed. My 31-year old liver that had been with me since birth, before birth, was taken away. I find that sad and maybe some part of me still wishes that its removal was avoidable. Yes, a silly concept where the useless wasted liver could somehow be left where it lay, and the young fresh vibrant one could be placed by its side and do the work. I can't explain – I just didn't want to lose a part of me. Nevertheless, it was detached from its blood vessels and my bile duct and removed forever from my body, along with my gall bladder. For the first time ever seen by a human eye, my liver was observed to be very large and swollen, in particular it caudal lobe. It also showed numerous venous collaterals, a sign that my body had struggled to supply new blood vessels to drain my liver, but obviously hadn't completely succeeded. All in all, it wasn't happy and appeared to have been struggling for quite some time.

I was then without a liver. I once read a book which describes the cavity occupied by a human liver 'the place where the surgeon sees God'. I know transplant surgeons become competent with the experience of seeing this type of surgery so frequently, but I think that, like some other experiences in life, every case is different and new - and they surely don't become accustomed to or overly-familiar with something as amazing and complicated as a transplant surgery.

Generally, a donor liver is prepared before a diseased liver is removed, meaning there is very little time when a person is 'liverless'; as I mentioned before, a person can't live for any length of time without a liver – unlike diseased kidneys where a person can survive on dialysis. When your / my new liver was put in place (minus a gall bladder!), my surgeons attached my blood vessels; vena cava, portal vein and hepatic artery and bile duct. Nothing happened. My blood was supposed to perfuse your liver and basically give it life, take it over and claim it as mine. (Does that sound voracious somehow?? I don't mean it to be – my body had to immediately accept it). So, they watched as your liver remained without blood. My hepatic vein, as well as my splenic vein and mesenteric vein were clotted, dry and useless, unable to allow blood to flow through them. I think they took out the liver again, no doubt considering using it for another person – someone with a healthier and more cooperative circulatory system. After some time, another liver surgeon, Mr. Donal Maguire, was summoned to the theatre, where he, in his genius and wisdom, created a conduit from my vena cava, bypassing my portal vein and essentially undertaking a procedure that, previous to mine, had never been done. Having a liver transplant is no small feat but there's some comfort at least in having an 'orthodox liver transplant', one that's very near to normal. And sometimes in life, it's important to stand out from the crowd and be different. Now, with hindsight, I can admit that that wasn't one of those times when I wanted to be different. I didn't want to stand out. This was a time I needed an uncomplicated typical liver transplant – like most other recipients. There were no data to pull from in terms of success rates or prognoses for me, and because my vena cava was used in such an unconventional way, there were some predictions that I would not be likely to walk following my transplant. There simply was too little known about the outcome of such an alteration in my circulatory system. Now, five years on, walking, swimming, running, driving, kayaking; I can confirm my legs are just fine.

At some point after my surgery, I remember seeing Dad sit beside my bed. I was thirsty, so thirsty and my back was in agony. Suddenly something was in my mouth; it felt like a soft sweet. A gloved finger scooped it out of my mouth after I bit it. It was an oral swab; a welcome and refreshing taste of water as my first food / drink in days. Mum was there too but I remember little but my back pain and thirst.

I felt as if I lay on a concrete wall. I couldn't move, couldn't change my position. I really didn't know why but later I realised I had little strength in my arms or legs and my abdomen was weak and newly stitched. I closed my eyes again.

12th December 2011

Dear James,

I've been having a busy yet, in general, good few days. On Friday night I went to a concert in Galway. I went on my own as it was a classical concert in a church in the city and I really didn't know anyone who'd like to go to it with me. As it transpired I met two people there I knew, and also got chatting to the people sitting beside me – whose daughter was playing the cello.

Over the weekend, I caught up with my family, began my Christmas shopping in earnest (who doesn't love Christmas shopping?!) and watched my all-time favourite movie 'It's a Wonderful Life'. As I was putting up some Christmas decorations throughout my house – no tree – just lights, snowmen, reindeer and other Christmas-themed animals – I became a little lonely about Christmases gone by. I have lovely memories of the festive time as a child – Christmas morning under the tree, opening gifts and giving much-wanted (or not) gifts to Mum and Dad, Mum with camera in hand taking pictures of her two daughters in their pyjamas and dressing gowns, eyes full of sleep. In later years, snapping her three daughters with their gifts from Santa, innocent, wide-eyed and full of hope for the future.

I became a little nostalgic, it's the time of year for remembering those who are no longer here, or times that were tough and memorable. Maybe today is a good opportunity to continue with my story, to take up where I left off – newly-transplanted and in the Intensive Care Unit.

As well as the urgent loss of my liver, and the unorthodox transplant I had undergone, the first few days, weeks and months of my post-transplant life were very difficult. Now, even now, years later, it's so very difficult to describe and talk about. So, since I undertook this project, this contract between you and me, I will try my utmost to describe the events in my post-transplant life.

I felt very enclosed in a tiny space, though realistically I was lying in a regular Intensive Care Unit (ICU) bed. I remember pain, intense, unbelievable back pain. I lay so still; every tiny movement causing my broken body to ache, causing pain to sear through every centimetre of me. I heard continuous beeping, dripping, hushed voices. My eyes remained closed and I welcomed escape in the form of sleep.

oOo

My surroundings changed – an unrecalled move to the High Dependency Unit of St. Brigid's Ward. Two windows to my right, blue sky, continued beeping, more voices and some TV noise above my head. I lay on a white fluffy cloud. Once, a girl opposite me, then replaced by a loud, aggressive boy. Again, alone? Another time Mum and Dad were there, talking at me. I needed to sleep but needed them close. Were they always here? The procedure? TIPS? Was it meant to hurt this much? They promised me it would be okay...

Such were my hazy memories of the first few days post-transplant. Everything was surreal, foggy and fuzzy. I was aware of some pain but more so of a heavy, overwhelming fatigue. I didn't know anything of what had happened. I went for my TIPS procedure but only regained my consciousness days later.

I was dangerously ill. Yes, my unorthodox transplant had been successful and I was alive but I was still fighting for more life – and not doing a fabulous job.

I was in acute rejection – my body's white cells fighting this foreign invader; your liver. My liver function tests (LFTs - enzymes which indicate liver health) were extremely high – in some cases over 50 times the normal upper limits. My bilirubin – the yellow pigment in blood and faeces usually cleared from the body by a healthy liver was over 500μmol/L – I was practically glowing with a luminous yellow that was no longer just 'jaundiced'.

My lungs were very congested; consistent right-sided pleural effusion and underlying atelectasis. I breathed through a mask – continually reliant on an oxygen tank to help my lungs. And nebulisers...terrible, constrictive nebulisers. A tube drained infectious fluid from my right lung into a glass jar beside my bed – apparently it filled the bottle with toxic liquid at quite an alarming rate; better out than in! I was conscious – trying to sleep at night but so so very afraid to close my eyes. I was so certain that I wouldn't waken up. For days, my family had prayed around me, presented me with myriad Mass cards from friends, relations and neighbours. At night, surrounded by medals, rosary beads and holy water, I feared that those beacons would draw the attention of a higher being – a being that would take me away. I was literally terrified to sleep in case I would die. So, I lay awake in the darkness, feeling suffocated and confined to my one spot; too weak and sore to move and change my position. To this day, I remember the tremendous relief of being moved so that I could shift a little in my bed. Two nurses would pull me up to the top to the bed by the bedsheets on which I lay, useless. Then they would prop pillows all around me to give me comfort. The joy at finding a comfortable position was ineffable. I couldn't move myself at all, my abdomen too sore and my arms and legs too weak.

I didn't know it but there were fears about my brain activity. I had CT scans and an EEG to rule out an inter-cranial bleed or some brain damage. I imagined things; I thought I was somewhere else, assumed I was an actor on TV, believed the year was 1996 and I was being born. Crazy thoughts and morphine-induced musings…

The days went on, punctuated by visitors, doctors' rounds, surgeons' rounds, nurses fussing around my bed, injecting, withdrawing, washing, changing my clothes and bedsheets (soiled or otherwise). I didn't eat, breathe, wash, move or urinate without help. A nasogastric tube was in place to feed me, providing nutrition to my gaunt, weak body. The tube bothered me, hanging there from my nose. Maybe it was a hopeful sign when I noticed its inconvenience? Maybe not. One day, I vaguely remember, but am constantly reminded; I'd had enough of the tube and pulled it out, gradual centimetre by centimetre. With it gone, I then hid my head under the bedclothes – somehow knowing I'd done wrong but not lucid enough to have left it. Within minutes, of course, I had a NG tube back in place; following a session of dry-swallowing on my behalf and feeding a tube down a small woman's oesophagus on a nurse's behalf.

The days continued; my condition apparently went from dangerously to critically ill. Mum, Dad and my sisters were there through it all. I was so scared of being alone and asked for them night and day.

My statistics improved little by little but the treatments and investigations – liver biopsies, CT scans, MRCPs, MRIs – continued. On a random Monday, 10 days after my life-saving surgery, Diarmaid asked me what day it was – a routine 'brain-test'.

"Monday" I answered, "Mum's birthday".

I was right. On Monday, 10th April, I guess I gathered some sense of awareness and reality. It was, at last, a step in the right direction.

oOo

I remember the day I found out I'd had an emergency liver transplant. It was days past the actual event and apparently I had been told by a transplant coordinator - on a number of occasions. Obviously it hadn't registered in my altered mind…

Mum and I were alone, me, lying motionless, her, fussing around my bed, fixing my bedclothes and belongings. By then, I had accumulated an astounding number of cards, a collection of books and magazines (which were pretty useless to me), an enviable supply of chocolates – and a hospital DVD player with a bunch of movies.

Mum was chatting lightly and casually mentioned the words 'your transplant'. I stopped her, shocked. She smiled and nodded, the joy she displayed not quite reaching her eyes. I then learned what had happened, what my parents and family had been through, the truth behind their elated 'happiness'. The truth of their tears cried outside of my room, their hair styled to camouflage sleepless nights and rushed showers, makeup to conceal black rings under their eyes… It hit me very hard and I just cried and cried with shock and numbness. It all made sense – the extreme pain, the feeling of being hit by a vehicle (over and over), the feeling of being turned inside-out – and back the right way again. Mum reassured me I was going to be okay, that I was so much better, I was doing really well, she said. It was exactly the lie I needed to hear. The truth would have scared me too much…

oOo

Physiotherapy was heart-breaking. That may sound nonsensical but it was no understatement. As I lay in bed, I imagined myself going to the bathroom, standing to look out the window, gathering belongings from my locker or even sitting on a chair by my bedside. It never occurred to me that this might be more difficult than anticipated.

Physiotherapy began with an introduction to a walking frame – an old person's tool. I was 31 and most certainly didn't need help to walk! With Joanne, the physiotherapist, and a nurse's help, I got into a sitting position on the bed edge, my hair falling like a crazy hair waterfall from the top of my head – plaited from bottom to top for my comfort in lying down.

The walking aid was placed in front of me – all I had to do was to use it to stand up. Easy! Right? I held the aid with both hands and tried to pull myself into standing. It just tilted towards me, useless in its role of 'aiding' me.

It was my fault, apparently. I needed to stand before reaching for it. Again I tried. No strength in my legs. I sat there, actually dumbfounded. I was a fit, young healthy woman, wasn't I? I swam, jogged, did aerobics…I was literally shocked at my legs' inability to function for me.

My arms, weak, thin and lined with cannulas and bruises then managed to eject me slowly from the bed and then grabbed quickly at the aid. Progress! I was on my feet. I looked down at my huge, bloated, yellow feet in stretched too-small slippers. What on earth? Holding the walking aid tightly with both hands I stood and tried to straighten myself. An ache appeared and a strange sensation of intense pressure pushed on my abdomen from inside. I moved foot one – with difficulty. Then the second one to meet it. They were working! Within minutes, I had taken my first few steps – and was ready to lie down, exhausted. Again, a shuffle to my bedside where Joanne adjusted my oxygen tank, held my various tubes (heart monitor etc) and untangled my urinary catheter. As if walking wasn't complicated enough!

I was exhausted. Previous physiotherapy sessions before walking had consisted of lung exercises and attempts by me to provide sputum samples. These were failed attempts in general as I couldn't quite manage to 'huff' like an old man.

I have an overwhelming memory of a walk which still brings tears to my eyes. I walked, again with my oxygen tank and walking aid, the length of St. Brigid's corridor – 10m? There is a stained glass picture of St. Brigid at one end – to which I walked towards. When I reached it, I heard applause and cheers. My family and some nurses watched my attempt and were delighted to see me do 'so well'. I cried – with very mixed emotions. It was a happy day that I was able to walk such a distance, but also such a devastating realisation that, because I had been so ill, this mere walk was something to be celebrated as a huge achievement. It was a huge achievement. I was walking – something the surgeons weren't certain would be possible due to the circulatory system changes. I was walking – after numerous days of immobility. I was walking – after a life-saving surgery which may not have worked. I was walking – using barely-functioning lungs. I was walking – I was alive. But I was so disappointed that I was now not the strong and healthy woman I was in my head. I had been reduced to a weak, dependant, unwell young woman.

I floated with April into May as tube after tube, line after line, began to be removed. On most days, my incision was freshly dressed by a nurse wearing surgical gloves and armed with sterile, disposable implements. I watched, fascinated, as she removed metal staples keeping my abdomen fastened shut (not really!). I watched as alcohol was applied, stinging me and my very large and impressive Mercedes-Benz-shaped incision. I watched as new dressings were applied to replace the old, as clean fresh sterile gauze was stuck to my abdomen to keep my wound clean, dry and infection-free. I watched, fascinated, with a detachment that now scares me. It was as though I were watching a demonstration, a 'how-to-attend-to-a-post-transplant-incision' movie. The incision, the wound, the staples and the sometimes oozing blood didn't seem to feel mine. I guess it took a little longer to accept the enormity of what had happened while I was sleeping.

8th February 2012

Dear James,

Today was a long one by all accounts. It mainly consisted of a trip to Dublin for my now-routine OLT (orthotopic liver transplant) outpatient's clinic. I got up at 05:45 and was on the 07:28 train in plenty of time – wearing my new coat and hat, with dress and winter tights inside. My appointment began with meeting Jane, one of the coordinator nurses. We chatted happily as she took my weight and blood pressure – both normal and completely fine. Jane is a reader like me so we always have book recommendations to share with one another. Then the phlebotomist took my blood – painless and routine. At 1:30 I was taken to a consultation room to meet with Prof. He still makes me smile when I am greeted with his "hello, young lady!". We discussed my blood results – nothing sinister – and I mentioned one or two issues, to which he raised his eyebrows and almost asked "Is that all that's wrong with you?". Then a friendly handshake and I was done. I actually enjoy clinic these days. They are, in general, happy events where I get to meet other transplantees and hear their stories (on many occasions, I'm happy not to hear other stories, but sometimes a nice chat with a friendly person can be very enjoyable). My outpatient's appointments these days are nothing like those first few appointments after being discharged from hospital in 2006. But I am jumping ahead of myself. When last I spoke to you, I was still in my early days of recovery.

My walking practise continued every day – still with oxygen and urinary catheter. I had begun to eat a little at mealtimes – recollections of jelly and ice-cream, mashed potatoes and baked beans – and lots of milk and orange juice. My NG tube still fed me overnight.

I remained in the HDU for weeks until one day, I was deemed stable enough to be transferred to a 'normal' five-bedded ward, in which four women lived. By then, I knew every nurse and doctor very well – and they me. I was introduced to all four women – and became especially close to two – a lady from Cork in the bed to my right, and a Dublin lady opposite me. The Cork woman had undergone a transplant and was waiting to be discharged, while the Dublin lady was awaiting a transplant. (Months later, I discovered she wasn't strong enough for the surgery and died in St. Brigid's.)

As well as a change of scenery, I also was allowed to alter my wardrobe – I got to swap my 'functional' hospital gowns for my own nightdresses. Almost every day Mum brought me a new bunch of nightdresses – with ribbons, flowers, stripes, embroidered stars and cute animals. One particular one got an unusual reception from Teresa, my Cork neighbour, who proclaimed that the green colour didn't do my complexion any favours; it wasn't my best look. I had no idea why until I saw myself in the mirror for the first time; I was still boasting a yellow luminous glow of jaundice – the nightdress literally clashed with my skin colour!

The day I first saw myself was the same day my NG tube was removed and my overnight feeds were discontinued. I was apparently eating enough to gain the much-needed weight I had lost in the recent months. Ali, one of the nurses gave me a hand mirror to see myself and to attend to my nose which had become raw and sticky from the adhesive to hold the tube in place. My first reaction to my reflection was sheer shock. My second response was more shock. I literally did not recognise the face looking back at me. In the few months of hospital life, all of me had just wasted away. My face, so skeletal, contained huge horsey teeth, gleaming white against my yellow skin, and my ears looked as though they belonged to a large old man. What had been a gradual weight loss appeared to me as a sudden dramatic decay of my entire body. At just 40kg, I had bony, bruised arms, a much undeveloped chest (where were my breasts?!), thin spindly legs and a wasted pelvis. I hope this doesn't sound in anyway insulting but I resembled a prisoner in a concentration camp – my abdomen was the only 'large' part of me – still swollen and distended from my surgery. (My legs, for so long equally as large and fluid-filled had at last reduced as the fluid oozed out of my pores and stained the bedclothes.) I understood now why sitting down after my many walking-aid-walks was so painful – I had absolutely no padding!

I suppose I settled into the regular ward routine of sharing a toilet and shower room, eating regular but small meals and chatting to my 'room-mates'. We shared magazines and discussed TV programmes, complained about food and gossiped about nurses and doctors. I was the youngest by far, but just got on with the daily routine – quite happily.

The day arrived when I was trained in the management of my own medication. It was explained by Sylvia, one of the nurses, that many of the pills I was taking one a daily basis were to be taken for life. Unlike my reaction to my anti-epilepsy medication, I accepted that this was necessary to maintain my liver function and to ensure I wouldn't reject it. Before then, I knew about anti-rejection medication for people who've had transplants but didn't understand (or know) how they worked. Between the pharmacist and my nurses, I was informed that anti-rejection medication worked by lowering my body's infection-fighting white cells. This meant that my white cells wouldn't jump to 'attack' my new liver as a foreign body because my immune system wouldn't be quite so efficient. Therefore, the medication I took to prevent rejection of our liver was basically immune-suppression medication – tablets to suppress my immune system or to lower my immune response. It would mean that I would be susceptible to general infections for the rest of my life and so I was trained in food safety and general avoidance of flus and infections. In the very early days I was taking medication at least six times daily, though many were reduced as my condition improved. I was on a high dose of steroids, but the concentration was gradually lowered over my time in hospital. I was also prescribed warfarin – an anticoagulant to ensure that my blood remained thin and less likely to clot than my 'thick sticky blood'. With warfarin, I was given a 'target range INR' or internationalised normal ratio, within which my levels should lie. For me, as a high-risk blood 'clotter', it was recommended that my INR should be between 2.5 and 3.5. A simple blood test would provide me with the result and my warfarin concentration could be adjusted to reduce or increase my INR. I have to admit that was quite daunting as foods high in vitamin K, such as spinach, broccoli and rhubarb would reduce my INR. Less than 2.5 was not good – my sticky blood might clot. Greater than 3.5 and I might bleed in my brain or abdomen – or anywhere. It became a delicate, scary balancing act - a steep learning curve, and actually a pretty big responsibility.

Additionally, I took an anti-viral medication to prevent a virus common to transplant recipients – CMV. Thankfully I never developed CMV or cytomegalovirus – thank you!

oOo

The weeks went on until we were in mid-May. So many of my friends visited me – so many of them had looked at me with shocked expressions – and told me that I looked great. The true friends were honest – I looked hideous and very sickly! I received so many cards and letters, books, chocolates, DVDs, CDs and flowers. The flowers, unfortunately, were always promptly removed from my room and taken to the church or oratory – there was too much risk associated with developing lung or other infections from flowers. My LFTs were still literally diabolical and my lung function quite poor when Diarmaid came to me with the news that I was to be discharged and allowed to go home. I would return to St. Vincent's outpatient's appointments on a weekly basis at first and gradually, I would be allowed to attend appointments on a three-monthly basis. What amazing news! What a fabulous concept to be allowed to leave the building that had been my home for over two months! What an exciting adventure to be leaving Dublin for my own home in Mayo, when I had only been outdoors once or twice in such a long time! What an utterly terrifying, startling, fearful journey he was proposing! I was petrified at the concept of leaving behind the now-annoying routine and my room-mates and the haven of St. Brigid's for a house with no life-saving equipment, no doctors or nurses – and no security! I was elated but so very afraid. I was assured that the experts were only a phone call away and I would be attending clinic so frequently that I should feel secure that nothing could go wrong in between appointments. I would have a visit from a public health nurse and would attend the Medical Assessment Unit of my local hospital for blood tests – particularly those to monitor my INR for warfarin dosing. And so, I accepted the general consensus that I was well enough to go home – and resume my life again, or maybe begin a slightly-new one?

I was set to go home on 19th May. My parents who had lived so close to the hospital for over two months had returned home to prepare my house – unlived in and generally unloved for a long time. They planned to drive me home on that special Friday.

On 18th May, I gathered a huge host of my belongings – enough nightdresses to set up a market, chocolates, books, cards and so many new toiletries. Mum had undertaken to bring a second suitcase for my stuff in the morning! I took my medication at 10pm, pulled the curtains around my bed and went to sleep, nervous but so excited.

The following day I woke at 06:30 for medication. I sat up in bed, still weak and frail, but adapting to my puny arms and delicate abdomen. I touched my nightdress where it felt a little wet. Blood came away on my hands. I startled, pulling over the bed covers to take a look, examine myself more closely. I was covered in blood, my nightdress dark red from old, cold blood, the sheets too, saturated from at least 300ml of my blood. I rang my alarm bell – shaking in fear. I didn't know from where I was bleeding! Was I dying? Would I bleed to death? I was so cold and the blood too was ice cold. Rosita came, pulled my curtain and looked gravely at the mess. Within minutes, two registrars were examining me, concluding that a scab had come away from my incision and, because I was taking anti-coagulation medication, my bleed was a lot more dramatic than that of a regular person. One of them pointed his finger at me, aiming a 'gun' at my abdomen. They claimed the scene was like a Quentin Tarantino movie. I claimed that this was not a hilarious moment – I cried when the surgical registrar recommended that I be given a blood transfusion and be monitored for a few days. I was not going home.

I was gutted and so disappointed. I felt so near and now so far. While I was so scared to go home, I had gotten used to the idea and felt ready. Now, I was confined to St. Brigid's for at least another five days. It seemed so unfair.

After yet another cannula was placed in my poor, wizened, tortured arm and my transfusion began, Jane, transplant coordinator, came in for a quick chat before she pulled my curtain to give me some much-needed space. What she said was, in hindsight, such a simple statement but to this day I still remember it and take courage when I think of her words. She basically told me that my life post-transplant would be full of ups and downs. Sometimes the downs would be so bad, it would be difficult to see past them, but I must remember that after the downs, there will always be ups. It's true – life has its peaks and troughs but when deep in a trough, one must remember and realise that there are still amazing peaks out there for us so don't despair on the tough, nasty days – there are always good ones ahead.

oOo

On Friday, 2nd June, a Bank Holiday, I lay in the backseat of my parents' car, in a makeshift bed of fluffy pillows and a sleeping bag, and we headed for Mayo. The walk to the front door of the hospital from Brigid's ward was difficult. The walk from the front door to our car was difficult. I was slow, breathless and so weak on thin, frail legs with almost-healed lungs. The fresh air was so overwhelming! I made it and we arrived in Mayo, where my front garden was decorated with potted plants and a manicured lawn (Mum and Dad had been busy!).

I climbed the stairs one step at a time and managed to haul myself into my quite-tall-in-comparison-to-a-hospital-bed large double bed.

The sun was still shining in the window and I left my curtains open – happy to sleep with the light streaming in.

I didn't sleep. I couldn't manage to sleep for a single hour even though I was shattered after the three-hour car journey. The room was just too silent. There were no noises whatsoever, no whispering nurses, no phones ringing, no monitors beeping or people snoring. There were no shouting patients – confused from liver disease and the build-up of toxins. The silence was deafening and sleep eluded me. I guess I made up for it in the weeks following.

21st February 2012

Dear James,

Today, a beautiful delivery arrived in the post from my friend Tracey. It was a memory book – a collection of photos and quotes – from our times last year. We, Tracey, Carol and I went to Kerry for a weekend in May, renting a house in a rural location outside of Dingle. We hiked, admired the scenery and seabirds, spotted wild flowers and rocks, beehive huts and sea cliffs. We treated ourselves to dinners out, homemade ice-cream and cheeky slices of cake. In September, the three of us went to Budapest where I got to celebrate my 37th birthday in a beautiful restaurant, and afterwards to sit outdoors with a cocktail (non-alcoholic, of course). We spent four days exploring the tourist highlights, walking, shopping, visiting castles, museums, synagogues and spas – and just holidaying as normal people should do. Tracey's book, a gift to both Carol and I, commemorated our fun times, our smiles and laughs forever captured.

I thought about our holidays, so relaxing and 'normal'. I felt the same as my friends, equally as energetic, and almost as fit and easily as happy. I am thanking you for that.

My first few months at home post-transplant were nothing like normal. They were trying, physically draining, emotionally convoluted and culminated in an unwelcome but necessary return to hospital, to St Brigid's Ward.

My initial days at home after almost three months in hospital were more difficult than I anticipated. My walking was very unsteady and painfully slow. I attended the Medical Assessment Unit of the local hospital daily to monitor my INR. I wore a mask over my nose and mouth to protect me from airborne infections – it made me a little self-conscious, as did my newly-frail frame with 'padded abdomen'. I was still extremely yellow and had black tired rings underneath my eyes. But, something I can't quite articulate, being a newly-saved person of the world, having undergone a number of trying and challenging procedures and faced death head-on, I was now afforded a new immunity against the stares and comments of strangers and acquaintances – I, for the first time in my life, could stand up and feel proud of how I looked, feel ecstatic to just be alive and feel completely certain that, considering all I had fought through, I looked amazing - while admittedly looking the least attractive and possibly the worst I've ever looked in 31 years.

Mum, who had moved to my house to look after me and drive me to all my appointments, and I walked in my street; a few minutes of fresh air was all I could take before I needed to rest – I easily slept at least 20 hours daily. I bought new clothes to hang on my bony frame – my old clothes were much too big and made me look like a scarecrow. I ate well and gradually became accustomed to my new routine of waking up to take some medication on an empty stomach, taking some with food and fasting again for others. I enjoyed being in my own house and being free to do what I wanted when I wanted. Showering was difficult though, as my large abdominal incision hadn't completely healed and I tried to avoid it, and some bandages, with shower gel. Showering was also difficult for another reason – the large mirror. I examined myself naked the first time I showered at home. My body was unrecognisable, completely new and foreign. To begin with, it was still bruised and heavily marked from the surgery. As well as its new 'streamlined' shape with larger abdomen, a huge audacious scar was now developing, complete with staple 'pimples'. An 'x' scar lay beside my right arm along my shrunken breast marking my lung draining episode, numerous little dents adorned my right side where multiple liver biopsies were undertaken and my arms were dotted with tiny cannula reminders. The skin at the tops of my thin, yellow legs, hung loose and floppy where my weight had been lost so dramatically. I looked silently at all of it, at all of me and breathed a large sigh. I was torn between deep sadness and loss, and a strange sense of pride that my body now contained all the evidence of the struggles I had recently battled – and won. I would never be a bikini model – would I ever wear a swimsuit in public again? Were my swimming days over for me? I stared a while longer before I looked away and decided that I needed my hair cut, my eyebrows shaped and my legs waxed.

The days continued as I negotiated my way through post-transplant life, visiting the hospital for daily blood tests, pharmacies, beaches and trying to enjoy my time. I returned to St. Vincent's for outpatients appointments, wearing my best clothes and, in hindsight, looking sickly and sticklike. Prof. and the other doctors told me I looked 'super'!

We spent the days, Mum and I, reading and sketching. I began to draw pictures of invertebrates and insects, giving them personalities and humanlike characteristics. I promised myself I would publish a book, using mayfly and stonefly larva as the principal characters but I inadvertently just kept reinventing existing childrens' books – Merry the Mayfly tried to get home with the help of Perla the wise stonefly (Wizard of Oz, anyone?). I gave up on the stories but continued to draw.

On my own, I couldn't acknowledge you, couldn't think that my liver was gone, disposed of as clinical waste and I was now carrying a stranger's liver in my body. I was unhappy and so guilty as I knew your liver had saved me, saved me directly from a silent death. But I still felt as I did the first day a transplant was mentioned in St. Brigid's – unaccepting and positively certain that I wanted only my own liver. It didn't help when most people I met told me how lucky I was to have a new liver, to have received a transplant organ so fast and not to have been on a waiting list for any length of time, as most people are. (Everyone I spoke to was an expert on liver transplants!) At first, I explained about the super urgent waiting list and how my time for waiting was short, purely because of necessity. I stopped as the comments continued about my luck and the 'miracle' – I began to just nod silently, too tired and frustrated to tell them the truth. I didn't feel lucky and sometimes I wanted to snap and scream that I had been incredibly unlucky to have needed a transplant in the first place. I guess I gradually became more sulky and angrier, confused about how I should feel; conflicted between guilt, anger and extreme worry. Most transplant recipients speak of their joy at being granted the gift of life – what was wrong with me? I am happy to be sharing this admission with you, considering there is, in effect, a happy ending to my denial or complete lack of acceptance of you in my life.

As the days went on, I became physically stronger and went to stay with my sister and her family for a few days' holiday. While there I became ill. Initially I felt feverish and tired, nauseous and queasy. After a few hours of feeling sick, I vomited and began to fall asleep. I literally began to drift off and couldn't stay awake. My sister knew something was seriously wrong so we took a very rushed trip to the local hospital. After hours in A&E, I was transferred to an isolated room where an abdominal infection was diagnosed. I kept sleeping; my parents arrived and tried to talk to me through my drowsiness. I imagine they were told that keeping me awake was likely to be important. After more tests, it was determined that my white cell count, one type in particular, my neutrophils, were extremely low. My ability to fight infections was completely diminished and so a simple stomach bug had turned into a medical emergency. I had neutropenic sepsis.

After almost two weeks in Mayo General Hospital, I really wasn't doing much better. Those days are now a haze of sleeping interspersed with questions and discussions with doctors, taking new medication as well as my own little batch, and a poorly-functioning airbed! (Basically, I was assigned an air mattress in a room on my own. It was meant to provide me with comfort given my still-emaciated state. It regularly inflated automatically night and day, sounding like a small plane. Unfortunately for me, I woke every morning lying on a bare bed, bars and metal sticking into my back – there was obviously a puncture somewhere in the mattress, leaving it flat every morning. I never said anything to the well-intentioned staff.)

Given my deteriorating status and my still-poor blood tests, a transfer to St. Vincent's was arranged. I have to admit now, that, unlike the last trip from Mayo

General Hospital to St. Vincent's, I was relieved to be going to a hospital where staff was very familiar with my new health status – Mayo General staff just didn't have the expertise to treat me, considering I was still a fresh, new, and very delicate, transplant recipient.

I remember little of my transfer from Mayo to St. Vincent's and little of the ambulance journey. Now, all that I remember is arriving to St. Brigid's Ward wearing my mask and walking from the elevator to be greeted by some nurses I had so happily said goodbye to the previous June. And that's when I began to cry – and couldn't stop. I was scared; back in St. Brigid's where I had almost died, back for their help to, once again, save me. And, worse than anything, Prof. was on holidays and Diarmaid had moved to another hospital.

The registrar who replaced Diarmaid greeted me and within minutes, my blood was taken and a cannula was in my arm. Then I began to feel safe and grounded – the familiarity and relaxed ambiance of St. Brigid's reminded me that this was the place where my life had been saved. This was where the experts on liver transplants were all located and this was the best place for me to get well - hopefully.

Within a few days, I was on new antibiotics and my medication was reviewed. Since my transplant, among my daily lot of tablets were two immunosuppressant medications. One was stopped for a trial period of a few days. The aim was to maintain my now almost-normal LFTs and to increase my white cell count slightly – in particular my neutrophils. Minding one's transplanted liver in this manner requires balancing – too high the concentration of immunosuppressants and one's white cells will drop too low, leaving a person susceptible to common infections, in addition to many cancers, while too low a concentration of immunosuppressants will result in increased LFTs and liver rejection. As everyone metabolises medication at different rates, getting the combination of medication and the proper concentration correct can be a case of trial and error. After a week off one of my immunosuppressants, my

LFTs were still excellent and my white cell count had begun to rise. So, I was discharged with a happy immune system, happy liver and as a happy Karol.

I was also discharged with a new attitude. Having spent almost three months in hospital previously, when I eventually went home I felt that I was 'fixed' or 'cured'. Sure, I had some medication to take and had to be more careful about infections, but I described myself as 'better'. When my infection reared its ugly head this demonstrated, once again, how vulnerable I and my health were, and I was gutted, terrified and reminded of the horrible days where I had fought for my life. I realised that I had become almost complacent; felt safe and invincible again, just two months after my discharge from hospital. Being back in hospital and confronted with a serious infection, it was brought home to me that I wasn't quite safe or free to feel completely 'normal'. I was still a liver transplant recipient, still a person with a long-term illness, and still someone who was managing an illness rather than just overcoming it and moving on. I would always have a donor liver, always needed to be careful about various choices I made in life, and, while most things I did and chose to do were the same as anyone else, my life now came with the responsibility of maintaining more of a routine than before in terms of my diet, medication and life habits. I resented this a little, and have to admit that, in general, my infection floored me. I felt levelled from the realisation that as a transplant recipient, I needed to be just a little more careful and cognisant of my suppressed immune system than others. I was also completely dependent on my medication.

One other thing that changed following my hospital stay was my attitude towards my new liver – your liver. For months I had complained about losing my liver and needing that of a stranger's, moaned and felt angry and sad about the loss of my own liver and the use of a second hand version – without my permission. Following my infection, that attitude drastically altered. I knew that the infection I had fought was not done alone. I fought that serious infection armed with a new liver – and we won. This time, unlike the battle I had fought previously, there was something a bit like camaraderie about this fight. It felt as though I wasn't alone. It felt as though you, and my new liver, and I worked damn hard together to get over the infection – and won.

I went home from hospital completely accepting my liver, loving the idea that we had battled together, loving the notion that I now felt close to it and accept it completely as mine, as the liver I needed. You could say that – cringe moment – I bonded with my liver in those few weeks – at last. I eventually accepted it as part of me, and something to be so proud of and take care of, to the very best of my ability. In a bizarre way, you gave me life and I decided to make certain I didn't waste a minute of it – both you and I deserve that much. I had earned my right to life!

5th March 2012

Dear James,

Just a short word today as, well, I'm not really in a writing mood – for no particular reason. I just wanted to tell you something more about life after transplant – my return to work. I returned to work as an environmental scientist a few days over six months post-transplant. In hindsight I was entirely crazy. I went back to work on my 32nd birthday – 3rd October – my transplant was on 31st March. I felt bored at home – during one particularly frustrating day I had asked Mum to leave me to live on my own again, certain that I could manage, both eager and ready to reclaim my independence. I had been allowed to drive three months after my surgery, and so I could go to appointments on my own. I was feeling fitter and more energetic; cooking, cleaning, shopping and, in general, doing everything I had been able to do pre-transplant. I was still having my INR analysed, but this had become a weekly appointment; the daily blood tests were no more. I was obviously still attending post-transplant outpatients appointments but these, too, had become less frequent. I looked less jaundiced, and, though my weight had begun to increase, I was still a little underweight at less than 50kg, but not noticeably so (donuts and chocolate bars had helped me to gain the weight – actually advised by the hospital dietician).

So, I aimed to take another step towards normality – and return to work. As I mentioned previously, my role had been taken and a new person had replaced me in my absence. I didn't worry too much about this – knowing I had a permanent work contract and couldn't be dismissed after being on illness leave. I phoned my line manager who advised a meeting with him and HR and within a few weeks I was preparing to return to work, on a gradual basis; no more than three days per week. I had a large amount of holiday leave to take and so I aimed to take this leave for the days I wasn't in the office. I was to be working with an engineer who would provide me with my work load (unfortunately the archaic system in local authorities always recognises engineers above scientist, though *some* scientists have fourth level education – a lesson I learned a few weeks after working for the local authority and the principal reason I aimed to leave as quickly as I could. Of course, fate with a nasty blood disorder intervened…). I liked the engineer a lot and we worked well together, although in hindsight, I was very slow and my brain was still a little sluggish after all I had experienced in and out of hospital.

My first few days of work began with a lot of hand shaking and welcomes from friends and colleagues, many eager (some nosy) to hear all that had happened to me. I felt happy, special and was sure my decision to return was the right one. After the first week, I was certain it was definitely the wrong decision. I was exhausted. I struggled with somewhat unchallenging report writing, finding myself grasping for vocabulary that had been so very accessible to my brain just months before. I didn't retain information and, each morning, found myself practically gutted that another working day was ahead. My bed beckoned after lunch and on most days, I went home and crawled up on my sofa at lunchtime for a much-needed rest. With this acknowledgement that I was suffering from extreme tiredness came the feeling of uselessness and helplessness. What good was I when I couldn't even manage a full day at work, not even a full five days? As has always been the case with me, I criticised myself and found fault with my inability to perform well and took this as a failure to rely on myself, a failure to be independent and self-sufficient. It's only recently that I've realised I've always been quite a perfectionist, aiming to achieve nothing short of faultless in my working life and my private life. I'm a bit of an 'all-or-nothing' person, so when things didn't quite reach the expected one hundred per cent, I consider that as bad as not achieving anything at all. This led, and has always led to very serious episodes of very low self-esteem, which transposed into other separate issues of self-doubt and, dare I say it, self-hatred. Basically, when I didn't do well, I didn't accept this as just a separate, minor failure, but instead I took these failures as severe weakness and inexcusable lapses in my target of pure perfection. While ambition and a little obsession are important and considered useful characteristics in everyday life, I took determination and drive to the extreme and become very self-critical when I didn't quite achieve the 'unachievable'. How does this transfer to the complete and utter failure of my body to perform the very basic function of staying healthy and well? I'm certain there's a cruel nagging voice somewhere in my mind, criticising me, at my very core, for my failing liver and my negative, poorly-behaving blood disorder....

And so, these first few weeks at work demonstrated that, for the first time in my life, I had to acknowledge that my work wouldn't be good, wouldn't even come close to what I hoped it would be; that I would have the guilt of being paid for substandard work. The irony in this statement is that, in many workplaces, there are people who don't perform well on a regular basis; those who, for one reason or another (but not due to poor health or a near-death episode) don't work hard or with any pride, who don't care about their performance and don't feel one inkling of guilt in getting paid for doing a substandard job.

After a month or two of working, eating and sleeping (and intermittently kicking myself for my lack of energy and enthusiasm in the workplace) I also acknowledged that people moved on, I became just Karol again, not poor Karol, not brave, strong Karol, the fighter, the new transplant recipient. I guess that's the nature of people –

they eventually find gossip or interesting news elsewhere and I, as old news, was left to my own devices. I kept my head down and noticed that life in the 'real world' struck me as cruel and unkind. In hospital I was shielded from this, protected from the trials and unfairness of the rat race. In work, back at home and as a woman trying to return to normal life, I found kindness and support only among my close family and true friends – elsewhere, as an anonymous person, life was very harsh, left me feeling alone, isolated, vulnerable, very defenceless and was moving forward - with or without me in it. I had to try to keep up!

My want to belong, my need to feel a part of something brought me to an event for the promotion of organ donation during Organ Donor Awareness Week in 2008. I flew to Dublin and was invited to the Mansion House for a reception hosted by the Irish Kidney Association. The celebrity promoting organ donation that year was Ryan Tubridy. We met, exchanged pleasantries and had a photograph taken together. After that, we regularly chatted and shared stories; he is so fun and witty, intelligent and warm, so unlike 'the personality' that I had imagined. After exchanging email addresses the next year brought many meetings, including a trip to The Tubridy Tonight Show with my friends, and another outing with Mum and Dad to The Late Late Show, both times as guests of Ryan and entitled to relax in the green room where we met quite a few celebrities. Following this I was asked to be a guest on The Afternoon Show, the then magazine TV show of RTE1. Apparently, I was deemed quite the ambassador of organ donation awareness. At this I refused. I knew that, during another year of Organ Donation Week, as a transplant recipient I would be expected to relay my story, discuss how unwell I had been and how I had been saved by a donor liver – I had been given the gift of life by you. But I wasn't the gift-of-life-appreciating, happy, relaxed liver recipient. (For what it's worth, I've always hated the gift-of-life analogy that transplant recipients speak of. A gift, for me, suggests a calm, gentle exchange of a wondrous gift. While a new liver is a remarkable, much appreciated donation, there's nothing gentle or calm about before, during or after a transplant!). I refused point blank because, as time was going by I was beginning to feel sick to death of the 'gift of life' happiness, the possibly-fake and dishonest smiles of transplant recipients and the joy they all seemed to elude following their life-saving transplants. I was an angry woman, had almost died and struggled through pain and suffering. I acknowledged that, without your liver I would have certainly died but I was still reeling in anger and pain of having been dealt such a serious blow in life that I almost died at the quite young age of 31. I couldn't appear on the show and be the happy, joyful, grateful transplant recipient the show's promoters wanted me to be. I was, truly, truly grateful for your liver but I was full of anger, regret and fury that I was this living-on-the-edge medication-taking woman who had stared death in the face - I didn't believe I had quite deserved that horror, when I was just trying to plod along with my thirty-something life; working hard, playing hard, holidaying and exploring relationships. The chat show audience wanted a positive, organ donation-promoting story, a happy-ever-after-story that members of the public are becoming so accustomed to hearing (and possibly are a little nauseated by / habituated to?). I felt then that I didn't have that positive story to share – yes, I was alive and well but they surely didn't want the angry, pitiful truth that my story had become more than a little tainted by anger and quiet rage, jealousy and self-sympathy.

After reading through what I've just shared with you over the last few years and following my undertaking to share my story with you, I realise that, I imagined that at the beginning of my letters to you, I would be portraying myself as a thankful and a smiling liver recipient. I hadn't intended to really open up on my anger, fear, sorrow and, consequently, hardened personality. I am sorry that I've done that. You saved me – I should be happy, simple as. But life is never simple or undeviating.

So, maybe I'll continue to talk with you. I've shared some of my story, the end of you and essentially the beginning of my second life and I could almost end my letters to you here and now. But do you know what? I would miss our conversations. I would miss sharing my stories, issues, dreams, hopes and fears with you, dear friend.

So, I think I will continue with my musings to you, continue to talk and keep you close as my friend and co-warrior. Let's keep this friendship going, with me as the protagonist of sorts, the sole voice and narrator, and you as the silent, yet ever so present, patient, hero.

13th March 2012

Dear James,

As I look back on the last few weeks of my long stay in Brigid's Ward, I'm almost astounded at how happy and elated I was. Once the days and weeks of immense pain and life-threatening struggles had passed, I was having visitors, enjoying chatting to people and really pleased to meet new friends in my five-bed ward – both old and young. I woke up each morning with a smile on my face and literally hopped out of bed to use the shower before the four other ladies. I greeted everyone with a cheery 'good morning' and looked forward to seeing which nurses were with us on each day. Food was pretty good and, though my appetite had declined over my time in hospital, I looked forward to breakfast, lunch and tea – and the chocolate I had between meals. In hindsight I was likely hungry because of the still-high dose of steroids I was taking. Before I was discharged from hospital, I was less than six stone, seriously underweight, had an extremely jaundiced appearance (my white teeth gleamed!) and I had an abundance of fluffy hairs on my face, arms and torso. Having my bandages changed was quite painful as the hairs clung to the dressing – every day I had my abdomen waxed!

Very simply, I was happy because I was alive and knew just how close I had been to not being alive. Every day, doctors, surgeons and nurses reminded me of how complicated my surgery had been and how the surgeons were not at all convinced that it would be a success. Their options were very limited and when they did bi-weekly rounds to my bedside their smiles and winks hinted that not every transplantee received the same attention and list of questions. I was treated with a little more care then 'regular' transplantees – I had given the team something very exciting and exhilarating to discuss.

I took joy from showers and being able to walk unaided, the fabulous view from Brigid's Ward – Elm Park Golf Club from one corridor and the Irish Sea and Sandymount Strand from the second corridor. I could read, rest, chat with visitors, watch DVDs and just enjoy life, knowing that I was safe, that I had undergone major surgery and I was now fixed or cured.

There was a great network of happy nurses there who were so positive and supportive. The nurse manager, Denise, a busy young nurse from Dublin told me that even though I had had a transplant, I should never feel that my life was limited. I should not behave any differently to anyone else. I'll never forget the day she told me there wasn't anything I couldn't do – even skydive or parachute jump. The world was mine and I should not feel that there should be no limitations in my life. I guess it was her way of telling me to 'live'. At that time I didn't know that Prof. Hegarty had hinted to my Mum and Dad that, though I was very well a few months after my ordeal, he really had no indication how long my liver would work successfully. He couldn't predict if, going forward, my convoluted and unorthodox new anatomy would hold out and function properly. I'm so happy I never knew this, as I had full confidence in my new liver and felt it was mine for keeps.

I realised that while I was lying around, day after day, it was a good time to think about what I wanted to achieve in my life. I should develop of list of those important things on my wishlist – or bucket list. In St Brigid's for months, there were two things at the top of my list. The first was to walk on a beach with the wind in my face, to walk along the sea with my shoes off, paddling and sinking my toes into the sand. The second thing I really wanted was to stand outside in a thunder storm and let the torrential rain fall on me, drenching me with cold delicious rain. Bizarre though those desires were, I expect it was from months of being indoors, in one ward, that I needed to feel freedom and nature's elements connect with me. I had been on one side of a large, sealed window for so long – at first not able to see out from where I lay and then, months later, happy to walk and stand by the window on my own feet, but not free to breathe the fresh air outside. For the safety of transplantees, the air in Brigid's is filtered of bacteria and viruses and no external air can circulate in the wards. This is because most of the patients are on medication to suppress their immune systems so are susceptible to infections – airborne infections from outside could be very dangerous. Because I was so long indoors, I yearned for the freedom of outside.

On two occasions before I went home I was allowed out of St Brigid's Ward. The first time, a lovely little nurse called Sylvia wrapped me up with a blanket in a little wheelchair and took me for a spin. Having been admitted in a very bad state I had no idea where the hospital was but also had no clue where Brigid's Ward was in relation to the rest of the hospital. Sylvia put a disposable mask over my mouth and nose and off we went. We journeyed from the fourth floor to the first, along a long corridor and towards the oratory. I remember seeing baskets of eggs and little rabbits in front of the altar – remnants from Easter, I guess. There were also many bunches of flowers and posies – gifts to patients who weren't permitted flowers due to infection risk. I don't remember saying any prayers but I imagine I did. We passed a vending machine on the way and I got a bag of mint chocolate Aeros. As I was still being tube-fed I guess I was craving sugar or something tasty instead of mashed potato, jelly and ice-cream I was becoming accustomed to. We stopped at a door into a small courtyard. I sat in my chair, looking at a big tree outside and breathing in the cool, fresh air. When Sylvia helped me back into bed, I was exhausted and slept for hours.

The other time I 'escaped' was only a few weeks before I went home, probably in early May. I had been advised by Jennifer that I could maybe go for a meal with my family. It would be a 'boost' for me to get dressed and go into the outside world – something I hadn't seen in a very long time. We went to a restaurant in Dun Laoghaire. I sat on a wooden seat, surrounded by my parents and sisters and smiled to all; I was in agony. My severe weight loss meant that there was little padding between the hard chair and I. My bones sat almost directly on wood and I struggled to get comfortable while we ate our meal. I got through the main course and, a combination of fatigue and bottom pain, was relieved to think I'd be going back to Brigid's shortly. My sister then announced she wanted a dessert! My heart sank and my bum ached! I said nothing, looked around and pondered life from outside of a hospital ward. To my right was a middle-aged couple. He had his back to me and appeared to be busy eating, while his wife / partner was facing me and had stopped eating to watch me. I decided I was paranoid and looked away, talking to my family. When I glanced back at her again, I was uncomfortable to see she was still looking, staring, straight at me. I became very embarrassed and sad. It struck me that, though I felt pretty normal by then, for the first time in months, I obviously didn't look normal. I didn't feel like I blended in, couldn't pass for regular 31-year-old woman. It make me realise I wasn't quite ready for the outside world and the perceptions of people. My gaunt, jaundiced face and body had given me the appearance of someone who should be stared at, someone to be analysed, to be pitied even. We left the restaurant soon after and I headed back to Brigid's. Before I got there I vomited up my meal in the downstairs toilet. I guess I wasn't quite ready for restaurant food yet either.

I needed a wishlist – that's what I wrote to you about today. I thought of one – a list with four items which would enhance my life, give me confidence and hopefully give me happiness. The first was a simple treat – an electronic reader, a kindle. I'm an avid reader and felt an e-reader would be just the thing for me to collect more books, subscribe to newspapers, allow me to highlight and clip interesting phrases and paragraphs.

Secondly, I promised myself I would invest in having my teeth straightened. Following years of constant thumb-sucking (at least 14!) there was an obvious overlap in my two top teeth. For years I had smiled with a closed mouth, or covered my face with my hands when I laughed – this would give me the confidence to smile without self-consciousness.

The third – travel. I love travel, always wanted to see as much of the world as I possibly could. I believe, as humans, we're all entitled to see as much of our planet as we want. Obviously, financial circumstances dictate, or curtail, the amount of travel one can do. I promised myself that, once allowed to travel one year post transplant, I would never deny myself, within reason, any holiday or trip to another country. The more I saw of the world, the more free and alive I would feel. While Canada was always top of my longed-for destination list, I also wanted to see so much more of Europe – Rome, Barcelona, Prague, Berlin Warsaw, Vienna and Nice, to name a few.

Finally, I would learn to play a musical instrument. I've always loved music of all types, amazed and awed by composers and musicians and the sheer talent it takes to compose something so brilliant it can move people to tears, laughter or just sheer joy. I decided on a wind instrument, purely because my lungs suffered quite a bit in the days following my transplant. Pneumonia and fungal infections caused my breathing to be very impaired and litres of fluid were drained from my lungs in the early days after my surgery.

Today, I am in Edinburgh! I've been twice before but this time I decided to bring Mum and Dad along and introduce them to one of my favourite cities. We're in a great hotel, right in the city and we've made lots of plans for the next four days – Edinburgh Castle, Princes Street shopping, city sightseeing and lots of nice restaurants. I'm loving it here and this year I also have plans to see Lake Garda, including Verona and the Dolomites. Rome is also on my 2012 list - maybe June!

At present, I have a brace on my top teeth but I am still a pretty good clarinettist. In just over a year, I've learned, from the very beginning, how to read sheet music, how to recognise notes of different lengths, different beats and rests. Initially, it was like venturing into a whole new world. Recently, one year on, I received honours in my Grade III exam, am preparing for Grade IV, have played solo in front of other music students and have joined the school orchestra. Life is good.

3rd October 2012

Dear James,

I intended to write to you today, to make time and ensure I put some words down on paper. Today is my birthday, you see. Today I am 38. What did I do to celebrate? It's Wednesday so technically it's a work day (I work Wednesday to Friday now – a three-day week). However, today I had my four-monthly orthotopic liver transplant outpatients' clinic.

I promised myself I would enjoy my birthday and attending my transplant clinic would not necessarily prevent that. Strange as it may sound, I still look forward to my outpatients' appointments. Today though, I'm struggling a bit. Well, quite a lot actually. Physically, I feel well. My liver is 'happy' and my all-important LFTs (liver function tests) are steady and if not completely within the normal range, they're very close. Prof. regularly tells me my LFTs are better than his own and that I'm doing really well. But today, I feel lethargic and sad, anxious and low.

I have to admit that today isn't the first time that I've felt this way. It crept up on me like a nasty shadowy figure wanting to cover me with its eerie dark cloak and hide me from light. I can pinpoint almost to the day when I first came to feel this way. At first I didn't recognise the symptoms. To me, being low was simply feeling sad and unable to be happy or optimistic. I didn't understand the huge spectrum of mental health issues and the plethora of stages and varying symptoms. I naively assumed that depression, for example, was just the inability to find motivation and enthusiasm for life. And, horribly, I thought that people with depression were weak-minded and should be able to 'snap out of it' if they really worked at it.

My first sign that I struggled a little with anxiety was in mid-2007. I was just over one year post-transplant and basically I now know that's exactly what triggered some complicated, misunderstood change in my body chemistry – my anniversary. One year. The short space of time – a little over 365 days post-transplant - that timescale that researchers use to plot survivors against the non-survivors. The winners against the losers. Medical research on liver transplant survival rates, at one time consumed so vigorously by me as if the more information I could devour the more armour I would be equipped with. One-, three- and five-year survival rates are decreasing numbers which, albeit have radically changed in a few short decades. The first paper I read following my own transplant offered 60% to 80% survival to one year, while over 50% will be granted five years. A 1989 paper I torturously found myself reading during my convalescence quoted one-, three- and five-year actuarial survival rates at 68.8%, 44.7% and 44.7%. (How morbid?) I now know that with better immunosuppressant medication, improved diagnostic techniques and brilliant follow-up care received, those figures have increased significantly. Today, I don't know what the figures are, but occasionally I find myself using mathematical modelling to forecast my own survival rate.

In 2007 I found myself in the scary situation where I had surpassed my one-year anniversary; that vital one-year fight which had become imbedded in my brain as my target. I had subconsciously worked towards one year post-transplant with a vigour and energy that I wasn't sure I had. I was back at work; a three-day week, I had developed a liver transplant and organ donation website – a now cringe-worthy site with health information which was supposed to encourage organ donation in Ireland. It also had an aim to seek like-minded transplant recipients as I had begun to feel alone and isolated; I felt that absolutely no one understood what being a transplant recipient was like and sought out others to discuss life with. I also endeavoured to become involved in the World Transplant Games – Olympic-type competitive events for those who had undergone solid organ transplants. I was aiming to participate in the Winter Games in Finland with a heart transplant recipient called Stephen who I had met through my website – as a snowboarder or skier (sounds like a throwback to that ridiculous movie about the Jamaican bobsled team, right?!)

Then when the all-important anniversary arrived and went I literally didn't know what my next aim was. It was as though I just cracked under the pressure of meeting and beating that date. It passed in an anti-climactic day of sitting by a lakeshore pondering on my life and its events. I don't think I've ever felt so alone and tiny in the huge world that seemed to be closing in on me. I felt lost, literally. I needed something to aim towards, another obstacle to strive for and overcome. But I couldn't find a suitable hurdle to focus on. Five years was too huge a jump from one year. It was a thinking that I just wasn't capable of – it was a lifetime away, an interval during which anything could happen, and if I dwelled on it, probably would. Three years also felt unattainable – it was three times longer than my difficult one year marathon. And so, one year post-transplant I found my life fumbling towards a new feeling, an unfamiliar defeated feeling of loss and disorientation. The unmapped territory of my one-year anniversary brought on this new unexpected episode.

At first, I thought I was just more grumpy and impatient than usual. (I've never been the most patient of people, less so as I've gotten older). Then came an increased anxiety that I'd shrugged off in my twenties. My noticeably-lighter sleep was disturbed by night terrors and horrible dreams and I became completely intolerant of, well, people. How is it possible to become intolerant of just about everyone? Well, it's a lonely path but one I took. I withdrew from my already-fewer social activities and almost cut my family out.

Now, only years later do I understand why I acted the way I did. My family was there with me when I needed them, but getting control back of my life post-transplant seemed to be somehow interrupted when my family members continued to 'look after me' and treat me as the 'weak one', the sister whose physical appearance made her look frail and delicate, the daughter who, though in her thirties, had to be fed and taught the skills of walking again. The more love and care they offered me, the more I angered and frustratedly rejected their help. It was a vicious circle; I needed lots of rest and welcomed help with physical work, but there was a line over which my Mum or Dad were not allowed to cross; I fought to retain my independence and fought to clarify that I loved them and *wanted* them but did not necessarily *need* them. Does that sound horrible or ungrateful? Maybe for someone who doesn't really know me it sounds like I shut everyone out. To me, I was reassuring myself that I could manage my life by myself; I was the one in control. I had some sessions of cognitive behavioural therapy (CBT) not too long post-transplant, that taught me that because of what I had overcome - I had almost died a number of times, I had become a transplant recipient overnight and woke up from a nightmare with epileptic seizures, an unbelievable fatigue and a body so scarred and altered that to me it was unrecognisable – I should expect to feel affected. My body had failed me. It felt like my body had turned against me and no longer behaved as it should – almost with some semblance of perniciousness – and I had absolutely no control. I still find the concept weird – the detachment between 'me' and 'my body'.

Anyway, I learned it was actually ok to be angry and if I wasn't angry and afraid then my sanity would be in question! I gradually began to allow the 'real Karol' seep out more often, overcoming 'passive Karol's' holding back on feelings and emotions. Basically, I learned how to articulate my feelings and learned that being angry, afraid, so angry and so very fucking crazy with anger was fine and completely acceptable. I began to write some of my feelings down. I'm not sure, maybe I didn't have enough sessions or maybe it was an easier outlet for me to 'speak to someone'. I found that diary quite recently and have to admit I was a little shocked by the entries.

There were lots of frustrating and anger-based ruminations. At that time I felt a huge burden on my shoulders to live my life, not just for myself but for you, my doctors, surgeons and above all, my family. I also wanted to be 'normal' while concurrently needed some sort of recognition from my peers of the huge ordeal that I had overcome, nothing like a C-section or a tonsillectomy. Thankfully, so very thankfully I don't recognise that angry person now. Crikey, I still have very angry and frustrating and sad days but I've acquired the tools to cope with the negative feelings.

First of all, acknowledgement is important. Then I know, always know that the dark feelings will pass. I know that there's some sort of inner conflict where I can't pull out of the quicksand I find myself in but I know that eventually I'll just break free. There's a little of the sadness and pessimism today. Just a sliver of sadness attached to the jumble of thoughts ranging from anxiety to extreme vulnerability to basic fear. In a rug-pulled-from-under-my-feet sort of way, my naïve faith in my world and my health evaporated in March 2006. I was flung into a parallel universe of living-one-day-at-a-time and deemed a lucky, miracle girl – a great save. I was returned to life from the far reaches of no-one-knows-where as a transplantee, a person with a new liver, one miles better than the old model. And I was expected to accept this and just simply acknowledge that a new liver from a dead guy who no longer needed it was perfectly acceptable and not a demanding concept for my emotional wellbeing (my apologies for that one). I'm not a rocket scientist and this wasn't rocket science. It was (and by 'it' I'm not speaking of the actual complex surgical procedure) a simple swap of organs. One-out-one-in. I couldn't grasp it. I couldn't begin to comprehend that I lost my diseased liver, my own liver, and it was replaced by an anatomically-welcomed-yet-Karol-rejected fresh one. I just couldn't reconcile this dramatic, frightening change in my life, Karol's life. It was such a surreal feeling. Imagine being told that gravity isn't true or that we actually don't breathe oxygen? That's how still unbelievable the whole concept was, is. It's simple – I had the audacity to assume, sorry, to completely believe that I would have a long and healthy life. That I would meet that 'someone special' (I know, how corny!) and be an extremely independent-yet-in-a-relationship careerist, juggling a successful, busy career with a happy, harmonious home life and maybe a few children.

In 2006, everything turned on its head and due to some delayed reaction and my clinging tightly to living for one full year, it all just became too much to manage in 2007. The numerous, fortnightly, weekly and daily appointments, the meticulous protection of myself from potentially life-threatening infections, the religiously-timed consumption of numerous multi-coloured toxic-but-necessary tablets, the self-injecting, the vital rests, light-but-frequent exercise – the routine and necessity of the robot-world just became too much. I had aimed for a successful one-year anniversary and when it arrived and passed, I was at a loss to know what was next. Was my whole life to be a dull routine of consultations, infection-avoidance and living in fear? It didn't really sound like a whole lot of fun, did it?

Treatment took and is taking time. Tears, anger, temper tantrums and deep-rooted fear of death by whatever means to finally begin to break free of the horrible shackles which I partly noosed myself to and were partly planted on me. I was and am a reluctant transplantee. There, I've said it. But in recent years, I've gained a feeling of acceptance and contentment. It didn't just 'happen'. It was a long process of difficult work, strength and if I do say so myself, courage. (Clap on the back, Karol!)

Today is my birthday and even though I don't really feel like it or might not summon happiness until a few days pass I now know what my aim is.

It's not about approaching milestones and numerical targets. I don't need an indicator to confirm that I've achieved my aim. My aim is to achieve contentment.

If I'm asked about my happiest time, I can think of a few but strangely, bizarrely, one of the happiest times of my life was during the period of a few weeks following my transplant. No, jeepers, not the days of chronic rejection or the seizing, the lung disease or the renal failure. I'm talking of the later stages, the weeks before I was discharged, when I woke up joyful and cheerful, when I was surrounded by my family and friends and when real happiness was in simple things; a compliment from a friend, having my hair washed or brushing my own teeth. I was happy because I could breathe, walk (unsteadily), talk and eat. I had the ability to think for myself and, though I was still very ill and taking medication at least six times a day, I seemed to understand 'it all'. The meaning of life, our raison d'être. The silly tripe that we all become consumed with just didn't matter. I was elated and in a state of consciousness where 'just living' was all that mattered. No work targets, no meetings, deadlines, complicated relationships. I was, it seemed, above that. I felt a happiness that was indestructible. I felt invincible and untouchable, able to accomplish anything. Maybe it was the morphine or the various concoctions that were in my system? Maybe I was sheltered from the real world, my only aim to focus completely on myself and getting well? But it was a brief phase that some days I yearn to return to. I know we, as humans, must work and need money to survive but there's a step back that we all need to take. The view from another angle is the one that really matters; life and living it for everything it's worth. It's the acknowledgement that however much we've evolved and advanced and improved our planet, we still must accept that we're organic beings, tiny fragments of a huge universe; temporary little vessels of life.

I want that back, that simple easy understanding that life is so brief that we can't waste it on material stuff that we've created ourselves or can't turn our backs on true happiness for human-created rewards of money and property, while ignoring, or worse still, not seeing the real world around us.

So, happy birthday, Karol – don't forget to enjoy your day. Honestly, I didn't really mean to launch into my deepest feelings and darkest secrets. But today, my letter just needed to follow that path. Now you know that the life of a transplantee isn't a straightforward physical acceptance of an organ, but it is also a series of hurdles, confusion, self-understanding and convoluted feelings – and sometimes bizarre epiphanies.

I'm happy to have survived, please know that's completely true, but some days (just some) it's more difficult to accept the whole huge transformation the event brought. And other days, I do feel like the 'miracle girl (woman)'!

5th February 2013

Dear James,

Well, I have to admit this year has begun with a challenge. Actually, there has been something which I have been avoiding for years and have been too afraid to face. I had a liver transplant almost seven years ago and now I am very stable, have great LFTs and apart from fatigue and some infections, a careful routine and good management, I am doing well. I tend to avoid the reason I was brought into the world of transplants and liver failure – my blood disorder. As I mentioned to you before, I have a blood disorder. It's called essential thrombocythaemia (ET) and it was diagnosed in 2001 – incidentally the year I was conferred with my Ph.D., affording myself the opportunity of a great career – in academia preferably. Teaching science students - and instilling in them my great love of the environment around us; of ecology, microbiology, water and earth protection and environmental management - was my ultimate dream. I digress – ET was diagnosed out of nowhere, identified only by my elevated (and ever-increasing) platelet count. I was asymptomatic as far as I was concerned. I struggled with severe fatigue but I blamed that on my age and my PhD work and its associated stress and worry. My age, incidentally, was 26! Now, at 39, I realise that at 26 I was a mere child – but that's the benefit (or not) of hindsight. I also had a high tendency to bruise – legs and arms mostly. I put that down to my clumsiness. I experienced burning in my fingers and toes, generally in the colder months – I diagnosed myself with chilblains and possibly Raynaud's syndrome. Finally, the weird symptom – I was itchy after showering or bathing. I literally experienced very itchy legs after contact with water. However, I discounted that as an allergy to shower gel or perhaps washing powder used to wash my towels. So, while I had symptoms which are now identified as those of ET, they definitely didn't knit together to form an obvious distinct diagnosis in my head; they were more a combination of harmless issues which most people, I imagined, contend with.

Following my unexpected diagnosis, my first questions were how long had I had this disorder and what had caused it. The first answer was unknown – until my 26th year I had never had blood taken so there was no baseline to refer to. My second question perturbed me a little more…had I done something to contribute to my contracting this blood disorder? Was it something I had eaten, or drank? Something I had breathed or encountered? There wasn't a clear answer. This was a blood disorder which appeared to be more common in older women, with twice as many woman diagnosed as men – and haematologists just didn't know the cause. I was questioned about medications during my lifetime, including contraceptive pills. There was nothing I had taken that pointed towards a cause. All I knew back then was that my platelets were too numerous – and also sticky and irregularly-shaped, making them more likely to clump together in smaller blood vessels and capillaries. This anomaly increased the risk of my developing a blood clot or thrombus. I examined my exposure to chemicals and had to admit that, during college and work, I had worked with a myriad chemicals – some hazardous, toxic and even mutagenic agents. While I took precautions, there were instances when fume cupboards in various laboratories I worked in weren't working – fumes weren't extracted as well as they should. Had I breathed in some chemical which resulted in this disorder? For whatever reason, clumps of platelets or blood clots form more readily in one with this disorder and it has now been shown to occur more often in the splanchnic area of the body (where all the abdominal organs are located) – exactly where my blood clot formed!

Four years after my diagnosis, after living with this mystery disorder which appeared to be relatively harmless – just something to be aware of - in 2005, a mutation common to over half the population of ET sufferers was identified – a mutation of a protein (JAK2) which regulates blood cell production and signals blood cell production in bone marrow. Should the mutation (JAK2 V617F) occur, the protein or enzyme behaves erratically and this behaviour results in the gross overproduction of blood platelets. I found out in 2006 that I am JAK2 positive or I have the mutated JAK2 protein, essentially placing me in danger of clotting or bleeding episodes because my platelets don't behave as they should. With this discovery came investigations into what exactly causes the mutation. Again, there were more unknowns but interestingly, the risk factors for mutations in general include environmental, lifestyle and familial / ethnic factors. Since it's not an inherited mutation – I acquired it rather than inherited it from one or both of my parents – I have struggled to pinpoint when it was in my life that one of my cells mutated and left me with a multitude of issues, whether it was exposure to ionizing radiation, or chemicals such as toluene and benzene and whether my career choice was a contributing factor. Why didn't my body recognise this stupid mutation as a mistake and just eliminate the rogue cells instead of allowing more and more to grow and multiply? I'll likely never know all the answers – it's likely a combination of causative factors I'll maybe never completely understand or identify. The research continues so maybe the answers will eventually be found.

I have to be honest about my reaction to my blood disorder. Initially, it alienated me and provided me with a scary secret; one that I needed to talk about and longed to share with similar people – blood disorder sufferers. I needed to know more, so much more about the disorder – but those were the days before ubiquitous internet access and simple search engines – library books held no further information for me. I felt like I was living with an invisible unfathomable illness completely on my own. I needed to hear of other peoples' experiences, their fatigue stories, their itchiness or treatment plans. I needed to feel less alone and less lonely living with this disease that may or may not result in blood clotting or bleeding somewhere, anywhere in my body.

I really didn't get that opportunity before my significant clotting episode that resulted in my liver failure and consequent transplant. Then I met my new haematologist – Dr. Murphy. That was the beginning of my greater understanding of ET and its relevance in my life. My first question, as one might expect was again where I had acquired the JAK2 mutation which resulted in my ET and subsequent clotting episode – my thromboses were described as extensive, spreading from my hepatic vein to splenic and mesenteric veins. Dr. Murphy frankly admitted that there remain a number of unknowns associated with this disease and the cause of my mutation. While I struggled to pinpoint the exact moment when I encountered the mutagen, she advised me to focus my energies on maintaining my platelets at a normal or near-normal number and to try to ensure that I prevent clotting as much as possible by not smoking, by eating healthily and exercising as much as possible. She explained that, a little like an airplane cockpit, a number of factors / lights have to be 'switched on' for my mutation to have occurred. While it's not a hereditary condition, there are familial traits which mean that some people, including family members, are more susceptible to these blood diseases than others. Environmental factors, exposure to chemicals and other unknown entities also likely play a role. All very interesting, but all very frustrating in the search for the cause… I realised I would have to just accept not knowing the exact cause and time of my mutation.

After our consultation, I understood ET more; I appreciated its unpredictability and almost sneaky evil characteristics. Treatment and management plans were then discussed and, having experienced a clotting episode, I was classified as a high-risk case – even though I was less than 40 and my platelet count was lower than 1 million at typically 900,000 (the normal range is 150,000 to 450,000 platelets per µL blood). I knew then that there was no cure for ET but its management as part of my life became a priority.

Since 2006 I have been taking warfarin but at the end of last year my haematologist discussed something new with me. I have so much admiration and respect for Dr. Murphy but I realised that I hate her clinics. While my liver transplant (OLT) outpatients appointments are generally happy and positive (generally!) attending her outpatients clinic brings home to me my blood disorder, the underlying reason I lost my liver and the underlying reason why I could just as easily clot another part of my body. My liver was a victim of my underlying blood disorder – and nothing else. ET literally destroyed my liver (in my real life ET is not the friendly little alien!) For what it's worth, the hepatic system is a little more sluggish than other circulatory systems of the body – it's like a secondary system so blood doesn't move as fast as in other areas. My theory is that, as we evolve as human beings, our hepatic system will alter to ensure that the blood moves along more expediently and prevents any clumping of predisposed platelets.

I digress…anyway, late last year, my haematologist and I discussed the merits of a cytoreductive agent or medication to reduce my blood counts in an attempt to control over production of platelets and reduce the likelihood of further clotting. She explained that while warfarin has its advantages, it merely acts like a band-aid and may not be reliable to prevent clotting. And I have quite the history. She reminded me that having had a serious thrombotic episode, it was more likely there would be another occurrence. Cytoreductive therapy is something a lot like chemotherapy, she explained. Chemotherapy!?! I was shocked and immediately panicked. My head spun as I listened to some facts about this treatment which cancer sufferers take; most people tolerate it well, there may be hair loss and nausea and careful monitoring, especially in the first few weeks, would be crucial. I could almost feel my head finding its way into the sand. Chemotherapy! Side effects! More medication! It all felt so overwhelming. She asked me to think about it but also asked me if I would be happy to seek a second opinion from a haematologist in Belfast. I agreed to both, wishing my long fingers were longer.

Time passed and I thought about it. My thinking led me to my initial opinion – I didn't want to begin chemotherapy and wanted to take my chances with warfarin as an anti-coagulant and hope for the best. I wanted to deal with it another day – forget the nasty possibilities and put it all out of my head. Surely, surely, it would be so unfair to have a clotting episode again? I had lost so much, come through it all and here I was faced with the possibility of another similar chapter!

I couldn't handle all of the pressure and worry but, on Dr. Murphy's advice, I sought the second opinion of a haematology specialist in Belfast. I made the trip into a midweek break; stayed in a nice hotel, explored the city, saw the sights, did some shopping – and went to a haematology appointment.

You guessed it – my second opinion concurred with the first – it was deemed a very good idea to begin and probably remain on life-long chemotherapy with the aim of preventing future clotting episodes. I was deemed at high risk of developing another thrombus – it might not happen but I was within a high risk category having experienced a clotting event and the odds of my experiencing another similar incident could possibly be reduced by new treatment. This was exactly what I hoped I wouldn't hear. I didn't want to admit to needing more medication with some possible nasty side effects.

I went home from Belfast quite sad and disappointed, and very preoccupied.

Within a few weeks, I met with Dr. Murphy. She agreed to discuss the effects of the proposed new treatment on my liver's stability with Prof. While it was deemed advisable to begin without delay, I procrastinated. We all agreed to re-visit this issue within a few months. Interestingly, Prof. wasn't entirely in favour of the chemotherapy because my liver was so stable and, as time had gone by, had settled well and was 'better than his own'.

I needed to make a plan, needed to make a decision but I just couldn't. I weighed up all the pros and cons, and knew, deep down, that proposed treatment was the right decision. The side effects might not be so bad – there might be none. Bizarrely, it wasn't so much the fear of side effects or new medication that scared me. It wasn't the weight gain or hair loss or nausea. It wasn't the close monitoring or the more frequent visits to haematology clinics. I knew that I should do everything in my power to prevent another thrombus. What frightened me, terrified me was the word - chemotherapy. I couldn't and still can't incorporate that word into my life. It shouldn't be a feature of my life. I have a blood disorder but is it so nasty and uncontrollable that chemotherapy is needed to help me? I need more time – much more time to think about this.

19th August 2013

Dear James,

Well, it's been a busy few months since I last wrote to you. Many ups, some downs and a lot of 'in-betweens' have gone in my life. Why don't I share some of it with you?

I had to say a very fond farewell to Prof., who has been my hepatologist for over seven years. I gave him a card and a little parting gift; he gave me a hug and told me I was 'one of the lucky ones'. I guess he has seen many of his patients lose their fights for life, he knows how complicated the human body can be – and he, more than anyone, knows how close I came to losing my own battle. He seems proud of my 'normality', happy to see me enjoy my life – but somewhat perturbed and troubled by my regular tears in outpatient's clinics. I am still so emotional, still struggle with the thoughts of how ill I had been – and I am continually plagued by concerns about my blood disorder and the treatment I still haven't begun – the cytoreductive therapy or chemotherapy to reduce my platelet counts. Consciously, I don't really think about it, can't think about it - but it's still causing me quite a lot of stress. In addition to this, my work has become increasingly stressful. I am writing two major reports supporting the county development plan which are taking up all of my three-day week. On top of these, though, I am responsible for examining planning applications, writing and appraising environmental assessment reports and balancing fieldwork with all-day sessions of report writing at my desk. Some days, I could scream from the top of my voice that sometimes, it all feels a little too much, all a bit too busy and stressful for me. My music is also causing me some stress; I enjoy it but it's very encompassing and time-consuming. I run to classes and practise every night - when I'm not at yoga classes or swimming – but melodic and harmonic scales have gotten the better of me!

75

I have noticed that headaches have become a regular part of my life and I am continuously exhausted. I struggle through the week, yearning for my generally-early Friday nights and my usually-quiet weekends. It's a struggle and I'm not certain if it's work stress, my age (!), post-transplant fatigue, my blood disorder symptom or a combination of a number of things.

For whatever reason, my reserves are low so I decided a few months ago to book a holiday – just for me. I enjoyed a really great holiday in Barcelona with Mum in May. The sun shone, the people were friendly, the city had so many attractions and the vibrancy of the city, as well as a complete break from the routine, was just what we both needed. We ate in great Spanish restaurants, took a walk in the nearby park every morning before taking off exploring for the day. We browsed Las Ramblas and Passeig de Gràcia, relaxed at Montjuïc, visited Casa Milà, Casa Batlló and – the highlight for me - La Sagrada Família. We shopped, relaxed and, all-in-all, really had an enjoyable break.

When I returned to work after my Barcelona trip, I began to plan another holiday – I completely believe in having a permanent carrot to look forward to and to focus on when things appear hard. That carrot became a break in Austria! Today, right now, I am a few days through my Austrian trip and really enjoying myself. It's sunny, warm and green - and there's something about the mountainous countryside and woodland hikes of Austria that makes me feel so free and energised. Being on holiday alone isn't so bad either – there's someone waiting for me back in Ireland. (I feel at this point that a wink or two should be inserted!) Yes, between you and me, I met a very handsome man a few weeks ago. He's literally tall and dark-ish too, but he ticks more than the physical characteristics boxes (you should know I'm not shallow – looks are only the start of the attraction). He's very smart and funny – and just interesting. We can talk for hours and laugh at each other's jokes. I do quite well in his company so have ignored the two dates I've been asked on since I arrived here as a seemingly single woman. One was an invitation for a drink in Kitzbühel, the neighbouring town to my base here in St. Johann and the second was an invitation to dinner from a friendly local ski instructor / historian. I really didn't have any interest in either man and so concentrated instead on exploring my surroundings – and doing a sky dive! Yes! I did a tandem sky dive here a few days ago! It was amazing, exhilarating, energising – but over too fast… There were a number of reasons for literally throwing myself off the side of a mountain with a mass of colourful fabric attached to my back! Three reasons actually – I'll share them with you, my constant companion.

When I was leaving St. Brigid's Ward in 2006, Denise, the nurse manager reminded me I was capable of anything and should never allow my transplant to hold me back. I certainly did not feel strong enough or confident enough for a sky dive – or anything remotely resembling a sky dive – when leaving hospital for the first time so I shrugged and laughed. Her words stayed with me, however, and when I saw the sign in my hotel advertising tandem skydives for tourists, I only thought about it for a few exciting minutes before booking a jump. The other reasons I made myself jump were to be impulsive and to take charge of my life – to be the opposite to always-thinking, planning, in-control, prepared Karol – and just do it! I made myself consciously do something that I knew I would find scary, challenging, exciting and, well, different to anything I had done before. The third reason was somehow an acknowledgement of you, and how you have given me life but sometimes I don't seem to appreciate it – the days I feel a little low or the days I feel very sorry for myself. So, by embarking on an exciting, exhilarating experience, I felt I was somehow honouring you and your memory by doing something 'real' that made me feel more alive than I had in years. It was amazing. Once I was hooked up with harnesses and canvas belts, I was advised by my instructor to run for a while with the equipment attached – towards the edge of the mountain. The wind would catch us at the edge so I literally didn't have to jump! Once in the air, we swayed and soared above the little town of St. Johann. I saw the town square, football and sports fields, the railway line and train, and lots of trees and green fields. We fell slowly, the instructor taking selfies to ensure I had lots of pictures to remember my jump. Within minutes, the trip was over – we landed in a football pitch minutes from the mountain I had jumped from. My initial reaction was to go again! I loved it. It's definitely been the highlight of my trip – tomorrow I'll be taking a leisurely look around Salzburg and am looking forward to doing the *Sound of Music* tour.

o0o

I'm conscious that I last spoke to you about my dilemma regarding the chemotherapy – my extreme apprehension about taking it, and extreme fear and dread about not taking it. I didn't begin the chemotherapy. I am still struggling with this – stupidly and irrationally – or otherwise. The fact that something like this was being proposed for me, already on a concoction of immunosuppressants and anti-coagulants, was and still is a tough one to take. I literally can't deal with the possibility of taking them, but I've also been worried incessantly about not taking them and the scariness of another thrombus in my body. I am worried for my lungs, my brain and obviously also fear that my liver may be targeted again. I am fretting over this horrible decision that is really only mine to make. It seems so unfair – so huge a choice to make – and I feel damned either way. I also feel that I can't tell my family. They had been through enough seven years before and Mum has lost a number of siblings in recent years – I know I can't burden anyone close to me.

So, I sought the help of a psychotherapist. I tell you this with a mixture of shame, apprehension, self-judgement and fear. I also have a sense of relief and happiness to be telling someone about my worries and my eventful life story.

He seems to be an understanding, clever, intuitive man and so far has admitted that I have quite the story (one worth writing down) but that my feelings of sadness, fear, terror and guilt are completely 'normal'. So, I'm normal…

So, my feeling of sadness and anxiety are understandable. He didn't tell me anything that I, deep down, didn't know but that's one of the problems – everything is just so far 'deep down' that I'm not completely in touch with my true feelings, my true self. That's okay; I want to believe I'll get there. I'm just not quite convinced yet...

He left me today with two thoughts. One, that my incredibly difficult introduction to hospital life in 2006 (today I don't want to refer to it as anything more descriptive than 2006) was such a huge event that it undoubtedly left its mark and took a toll on my perception of myself and the life in which I exist. And he believes my actions now are similar to someone who has undergone bereavement. And, his second comment was on my two traits – unrelenting self-judgement and my constant need for perfection in all parts of my life. I want to open up to this stranger (he's still a stranger) because he's not part of my family of circle of friends and I feel happy that I'm not burdening anyone with their own issues. As I answer some of his questions on myself, I preclude my response with "this is going to sound awful but". . . or I cringe and look away as I reply. He's asked me to be myself and, while noting my own reaction to my feelings, to try and not be judgemental. Speaking without judging my thoughts or feelings is a new concept to me.

So, that's, hopefully, been a positive step towards self-exploration and self-healing. I also hope that the anxiety and stress that I feel a little more acutely in the last while will become more manageable for me. I am quite positive about the changes I can make, the progress I can make if I truly want do – and I do.

Interestingly, this isn't the only positive step towards self-help that I've taken in recent months. I have a blood disorder. True. I had a serious blood clot which cost me my healthy liver. True. I know absolutely nobody with this quite rare blood disorder. True – until a few weeks ago! I have been searching online for helpful websites on my essential thrombocythaemia. I've found out information – material I already know. It's quite a rare blood disorder which results in the production of too many platelets. Approximately 50-60% of its sufferers are JAK2 positive and symptoms of ET include severe fatigue, night sweats, itchiness and erythromelalgia (burning, redness and irritation of my fingers and toes). There's been nothing new but recently I serendipitously stumbled across a website called *MPN Voice*. It's a UK-based support site and charity for people with blood disorders including ET. (MPN stands for myeloproliferative neoplasms). The site includes information for newly-diagnosed, shares advice for fellow sufferers, discusses medication options and, best of all, shares stories from lots of others with ET. They talk openly about their symptoms, their issues, medication choices and how ET blends with their daily lives. I am not alone. I knew, obviously that there were others but this lifeline, definitely a lifeline, has given me the feeling of being part of a group, feeling as though I am not the abnormal one with dodgy blood that doesn't behave. I now have the option of discussing my little, or not-so-little, ET problems with others – others who'll understand, who can empathise without being patronising, who can be useful and helpful to me – and I can be useful and empathetic in return. Having found the website, I feel human and 'real' again. I feel that I am no longer alone, no longer wondering, alone, what's next for me. Is this going to progress or is there more for me? Are there other treatment options? Can I manage the fatigue a little better? Can I do anything different in my life to improve my chances of not getting another blood clot? Who knows? All I know is that I need support from people who understand and are going through bits or parts of what I am going through. Understanding - there are others alive and taking the same medication as me, or have been on cytoreductive therapy or chemotherapy, others with ideas or theories about why they developed ET, or thoughts on how to live a more normal, happy and optimistic life. It feels like a huge support for me – and it makes me feel so much happier and less alone just thinking about my chance find.

9th October 2013

Dear James,

I feel like crying – with joy. Today I met the equivalent of a family member who's been away, a person who's been missing from my life. It's as though I've slotted in a missing piece of my life with a steady, confident, caring, intelligent man. I've known for some time that Prof. would retire soon. Whenever I thought about that, I felt sick, worried and so anxious. How could someone new know about the intricacies of my case and how hard I (and my entire team) had to work to put me back together? There would be someone new, someone who would glance at my file and note that I'm seven years post-transplant and doing very well. He/ she wouldn't appreciate the complications, the huge battle and, if I'm honest, the completely new and so delicate procedure which attached my liver to my vena cava (I still have the sketch Diarmaid drew for me on a brown paper bag in the weeks following my transplant). A new person wouldn't really care, would not know me, just be vaguely aware of my case as yet another in a pile of transplant recipients.

I've been putting all thoughts out of my head but when I imagined my goodbyes to Prof. Hegarty, my liver was good but my heart was sad. He saved my life and though it was his job he always reminded me that because of me, he hadn't slept properly in one full month of 2006. His "hello young lady" and his pseudo-lackadaisical attitude and sharp wit would always be with me.

I knew he would miss his work and truly hoped that he would stay well and enjoy his retirement for many many years.

Anyway, today at clinic, I waited my turn to be called, knowing Prof. wouldn't be there. There were a number of registrars and some younger doctors calling patients to consultation rooms. I sat for hours. People generally complain and moan that they can't afford to waste such time at appointments; I sat and relaxed, knowing that, since I was in Dublin until the evening train at 18:15, I really had nowhere else to be.

Suite 4 consists of two waiting areas separated by a long corridor of six or eight consultation rooms. It's part of the new wing of St. Vincent's, the wing that, during its building, I lay in a room alone, unable to move much and very unsure of my location in Dublin, let alone in the hospital. Today I sat in the very familiar waiting area, trying to avoid listening to the painful moaning of attention-seeking transplantees (some people insist that everyone in the room know when they were transplanted, how ill they were, what medication they take now and how they are coping). One man today insisted that he is curing himself with some herbal crap and assured the bored lady at his side (presumably just another outpatient) that medicine is not necessary. She shot me a glance to which I returned a smirk-with-raised-eyebrow.

After even more minutes, the area was almost empty. I was enjoying my book when my name was called, the second last patient left waiting.

I stood and turned the corner to approach the consultant calling my name. It was Diarmaid Houlihan. He stood and looked at me and gave a wide smile. I gasped and, overwhelmed with emotion, I began to cry. Diarmaid is back. He looks the same, a little less hair but same dark eyes that used to smirk at me as a registrar. He is Prof. Hegarty's replacement and from my viewpoint, there is no one else who I would be happy with, now that Prof. has left.

Diarmaid rhymed off my history and again reminded me of the amazing work undertaken by my surgeon and particularly Mr. Maguire. He remembered how I picked up every infection possible, how I was dangerously ill for weeks and how he, as well as Prof., had worked solidly for weeks to keep me alive. I was a 'great save'! I just listened and knew that I could trust this man in front of me to care, to work hard again and to understand how much I want to live and continue to stay healthy. He concluded my bloods were fantastic and that he will see me at clinic until he retires. I couldn't have asked for more from this clinic.

I know that I will miss Prof. desperately but Diarmaid is the only substitute I could ever trust.

I'm back to clinic in three months and he has proposed to work on the reduction of my immunosuppressant medication. This is fabulous news. Of course, I will remain on warfarin and am still considering the chemotherapy but to reduce my immunosuppressant medication would be amazing. I know about its side effects –

hair loss, kidney failure, numerous cancers…it's a lifeline but after being on immunosuppressants for seven years, my body might have accepted my liver as completely my own, enabling me to be weaned off my high tech drugs. I've become accustomed to taking medication to literally keep me alive. The fact that it's described as life-long hasn't bothered me as much as I imagined. Post-transplant I would have agreed to absolutely anything to stay alive – life-long medication wasn't a huge sacrifice. I've adapted to daily medication – it's a habit just like brushing my teeth or showering, just part of my daily routine which I've done without too much thought. At times, it's been a little inconvenient if I'm meeting friends or family for late dinners, Christmas parties can be awkward (who stops eating and drinking before 8pm?) and staying at other peoples' houses (I must eat, fast for two hours, take medication, fast for one hour and not eat after 8pm).

So, with reference to stopping one of my daily meds it'll be a challenge – for me and my liver. We'll tackle the change slowly, one reduction at a time. Should I begin to reject my liver, I'll increase the dose immediately. I trust Diarmaid; today I'm leaving clinic with a big smile and huge peace of mind.

23rd December 2013

Dear James,

Well, this year is ending on a nice, high note! I recently met a man I quite like…. He's nice, clever, ambitious and fun (actually he's not tremendously good fun – I joke that I bring the wit and sense of humour to this budding relationship!) Now I'm home for Christmas after meeting him on just two occasions.

It's given me a little 'pep in my step' following the disappearance / loss /dismissal of the tall, handsome man I mentioned a few months ago. So, I'll keep you posted on this one….

So, home for Christmas following a very busy and extraordinarily stressful and anxious month. Work really has been chaotic and I've been finding it very difficult to even climb half of the mound of reports I must complete as soon as possible. It's never-ending and, working a three-day week, impossible to ever see beyond a pile of documents. They continue to increase as I continue to clear them – a permanent mountain of work. I guess it didn't help that I was on sick leave for over a week in November. I contracted an ear and throat infection, felt as though it was the flu, with pains in my bones and headaches. I had, as always, the flu vaccine so I imagine it was just a bad infection, which responded to antibiotics.

At least it didn't interfere with my plans to celebrate my friend's 40th birthday in Limerick. I cannot believe that one of my best friends, Carol, is now 40. It's a huge age, sounds horribly middle-aged and old – and its only 10 months away for me! Being 40 brings obligations to have a gaggle of children, wear an apron and bake cherry cakes and brown bread! That couldn't be further from my current life. To celebrate her birthday, we, a small bunch of friends and her siblings, had a fabulous dinner in Adare and afterwards a fun night in a nearby pub. We met lots of people, had lots of fun, shared humorous stories and, all in all, enjoyed a great night. I stayed at Tracey's house in Clare and we stayed up late, chatting and discussing my 'new man', analysing and pondering over true love versus disastrous relationships.

Friendship is very special and I cherish my time with friends and family.

I'm a little concerned about some news Mum and Dad shared with me recently. Dad had a prostate biopsy after routine blood tests revealed a raised PSA test. This does not necessarily mean he has prostate cancer but the biopsy was undertaken as a precaution…a just-in-case.

So, while we're all a little mute and worried about the c-word, we're agreeing to enjoy Christmas and all that entails – nice food, presents, Christmas carols and visits to and from my sisters and their families.

Let's hope 2014 will be a good year.

10th May 2014

Dear James,

I can't sleep so I decided to write to you. I am just in bed after marshalling at the *Darkness Into Light* walk at Westport House. All funds raised go to Pieta House, the suicide support and awareness charity. It's a great cause but the enjoyment and happiness I got from my entire night was so special. It was undoubtedly a magical experience. I was basically on patrol at a junction along the route and because of the darkness (before the beautiful dawn emerged) I guided people along the correct pathway. The stars, the cool night air, the laughs, screams, chat and camaraderie of the other volunteers and participants was literally something to be experienced to be believed. I loved it and can't sleep as my head is spinning – in a good-elated-type-of-way. Maybe I'm crazy and people might say I need to 'get a life' but recently I signed up as a volunteer within my county and have been involved in various little projects almost every weekend. Already I've marshalled at cycling races, fundraised for oesophageal cancer support charity and – so much fun – tutored some young children at a Science Fair. I basically helped them to solder little musical instruments and funky alarms.

I needed to get involved in something fun, something less serious but also something meaningful and altruistic. Basically, I'm so busy with my work that there never seems to be enough hours in any day and I'm always exhausted trying to fit everything in. Work is at a critical juncture regarding some pretty large reports I'm compiling. A three-day week just isn't enough and so, I'm working outside of those hours to help myself along and take some pressure off me. That isn't an ideal situation either but it's helping me somewhat. I've recently made a pact with Mum that my working day should be the allocated 9am to 5.30pm and I promised her I will walk away at that time; work completed or not (for what it's worth, it's never completed – there's always a mound ahead).

Added to the intensity of work is my constant music practise which I absolutely love, but find hard to enjoy at times. These days, I'm working on dreaded scales and, as before, they are my Achilles heel, my downfall, my enemy. I can't do them! Yet, I know I have to if I want to proceed with my exams.

Spending so much time at music has taken so much time from my exercise regime. I always walked at least three miles every day; now I'm either too tired due to work or I have to spend time on my clarinet that exercise comes second. Consequently, I'm gaining a little weight…

I'm actually becoming a little stressed as I read back over what I've written. I began on such a high note, a happy note and now I'm listing the various pressures which are in my life at the moment. Maybe the main one right now, above work and the other stuff, is that, in January, Dad was diagnosed with prostate cancer. He, I think I mentioned before, had an elevated PSA level and so a small amount of cancer was detected on his prostate gland. It's worrying, scary and I feel so powerless and useless. His prognosis was good in January and in April, he had a 30-day round of radiotherapy and brachytherapy undertaken. Brachytherapy is bizarre – it really is internal radiation in which tiny radioactive particles have been placed into his body. As they degrade, they will emit radioactivity, targeting the cancerous cells and, hopefully, eliminating every single one of them. I find is amazing, praying and hoping that it will work.

I'm still seeing my boyfriend and it's an education - being part of a couple. There are still lots to learn about him, this still-new man in my life.

I did manage to survive without him though, when Mum and I headed off for Prague a few weeks ago. I visited the city before and, fascinated with the scenery and amazing architecture, convinced Mum to holiday there for five days. It was Easter and the atmosphere was very special – markets and delicious foods in the main squares, visitors and tourists sitting around, soaking in the atmosphere and the beautiful weather. I'd easily have stayed there for a few months!

Now, I am relatively tired and wound down after my exciting and interesting evening / night / morning. Tomorrow I have no major plans until the afternoon when my beloved clarinet will obediently play perfectly remembered and practised scales; major, minor, melodic and harmonic.

8th September 2014

Dear James,

Wow, wow, wow. Today I am exhausted, lethargic and my mind is not at all sharp. It's pure tiredness, pure lack of sleep and still excitement. I have just been on my dream holiday. For as long as I can remember, I have been fascinated by Canada – the accents (out!), the scenery, the pride at not being American, the scenery, Mounties, beachcombers, Vancouver Aquarium (*Danger Bay* was my favourite TV programme as a child) and the scenery. Did I mention my love of imagined Canadian scenery – high snow-capped mountains, waterfalls, glacier lakes, maple trees – and the potential for wildlife? Well, I'm just back since yesterday morning and it's been a dream holiday – all I imagined and more.

We flew to Vancouver and I was quietly excited to board such a large plane. The journey was nerve-wracking to begin with – a dash through Heathrow to catch our direct flight to the west coast of Canada. I feared the long haul flight and the threat of deep vein thrombosis so I was as active as possible on the flight – walking and rotating my ankles, stretching both in and outside of the ladies'. I drank lots before the flight and stayed as hydrated as possible. I also wore the ever-so-attractive flight socks. So, heeding all medical advice offered by my haematologist and other consultants, I tried to remain relaxed and calm about my blood circulation during the long flight. We watched *12 Years A Slave* and lots of episodes of *Modern Family*, ate interesting but enjoyable food and arrived to Vancouver Airport pretty energetic. Having rented a car, we made our way to our accommodation – and slept.

The plan was to drive from Vancouver into Alberta, staying at hotels, guesthouses and inns along the way – for 14 nights!

I don't know where to begin in describing our days as the holiday took in numerous national parks and so much wildlife. We saw wild elks, mountain goats, chipmunks, squirrels, buffalo and even timber wolves and grizzly bears that were orphans and rescued from the wild. On most days, we started the day with a good breakfast and drove to a national park where we would kayak, hike and climb to waterfalls or through canyons. Overlooking Peyto Lake, a chipmunk ventured over to me and came so close my breath held. I tried to have my camera ready but didn't want to move too much. Within a few minutes, the cheeky little thing was perched on my shoe, looking at me, possibly hoping for some food. It was the cutest experience. After days of 'living the wildlife', we made our way back to Vancouver for the final four nights of our holiday. Our hotel was fabulous and overlooked Vancouver Pier and the seaplane route which taxied people to the city centre. Vancouver is a really beautiful city – vibrant yet somehow familiar and local-feeling. People were so friendly and everyone was happy to help – maybe the tips were attractive?

Two highlights of my trip which will stay with me forever include an incident in Golden, Alberta and some 'alone time on a pier'. In Golden, we stayed in a fabulous log-cabin-styled guesthouse run by a lady from Scotland. We stayed there for three nights and I so wish it was longer as I enjoyed every single minute of that stay – including the chats around the breakfast table with couples from California, Germany and Spain. The sun beamed down and we spent lazy days wandering Golden and enjoying leisurely lunches. One early morning we were sitting on the porch, listening to the crickets chirping and birdsong. We planned to visit a wolf conservation centre later in the day, but took some time off that morning. Two hanging baskets decorated the porch, bright flowers trailing from them. Then I saw it – the tiniest bird I had ever seen. It stuck its long beak into a pink flower and lapped up some nectar, its wings beating and fluttering faster than my eyes could see them. It was a hummingbird – the most beautiful, petite and seemingly pertest creature I had ever encountered. I watched in awe as it moved to a second hanging basket and its vibrant flowers. Then it was gone. Within minutes, a second hummingbird appeared, took its fill from the flowers and left us. I was so energised and excited about my sighting. I had never seen a bird so tiny – smaller than a large dragonfly. Those little independent, self-sufficient birds have remained with me – and my strange and unexplainable admiration for them still makes me smile.

On one of our last nights in Canada, in Vancouver, I took a walk alone and was drawn to the pier. A Mexican tall ship was moored there and visitors streamed in for tours. I people-watched; noting all people, Chinese, South American, Indian, presumably Canadian and American. Some were in bunches, couples, with children, alone, some carrying cameras, some with knapsacks, happy and bored faces, young, old, fat, thin. I just watched, sitting on a step at the top of the pier. For a few minutes, I reminisced about the path my life had taken and how I was just here, in the present, in a beautiful city so many miles from home – the other side of the world. I felt you with me. I had come so very far – not just in a geographical sense but in an emotional and a psychological sense. I felt well, strong, whole and so very proud of me and who I was at that very minute. I could have stayed there on the pier for hours and hours, sitting and just being, feeling alive and feeling you there with me.

So, today, back in Mayo, back to reality (I trimmed the hedges yesterday!) I really want to retain that feeling of happiness, wholeness and pure contentment. I'm not sure exactly how to but that time on the pier has alerted me to the possibility, the knowledge, that the potential to 'just feel good' is within me, is mine to tap when I want to, need to. And I know I'll never feel alone – you're here with me.

There's just been one low point to today. I had my INR analysed before I left for Canada, and went on holidays taking my daily warfarin tablets to ensure my INR remains between 2.5 and 3.5. I saw my GP first thing today and hoped that after over two weeks of new foods, upset routines and one incident of severe diarrhoea on day

2, my INR would still be behaving itself. It isn't. Today, my INR was a very disappointingly low - 1.6. Basically, this means that at less than 2.5, my blood's ability or propensity to clot is increased somewhat than if my INR is within range. I'm annoyed with myself for letting this go unobserved and annoyed with my body and its metabolism for letting this happen! I have to increase my warfarin dose immediately and hope for the best, hope that my INR hasn't been less than my lower limit for very long and hope that nothing sinister has happened within my blood vessels over the last few days.

Now, it's time for me to rest – it's bedtime. I don't return to work until the day after tomorrow, but I still have clothes to unpack and family and friends to catch up with. Goodnight, friend.

2nd October 2014

Dear James,

I could scream – or throw plates, or take something extremely precious and breakable and just break it – into tiny, sharp, bitty smithereens… Crikey – I feel so frustrated and my hands feel tightly tied behind my back.

I am a scientist. I never saw myself doing anything very different – I've no interest in finance, accounting, computers, programming or perish-the-thought of Karol the hairdresser (my sister Paula has a great story about my one time with her hair and my scissors…). So I've always, always known I've wanted to do something REAL. Something useful, helpful, tangible, natural! A number of possible careers were attractive to me as I hit the age where I had to decide. At 17 I considered being a teacher (inspiring young people), a doctor (diagnosing and saving lives – I didn't have the confidence to know I really did have the ability and intelligence to be a doctor when I was 17), a nurse (a career in which I could eventually combine a knowledge of human health and teaching skills), a vet (ditto about my lack of confidence and fear of emptying Dad's bank account) and a scientist (working with chemicals, encountering animals and inventing things). I also considered law, but the pilot and camera operator / film maker proposals were too much for my boring and unhelpful careers guidance teacher to handle so I opted for a career as an environmental scientist. This was purely because of my desire to change the world, solve water pollution problems, save endangered species and habitats and, quite simply, to make a difference to the earth. Having spent four (wonderful) years at Sligo Institute of Technology I was conferred with an honours degree. It wasn't an extremely difficult degree and if I'm honest I didn't really work so hard to get it. I went to all my classes, did all the laboratory practice hours, undertook a 3-month work placement and, in four years, failed just one exam. (It was a midterm assessment in organic chemistry and I just couldn't warm to organic chemistry...). I was clever, listened in class and remembered. I didn't need to revise too much and happily knew getting my degree wouldn't be a huge challenge. I really didn't challenge myself during those four years and now I see those days with more clarity. I chose a degree course in an IT, a third level college where the emphasis was on practical experience and less on developing into an adult, finding my potential and reaching for it, attaining a good degree that I could be really proud of. You see, my degree wasn't ever something I was overly proud of, purely because I knew I was capable of more. I sat on my laurels and enjoyed my college days, partied like a professional, watched TV in the afternoons, had long insightful chats with my classmates and, somewhere in there, fitted in a third level education. While in college I met so many wonderful friends, some of whom are still the very best friends of my life. However, I frequently concluded that I should leave and apply for a degree course more suitable for me. A course where I would feel challenged and where I would struggle, but my eventual degree would be worth it as it would signify real, hard work, true grit. I always knew I should have applied to a university instead of putting an institute of technology as my first choice. My friendships were always the main reason I didn't move but continued there; I knew I may not meet such good friends elsewhere – and making friends has always been very difficult for me. I remember feeling so conflicted when I went home at weekends and spent time with other friends. I was generally embarrassed talking about where I was studying for my degree – people assumed I didn't get enough points in my Leaving Cert for a university course; this couldn't be further from the truth, but the snobbery about universities and institutes of technology was ever-present.

So when, with my degree and working in my first real science job, I was offered the opportunity of doing an MSc I jumped at it, grabbed that chance with both greedy hands. I had no mortgage, a small car loan and, following living as a student for four years, I was rich! The MSc was ideal as I could stay working fulltime and use my work findings as the basis of my research. Better still, I would eventually be conferred with a Master's degree from University College Dublin, while based in the Environmental Protection Agency in Mayo. An MSc from a university would 'redeem' my educational choices, 'fix' my degree I had regretted occasionally, would challenge me and eventually make me feel proud of my achievements. Without too much detail, my MSc of one year transformed into a PhD of four years, the final two of which were cruel, painful, frustrating, tiring, stressful – and challenging! I was conferred with my PhD in 2001 – a good day, a proud day when I felt I had truly achieved something really worthwhile. My dissertation didn't save the earth or leave a huge dent in the environmental research world but it put a Dr before my name – unimaginably more difficult to obtain than a Mrs!

My PhD changed me – I knew a lot more about a little topic – but I also learned how to learn, how to apply myself and undertake research efficiently. It made me see my potential and it made me greedier for knowledge and learning. I had struggled and succeeded. I was so proud of that achievement. I continued my research with a four-year post doctorate fellowship with the EPA and National University of Ireland, Galway. It was a mixed post-doc – physically- and mentally-demanding work, with long hours but amazing experiences of boat handling, lake monitoring and species identification. I qualified with my powerboat licence, drove a large long-wheelbase

Transit van (sometimes badly) and became completely proficient at boat handling and lake monitoring. I also learned so much more about limnology but there was a negative aspect to my continuing career with the EPA. Regular clashes with a difficult person are all I will say on this. It still pains me to recall being bullied as a woman in her late twenties...and I still cannot talk about the horrible and unimaginable repercussions of my plunging self-esteem – and consequential self-loathing.

And so I needed to leave, I just had to escape from there – regardless of my career prospects. I deemed life was too short for waking up daily with fear and stress about the day ahead. Life was too short to stay in a place where I was deeply unhappy. I opted for the first job that suited me – I had a new house in Mayo and wasn't prepared to travel away from that and my family and friends. I took a job as an environmental technician in Mayo county council in late 2004 – with the intention of staying there for <u>one year</u>. I had been offered an assistant lecturer role at Sligo IT – a dream job then. Having worked as a project supervisor and laboratory tutor at Sligo IT while I worked on my PhD I knew it would be a fabulous opportunity for me – I loved teaching and educating young interested (and not-always-so interested) young people. However, I had to turn it down as that job was part-time, with no holiday pay and really no guarantee of a steady income. It broke my heart to say no to that offer – but I was happy enough to work for the local authority and prepare for moving to better, more exciting things after one year. I was over-qualified to be an environmental technician, and knew it.

Fast forward 10 years and I'm still in Mayo county council. I got stuck. Post-transplant and having been on sick leave for over six months, I was happy to have work, happy to be paid to do a good job (or in the early days post-transplant, a not-so-good job). Fatigue was a nuisance; more than that it was debilitating. Mayo county council suited me as I had good and bad days. I had no strict targets, no major stresses and I coasted along for a few months until my energy began to return.

Now, though, my role has completely changed. My work is ecology-oriented and I work as an environmental assessment officer with the Forward Planning section. Simply, that means I assess proposed plans and projects for their potential to have negative environmental consequences. It's a busy role, a stressful role in which I feel as though I have to be the enemy. I'm quite frequently torn between my role to protect habitats and species, morally and legally, and the need (or want) for development. On a national level, many projects and plans are based on stupid ideas, useless policies or just a desperate need for economic gain without the foresight of environmental destruction. It's my role, in my three-day week (all I'm capable of now) to compromise, and to tweak projects so that they'll progress as planned – but with no or few environmental negative consequences. It's often a struggle to strive for sustainable development – when each project is like a battle with my conscience. I said I'm an ecologist but, years later, I'm still employed as an environmental technician. I earn little (even less because of my three-day working week) and I am junior to engineers, planners and most other technical staff who I work with on a daily basis. I've discussed, asked, almost-begged to be considered for another grade so my salary – and hopefully my status – can be amended. I arranged meetings with four directors within my section, a senior engineer and my immediate boss – who promised that in time a role would be made available for me to suit my qualifications and the new work I undertake. I'm still waiting at least three years later. Because I work three days I feel that I don't have a great argument for demanding more; my circumstances prevent me from being as reliable as I would always have imagined I would be. Or maybe I'm being too passive?

Today, not for the first time, I decided I am being too passive so I spoke to my manager about my now-overdue promotion. Weeks ago, I submitted my CV to him along with a well-structured letter pleading my case, demanding even, yet again, that my work, always so thoroughly-researched and well-prepared, be acknowledged for what it is; a good job that deserves some recognition. His response with regard to my promotion was, once again, a negative one. He acknowledged my work and had recommended me for a promotion, endorsed my letter and CV, but his honest answer today was not to hold my breath.

So, that's how it is. Right now, I am still reeling, still angry and still feeling my face redden with anger and frustration and annoyance and exasperation. How bloody unfair? How bloody cruel and horribly, incredibly unscrupulous of them? I feel so annoyed and small; like someone has walked, no, trampled right on top of me. I just feel that there's zero respect or appreciation…

But, tomorrow is my birthday and I've got my 40th and a well-deserved day off work to look forward to.

Low

12th October 2014

Dear James,

Life for me has been busy – in a good way. There have been quite a few events so in the first nine days of my 40s I'm proving that life doesn't slow down or become boring! I've always been an enthusiast for celebrations. I like to mark special occasions with cakes, cards – and moments. I'm unlike my sisters and my parents who actually dread birthdays, allow certain dates to just pass by and, worst of all, really don't enjoy Christmas!! I call myself Christmas Karol in December, loving Christmas music, movies, decorations, food and the special ambiance that only happens at that time of year. There's always a warm and cosy feeling too, when people become nostalgic, a little more emotional and kind for a few weeks once a year. So, I go all out, spending money I don't really have on gifts people don't need (or want) just because. . . I also love recognising the first day of spring, anniversaries and Easter, and I love birthdays! Birthdays are personal celebratory occasions when you get to feel special for just being born, to be treated because it's your once-a-year special day. My fortieth birthday was amazing. It happened on a Friday so instead of spending my special day with work colleagues who may or may not know the significance of the event for me (big 4-0) I took annual leave and spent the day doing exactly what I wanted.

I got quite a few cards in the post, and literally just spent the day doing what I liked – visiting the beach (still warm), having a nice lunch and blowing out 40 candles on a cake! My boyfriend also gave me an amazing present – the details of a trip we're to take in December – to Reykjavík! We are going to Iceland to see the Northern Lights, the Blue Lagoon, the Golden Circle and whales. I'm so very excited! The prospect of visiting a country known for geysers and volcanoes, short days and interesting animals is just so exhilarating. It's a place that's always fascinated me and fabulous to have something really cool to look forward to December.

One of my movie heroines is Katniss Everdeen – of the Hunger Games. She fights for her life in a movie trilogy – using her bow and arrows. I took an archery lesson as another birthday treat. It was so fun and actually quite challenging. After a few hours I was quite proficient, whether by luck or talent! After I got my hair done before we met my family for my dinner party. I organised a family reunion / birthday party for Sunday afternoon. It was an excuse to gather my immediate family and boyfriend to mark my special day or weekend. (It was also an excuse to have a birthday party my reluctant family wouldn't have otherwise organised – I didn't mind).

So, that is how my birthday festivities went. Fun and happy!

Yesterday we were at a wedding, and it was a fun day, sunny and so enjoyable. We began our journey before 10am and were still standing around chatting at 2am. Weddings are such long days though. I still have to be convinced about the merits of a traditional Irish wedding. Church, large gap in the middle of the day where drinkers get drunk and non-drinkers chitchat, dinner, speeches, wedding band (cringey or otherwise) and DJ. Long day – drawn out event or a welcomingly extended bunch of hours of bliss for one bride and groom – and their happy families and fans? Either way, I had a good day. I felt pretty; hair up, nice jewellery, minimal-yet-adequate amount of fake tan – and a beautiful new blue dress with a cowl neckline and diamantes I first wore to my cousin Norah's wedding in July. I am definitely not in a relationship with a dancer which is disappointing – I've tried again and again to take dance lessons with him, but it still hasn't happened. So we danced, but not well. As with every social occasion, questions were asked about my non-drinking – I'm still wondering why he hasn't said anything to his family about my historic liver transplant and the reason I don't drink. I find myself taking tablets behind closed doors, or at opportune times when I think no-one is looking. I have no problems in admitting I had a transplant in 2006 – and the reasons why. I'm proud of how far I've come and happy that I can live my life practically normally as a transplant recipient. This bothers me a little, though he just claims its no-one else's business to know. When I'm away for weekends, my routine, so carefully adhered to at all other times, is completely thrown out with late breakfasts, early lunches and not fasting for long enough periods between food and immunosuppressants. I'm a fool for not standing up for myself – for changing my careful routine just to blend in and cover up. If they knew they'd completely understand. It's my business to tell if I wish, I have no problems with people knowing...but he's just so secretive about it...is it embarrassment?

I digress – I ended the night with a strong desire to escape my dress which appeared to have tightened considerably around my middle during the day. I stood at the bar talking to other wedding guests, feeling very uncomfortable and self-conscious of my fatter tummy. I am still large today, damn it. It must be a food allergy or symptoms of irritable bowel syndrome. I drank a stupid amount of coke yesterday too – maybe I've gas? Whatever, I hope it goes down over the next few days. It's not exactly flattering.

20th November 2014

Dear James,

Today I caught myself wondering if I'll live to see Christmas.

You see, some things have changed for me in the last few weeks. In October I was plunged into the nightmare I always feared returning but always hoped wouldn't. It returned, not necessarily in the form I had imagined, but in another form, equally as horrendous, dreadful and ominous. Since 2006, I've imagined myself as being in a grey room / space. Once I had undergone a liver transplant, I was moved from a white room with everyday normal people into a grey room, waiting movement into the next place – a darker room with little light – or life. It's like once I had a transplant I became somewhat detached from other 'healthy' people; I found it harder to relate to them as there was a lack of understanding on their part of my life and how it had changed and consequently changed me. Yes, I had a transplant, but more than that – I had faced death, acknowledged that my life had almost ended and there was almost no hope for my survival. In the early months and years after leaving hospital, that was what I struggled the most with. I couldn't relate to other people. I felt different, almost nervous and deeply irritated by other people, impatient and quick to get angry. I wanted to scream at the top of my voice at people to listen to me, to hear what I had been through and to learn from me that life is so short, so unpredictable and so uncertain. They seemed to be 'sweating the small stuff' – I felt above that, recognising, and sometimes suffocating in life-and-death worries and fears. I knew that it's necessary – vital – to live every day, to make life count and be aware that life is finite – and really brief.

Initially, while I strove to be continuously positive and optimistic, I found myself rushing to fit as much into my days as possible. I wanted to 'live' every day, to make my life matter, to 'use' my life and make the most of the chance I was given. Sometimes that meant I ran out of energy or wore myself out trying to fit so much into every day. Eventually I realised, or time forced me to realise, that living meant doing normal stuff like spending time with family and friends, enjoying holidays and trying to acknowledge life going on around me. It also meant just having ordinary days with no rushing, no frantic attempts to make special events occur every day – that's not the way life is. A normal uneventful day can be a day with better memories than a frantic day of struggling to 'make it count'. Being mindful became very important to me – being aware of the present time, of me in the present. I learned that being mindful is another way of living life to the full.

I'm avoiding the real reason I chose to write today, so here goes. . .

On Thursday, 16th October, I went to my warfarin clinic to have my INR analysed (you know, how thin my blood is so I'll know what concentration of warfarin to take). I had noticed persistently itchy feet for a few days, so much so that I woke myself from my constant scratching. Because of this and no other reason, I requested that my liver function tests (LFTs) be analysed also. My LFTs have been very stable recently; they became a little unsettled as my immunosuppressants were reduced, very gradually, all the way to 0.5mg. At that level, it was determined by Diarmaid and his team that my body still needed to take a low dose to prevent rejection. Diarmaid's plan to wean me off them completely didn't work in my case, as it had in others. I didn't mind; 1mg twice daily was a very low concentration of immunosuppressants to be taking, and my liver remained well.

Before midday, a call came through from my local hospital; Ita, one of the staff nurses told me that my LFTs weren't so good. My liver enzymes were, in fact, pretty high. They were erratically detached from the normal range. My ALT, generally in the range of 4 to 50 was 308; my ALP, normally less than 129 was 288 and my GGT was 270; it should be less than 36.

I didn't quite panic at first but I did phone St. Vincent's immediately, requesting Diarmaid's registrar. Within hours of that call, I was in the A&E department of St. Vincent's University Hospital with Mum and Dad by my side, Dad having driven the three-hour journey. Hours later, probably about 2a.m., I found myself in a five-bed ward.

The following day, Diarmaid came to see me, smiling and looking unfazed. He suspected a non-too-complicated form of organ rejection. I'd have some IV steroids for a few days but that would likely resolve the issue and get me back to normal. In the meantime, some tests would be run – CT and X-rays.

But, day by day, my LTFs got progressively worse. I had a CT in the much-remembered Radiology Department that I visited so frequently in 2006. At least I had the ability to walk there and manoeuvre myself on the trolley, unlike my weakened, helpless state in 2006.

Then a Thursday morning.

Diarmaid came to see me. I remember I had just washed my hair. It was still damp and in a long plait but it smelled nice and fruity; living in a hospital doesn't always allow one to feel fresh. He sat beside my bed, looking down at the shiny floor. The registrar, SHO and Jennifer, liver transplant coordinator, stood beside him. Someone, I'm not sure who, pulled the curtain around my bed. My heart throbbed and I felt my face become white. They all looked serious; I knew they were delivering bad news.

Diarmaid told me the scan revealed a blockage – complete blockage – of my hepatic artery, a HAT (hepatic artery thrombosis). Once again, a blood clot had wreaked havoc on my body. Now, I don't remember much else of what he said. I did ask how it would be unblocked, dissolved, bypassed and he bluntly said that from my aorta to my liver was entirely blocked with a coagulated hardened bloody rope. I had imagined a spherical clot, a small blob. Somehow, I imagined a small blob could be bypassed or 'blasted away' but a complete blockage didn't sound so 'blastable'. I wondered how my liver was surviving, and he mentioned a great network of collaterals – tiny blood vessels supplying blood – apparently enough blood to keep it adequately healthy. The increase in my LFTs demonstrated that it wasn't quite healthy enough and was 'giving out'.

Then they all left me with Jennifer and an illustration of a human liver. She remained, silently willing me, I guess, to ask questions, shout or cry. I had nothing to say, no more queries, no more energy; I just felt flattened – and scared.

She didn't stay long and when she left I sat in a cold sweat. I didn't cry – I was so calm. I felt my heart pounding in my chest. I had dreaded this day for over eight years – the day when my liver would give me reason to be back in hospital, the day it would stop working as efficiently as it had been, the day I would be awaiting another transplant or maybe just awaiting death. In a bizarre way I felt prepared, I felt almost eerily relieved that the day had come. Bizarrely, the uncertainty of when it would come was almost more difficult that the actuality when it did arrive. Is that strange?

I sat on my bed, staring into space – nothing to say, nowhere to go, nothing to do. I felt so powerless at my body's stubbornness in clotting its own blood supply yet again. I couldn't do one single thing. I had no control over what was yet again happening to me.

I'm not certain if the dizziness and room-spinning began that day or a few days later. I'm not sure when my eyes stopped focussing properly. I began to have episodes of unfocussed eyes and severe dizziness. I was certain I was deteriorating rapidly. Now, weeks later, I know that it was shock; my body's reaction to something so overwhelmingly terrifying that I couldn't bear it. I thought it was the end. I thought I was days away from dying. I felt that death was very close.

I obviously didn't die then, but a little of my spirit did. Even though I always knew that my transplant and unprecedented blood vessel manipulations would result in my being ill again, I just didn't know when – or how. Recent clinics up until that day had reassured me and the consultants that I was likely to live a long and normal life; with little or no difference to my life expectancy from that a non-transplantee.

But I never really relaxed. In the months and years post-transplant I read about one-, three- and five-year survival rates. Subconsciously I really never felt safe or confident until 2011, five years on. By relaxing and being more confident about a normal life expectancy somehow always made me feel as though I'd jinx the possibility but that by being constantly alert and expectant of illness and a relapse, I would stay safer. I guess that was the deal – be on alert and never get too confident or cocky about how good my health actually was, and that way I would stay well.

That morning, once I was left on my own, I began to make plans. I contacted my solicitor about updating my 10-year-old will and texted some friends. I also paid off my credit card bill and compiled a list of songs to be played for me during my funeral. I wrote some letters – to my family, and one to be read out at my impending funeral. It was very angry and hot-headed. I read it again recently and it definitely wasn't an appropriate insight into the real me. It was just too irate and enraged. I destroyed it.

Dr. Murphy came to see me and, genuinely saddened, likened my situation to a bolted horse. Basically, too late and too little, I agreed to the cytoreductive therapy to reduce my platelet counts. The irony! The fucking horrific, nagging, cytoreductive agent / chemotherapy that I could have been taking for months – hindsight was having the last laugh. I was placed on prophylactic medication – after the horrific damage was done. I agreed to taking it – what was left to lose? I began a tri-weekly dose of hydroxycarbamide or hydroxyurea, acknowledging that the side effects would be very closely monitored and taking it last thing at night was probably the best option, given its tendency to result in fatigue. More fatigue!? I was already tired and lethargic.

I left hospital almost two weeks later; in the intervening time I had more scans, ultrasounds and they tried hard to stabilise my INR which had become very erratic. It did not help me one bit that there were a number of little doctors prescribing the completely wrong dose of warfarin which I had to fight about daily to get a more appropriate dose. Eventually, they just asked my opinion on what dose I thought I should take.

My temperature spiked a few times and my feet continued to itch. But it was my dizziness that scared me – and baffled the doctors. I had a normal blood pressure and neural responses but I kept experiencing severe dizziness and 'blackout' type sensations. Now, I think they might have been symptoms of ET – vision disturbances and transient ischemic attacks – I may be wrong.

I wanted to go home – as soon as I knew that I wasn't going to die immediately. I wanted to feel the normality of home – and escape the drama of other peoples' issues; and, I guess, come to terms with my own new issues.

The SHO who discharged me was a lovely boy from Cork. He told me that when my liver begins to give up on me, it will be gradual – there will be time to make decisions and plans; it will be a much slower process than before. My experience is not likely to be anything like before. So, maybe I get to experience liver transplants from two angles – one a hurried emergency and the other a gradual, slow, painful (?) loss of my liver function. I'm not certain if this really reassures me, but that's the truth of the situation I am now in and I aim to know as much about my health as any doctor – that way I can be involved as much as possible. I need to feel in control – that way I can be more prepared for whatever happens to me in the near, or maybe not so near future…

5th January 2015

Dear James,

It's been a while since I've written. I've thought about it, meant to get some of my meanderings and feelings down on paper – but I truthfully didn't know where to begin. I still don't, I guess, but I'll give it a try. I feel it would be good for me to just explain some of what's been happening; these days I don't feel like I can be completely honest with anyone without fearing repercussions or well-intended advice or looks of pity or worry. I don't want anyone to feel as frightened as I do.

We went to Iceland in December. We flew out on a sunny Friday and I admit I was full of apprehension. I wanted to go, obviously - I just wasn't certain that a foreign trip which promised to be quite active would be such a good idea. Before the delayed flight I pulled on my 'beautiful' compression stockings, drank lots of fluids and took as much exercise as possible. The last part wasn't really difficult – we carried our bags onboard so that meant a lot of wheeling, hauling and lifting. The trip was not really what I envisaged. I imagined Iceland as a country similar to Austria with meadows, Northern lights dancing in the starry skies and geysers bubbling up from random locations. We got an idyllic snowy Iceland with Christmas lights twinkling in every window, a quaint Reykjavik with happy people - and a lot of bitterly cold days. But, we wrapped up well and had a very busy few days of whale-watching (unfortunately no whales), Northern lights-chasing (we got lucky and I can say that I experienced the aurora borealis in Iceland!) and photographing geysers, sub-zero waterfalls and snowy landscapes. We had fun, laughed, enjoyed some good food (not always - who wants to eat smoked puffin or cormorant?!) and, despite the 24-hour delay in getting home, a beautiful break.

Sort of.

I tried to ban hospital, blood, livers, transplants and medication from my brain and from my holiday. In truth, I didn't completely succeed. I was in a surreal environment, a yearned-for break in a magical setting and I spent my trip feeling and looking like a heavily-pregnant woman. I'm talking six months pregnant-can't-fit-into-regular-clothes abdominal distension. For the few days before I travelled I was kidding myself by taking laxatives for my 'constipation' but deep down I knew the truth. I had ascites. I should remind you that ascites is a leaking of fluid into the space that separates the inside lining of the abdomen from the area storing the abdominal organs. That's the medical definition but the way ascites feels is something that few consultants or hepatologists have or will possibly ever experience. Ascites feels like a ridiculous amount of liquid has been poured into your abdomen and your back aches from the pressure of supporting it. There's no escaping the sheer discomfort of carrying a tub of liquid and, in bed, turning over involves supporting your tummy while you try and swivel your back around. I get cramps too – like my body resents this invasion of unwanted heavy fluid. Walking is also difficult as the fluid pulls from side to side and you feel like you've a full bladder and a need to use the toilet very quickly. I'm too much of a lady to discuss the difficulty in wiping one's rear with a huge abdomen and short arms and will also refrain from describing how ascites seems to have added to my bra size.

I'm generally a little over 50 kg but my weight over the two weeks prior to Iceland had increased to 53.5 kg. I knew this wasn't just regular bloating and not likely to be constipation either. I ignored the signs to go to Iceland. When I got on the plane, I felt terrified that I'd made the wrong decision – that if anything was to go wrong I would be in serious trouble, stuck in quite a conservative country where, I'm certain, the liver transplant record isn't as advanced as Ireland or elsewhere. I hadn't travel insurance either – scarily, a few weeks before the trip I discovered that no insurance company would take me on. However, apart from one episode of severe cramping and tummy pains (which passed after a few hours and many minutes on a toilet in a quaint bar) and the ridiculously huge abdomen aside, I survived the trip unscathed and without any medical intervention. But, while I had an amazing experience, there was a strong feeling of relief when I landed back in Ireland.

The day after I came back I met with Dr. Murphy. She began my appointment with a chat about Iceland but within minutes delivered some news. I had iron-deficiency anaemia and my platelet count had dropped to less than the recommended minimum limit. The anaemia meant that my bone marrow was producing small red blood cells with less haemoglobin because of a deficiency of iron – no wonder my nails had been breaking so much and my energy levels weren't particularly great. The drop in my platelet count was due to my newly-introduced and previously much-discussed medication, hydroxyurea. For most people who take hydroxyurea or another cytoreductive agent, their platelet count is at a concentration significantly above the normal range at 1.5 million, and hydroxyurea (HU) aims to reduce the blood cell count, ensuring fewer clotting-platelets. For me, frustratingly, my platelet count has been in the normal range since my transplant (or since my extensive thrombosis) but it is deemed likely that these excess platelets are pooling in my spleen. The hydroxyurea was fulfilling its role in reducing my platelet count in my circulatory system shown by a regular blood test but how could my haematologist manage my platelet count based on only those in my blood vessels when the remaining excess platelets produced by my over-enthusiastic bone marrow appear to be in my spleen? My platelet count was after my trip was 145,000 /µL so hydroxyurea was suspended. I can only imagine that such a low platelet count, in addition to aspirin and warfarin would be a horribly dangerous combination should I fall or cut myself. I'd burst rather than break if I was in an accident! I could see the frustration on her face; showing, I think, her annoyance that my disorder was proving very difficult to manage. I also saw sadness or pity - or both. Me; I just felt angry and sad – hydroxyurea, despite the huge list of known side effects, seemed to agree with me; I was tolerating it very well so the possibility of a new / alternative drug meant more guinea pigging for me. . .

Before my consultation ended, I mentioned my distended abdomen and my 'constipation'. She examined me and, yes, it certainly was ascites and my spleen was also quite enlarged (more so than usual). I felt like I had just admitted to stealing. I knew that the swollen tummy was ascites for over two weeks but I also knew if I said something that it wouldn't be ignored any longer. So, I had decided to say nothing – so I could travel. Immediately she tried to make contact with Diarmaid. Within a few hours I was making my way to St. Brigid's Ward, the National Liver Unit. With me I had a case and rucksack – both almost entirely containing dirty laundry from my trip.

The last time I stayed in St. Brigid's I had a happy time – in August 2006. I had an infection and there was no danger to my liver. I met some new people and, in general, my experience was fine. I couldn't describe this time as a happy experience. St. Brigid's has changed. I had a bed in a ward with three men, one of whom barely left his bed and when he did, he walked with his eyes closed and his dishevelled hair covering his face. He groaned all night and shouted at the doctors and nurses, abusing anyone who tried to help him. He was 38 and recently diagnosed with cancer.

I hoped to leave him the following day, Friday, once my CT was done and reported on. Christ, I wonder how many times I've had that weird sensation of hot fluid flowing through my body and the metallic taste, the voice telling me to "breathe in and hold your breath" and then "breathe normally"? In the waiting area I was asked by another patient if I was expecting! That hurt! It should be a rule that you never ask a woman when she's due! Back in my bed, Mum arrived to travel home on the train with me, my laundry and my distended abdomen. It didn't happen. Friday evenings are busy and since there was confusion over exactly why I had ascites, I wasn't discharged. My LFTs were still slightly elevated but they were pretty good. This was the Friday before Christmas – the time for shopping, Christmas music, wrapping the last few presents, parties, catching up with friends and just enjoying the nice build-up to the festive season. Instead, I got to spend a weekend with three strange men, dodgy food, no TV and uncomfortable pyjamas.

I didn't see Diarmaid or his registrar over the weekend. I saw two consultants who admitted they were baffled by my distension since my liver was seemingly stable. The CT revealed no changes to my October scan – hepatic artery was still blocked but there were no new clots and my collaterals were still well-organised and established. Other reasons for ascites are kidney or heart failure – it didn't seem like I had either but they weren't happy to send me home with no true diagnosis. . . I was prescribed diuretics and a low-salt diet (try that when your hospital tea consists of rashers and chips!) and advised to get out of hospital for a while over the weekend.

I won't share with you the experience of my shopping trip as my hospital leave. I'll just say I was like a briar – a frustrated, angry, sad and tired woman who just wanted to go home... I eventually did, the day before Christmas Eve. (The consultant responsible for my discharge claimed he couldn't be responsible for the tears of a young woman!)

During Christmas with my parents I continued with my crankiness but let me enlighten you as to why. While my ascites was responding to the diuretics and my tummy was looking more like the one I knew and recognised, I began to have cramps and an upset stomach. Maybe it was just a cold but on a few occasions the toilet bowl was filled with fresh blood. On another few occasions, my stools were 'tarry' or tinged with blood. Every change brought something new to deal with and I knew that mentioning these issues to any of my consultants would bring me straight back to hospital. Telling my parents or sisters would be worse, so I said nothing, buried my head in the sand and hoped it would resolve itself.

Today, though I'm on a course of diuretics or water tablets, the ascites is back with a vengeance. My back aches and my clothes don't fit. I feel like I've eaten a ridiculous amount of food but it's just stuck in my intestines. I saw more blood in the toilet today and my body is covered in huge blue, brown and red bruises. This is so very hard. When did my life turn into an unmanageable nightmare?

I saw a movie at the weekend and the main character is fighting cancer. He's been sick, undergone chemotherapy and radiation and is described as in remission; his lung tumour has shrunk by 80%. I found myself wishing I had cancer! I know it's a horrible, dangerous and sometimes-fatal affliction but with cancer there are many sufferers, many years of experience in fighting and controlling the disease – and there's generally a management plan with cancer. I don't have a plan. I don't know if my consultants have a plan. They are monitoring my bloods and treating my ascites and blood disorder but I feel so lost that I haven't a clear and definite plan. It strikes me that they're waiting for my condition to deteriorate to the point where I need a re-transplant. I don't like that plan; waiting to get worse before I can identify what I'm fighting for. Right now, I just go from week to week with a desperate hope that my LFTs continue to reduce. They do. Is it possible that my collaterals will serve me and my liver for months or years? I don't know. Is it possible to replace my hepatic artery? No, I know the answer to that is a definite no. Is it possible that everything will eventually settle back to the way it was and I can go back to living as a regular liver transplant recipient? Or a regular ET patient? There are no people with a story like mine within the MPN Voice community. They have ET and its symptoms, associated fears and concerns. But I've not found anyone living with a large inoperable blood clot. Is it possible to find someone, anyone I can relate to? I don't know. I don't know what I'm fighting for or working towards. I have no control over my collaterals or my LFTs. No control over my bile duct and the pressure it is now apparently under. I am literally at the mercy of my uncooperative body and while I need a plan and want to focus on my goal, there doesn't seem to be one for me right now. Mum and Dad are praying. I'm doing a little too, but I want to do something a little more proactive. I want to fight for my life. I want to fight and win.

But today, when I woke up and sadly saw that my ascites was still there, I decided to eat chocolate with my breakfast. I had a chocolate flake and branflakes for lunch. Fuck it, I worked so hard for almost nine years to stay well and keep my liver and my body happy. Now, it's become unhappy and is trying to pull me back into that known and much feared territory that I feel like all of my careful routines have been pointless, my avoidance of anything 'liver-harming' have been in vain. Today I feel reckless – and also so very, very sad.

3rd March 2015

Dear James,

I feel like I've had enough. I'm tired, unfocussed and so frustrated. Five months ago, I turned 40, I had a fabulous weekend – and I hadn't felt so happy such a long time. I felt like I had so much love and joy in my life – and I recognised it. I felt loved, cherished, spoiled and, apart from a lot of hassle at work I felt like I had few problems. I was beginning to relax and feel healthy – that my liver was now my own; it was settled – and maybe I was one of the lucky ones who could expect to live into old age. I had undergone so many challenges, had won my fight and felt I truly deserved to relax and feel 'free'.

Within two weeks of my birthday, I was thrown into a bloody mess of a world, and left reeling with the news that my liver was deeply unhappy. The prognosis then was vague – weekly blood monitoring to establish how fast the likely deterioration would happen. Now, five months later, I'm still reeling, still monitoring, still not working; the only prognosis is in the escalation of my mental state from good to not-so-good. Today, I feel frustrated. I am definitely much more tired than before – be that from new medication or the 'ramping up' of my blood disorder. I feel unrested after eight or nine hours of sleep and look forward to bed after I eventually manage to get up in the mornings. I am struggling with the management of my it all – keeping my bloods in check, my diet healthy, my mind healthy and balanced and my medication cupboard topped up. Every day is a day of worry about what my future holds, if my collateral blood flow will be sustained for weeks, months or days or if I will be facing a re-transplant in a year or in a few short months. My main fear now is of dying. I am terrified and so not ready but – and I hate hate hate to admit this – I feel I am facing it and am in a place where I'm closer to death than I was ever before. I don't want to go but I find myself thinking of my funeral so often and imagining if I will be with my aunts and uncles who have died (unfortunately, I'm not certain I'm convinced about life after death). I think of James Stewart, Corey Haim and Leonard Nimoy and my grandparents and struggle to imagine a 'place' where they all exist alongside each other. . .

The worst thing about this worry and anxiety is that there are no certainties about when it will all end – or be resolved. I have no idea if I'm 'stable' for the medium term or when my liver or bile duct will eventually 'pack in'. I don't know if I'm worrying unnecessarily right now about something horrible that might not happen for another 10 years or whether the very thing I am worrying about might not even happen – there's always the possibility of another thrombosis – in my lung, leg or elsewhere. Okay, that is morbid!

Generally, I try to be positive, pray a little, hoping that I can beat death again – maybe my clot will clear (unlikely) – and try to live in the now.

But today (and some other days), I have a very short fuse and am so frustrated by the uncertainties that I am facing.

I also feel so very alone.

Mum and Dad are great – they think about me all the time and offer me support in so many ways – including financially (which makes me feel so inadequate and helpless, a failure even). My sisters too and friends care and offer advice, love and support.

While I appreciate them so much, I don't find the solace I need in their support and love. I want to be strong, healthy, independent, successful, ambitious, and energetic and now I'm just sad, weak and tired – and I feel so alone in this. There is not one person in my transplant clinic who can associate with my story. No one with essential thrombocythaemia had a transplant and is now the owner of another liver clot. It doesn't help that my consultants always told me how special and amazing my case was – now I'm an outlier in a statistical database. Last clinic I looked at the women and men pre- or post-transplant and felt so alone. Some had jaundiced eyes and skin, gaunt faces and large ascitic abdomens – I felt sorry for none of them. Is this what I've become? A cold heartless selfish creature who cares about no-one but herself. I just felt sorry for me. I felt sorry for me because my transplant will be a very complicated surgery. An improvised hepatic vein and a non-functioning hepatic artery; who would want to face a life-saving transplant with such shit odds?! Not me.

I felt so alone in clinic. Many cases are complicated but most people appear to have a clinical management plan. Again, it feels like I have no plan, no knowledge of what to expect, when or how. I'm just rolling along, like the proverbial piece of tumbleweed. What sort of life is this?

If there is one human being out there who is facing the same unknown territory? I need to feel that someone, just one human being understands and walks in similar shoes to mine.

I wish I had a known, understood and more clear fight to face, not this vague, stupid fucking unsureness (is that a word?) where there are fuck-all answers and no peace of mind.

Today I am struggling with a scrambled mind full of unanswered questions and tasks I feel I must undertake. That leads to pressures and anxiety when I don't meet my targets on my bucket list. I will try to be nicer to myself, to go easier on myself and to try and slow down – to 'be' and not to 'do' a little more. It's proving difficult, so frigging stressfully difficult when I wake in the morning and my mind is whirring with stuff to do and tasks to address before I. . . before I what? Get better and go back to work? Become sicker and die?

No idea, no clarity. That's what's killing me now.

26th March 2015

Dear James,

I feel happier. Over the last few days I've experienced little flutterings of joy which I haven't felt in – well, it seems like years. I haven't felt this well in ages (since October and my diagnosis, I mean). I think the reason for this joy is the most basic of human emotions – love. I feel loved and cherished by my family and other people in my life. They literally are as empathetic as possible, putting themselves into my shoes and trying to understand what I'm going through; sometimes expressing my emotions of frustration and anger better than I can.

Recently, for whatever reason, I've been cleaning my house of all its clutter – momentos of previous relationships, old clothes and books, bills, payslips. . .the list goes on. I was a hoarder; now I've become a ruthless disposal expert. There's a real feeling of control and satisfaction in throwing out ridiculous amounts of junk that's been cluttering my home for years. It's liberating, I suppose. Thirteen bags of waste, recycling and charity items – and counting. Bizarrely (and thankfully) I seem to have overcome my debilitating energy issues to pursue my goal to have a more spacious home.

Last weekend I met with my very dear friends who I have since college all those years ago. We went for coffee, got ourselves ready for going out (always fun for women) and went for a beautiful dinner. Unlike the not-too-distant past we all opted for a quiet pub in which we could chat – no ambitions to dance or be exposed to drunken idiots looking to score. As with every time I meet the girls (women?!) I learn something new about them – something that certainly wasn't there when we were in our twenties. There's a new anxiety associated with adulthood – so many worries, so many issues. How different we all are now! In college, we fretted over exams, cramming, rent money (trying to get serious value for money!), job prospects, our life decisions – and boys - or, in some of our cases, the lack thereof. Don't get me wrong – I admired and was admired quite a lot but my crippling shyness prevented me from acting upon it. Shyness and low self-esteem; I dodged the slow sets by disappearing to the ladies', said "no, thanks" if any man managed to get a word in en route and sometimes I even pretended not to hear dance requests by ostentatiously engaging in 'deep and meaningful conversations' with my girlfriends.

Last weekend I noticed that we have aged – physically of course – but also in our attitudes, our aspirations and our core values. Me, now I feel trapped in this time, unable to grow or develop any more than I am – I feel I'm being pulled back from progressing by the thing that takes up the most time, space and energy in my life – my health issues. The others' worries have evolved into 'mother responsibilities', spirituality, education and career progression (I would have deemed myself the careerist of the bunch at one time), house issues, financial pressures - and fashion / accessories.

I feel left out, excluded from the regular worries that most women my age have. I don't for one second make light of their concerns but I envy them. I envy the luxury (does that make sense) of worrying about money, career and children. I felt alone with my crazy worries of frustrating blood, side-effects from meds, my fragile liver and all the other unforeseeable worries that I don't even know are possible (what is this horrible cramping that hits me regularly or this tightening back pain that prevents me from moving my right arm?). I know that my friends aren't invincible and I know they won't be and probably aren't perfectly healthy, but their worries are 'common' and familiar – mine are fucking rare and unusual – even at my hospital consultations.

Now, in the company of my friends I don't know who I am. The careerist? The intellectual? The logical-minded one? The introvert? The sometimes-rebel? The straight-talker? Or just the poorly one? I'm not sure. I think I like to be thought of as some of the above.

I am trying to focus on the positive stuff as my psychotherapist is teaching me how to do. It's important to try to be hopeful, positive and to keep 'healthy' and active. Sometimes, but maybe not today, the hopeful positivity is waning. I realise I must try to balance the uncertainties (the future / my collaterals / liver health) with my life's certainties. I struggle with this but it seems like the logical thing to do, the healthy way to approach life.

I am alive, I can breathe, I can drive, I can cook, I can eat, I can enjoy music and I can love. There are certainly others on that 'can do' list but I can't think of any right now.

Anyway, I tried to take that girly weekend off from my worries and tried to have fun with my girlfriends; chatting, laughing and reminiscing. . . While it wasn't a very late night, the fatigue kicked in on Sunday evening and continued into Monday and Tuesday (when I felt like a zombie). It was worth it though – it felt so warm and familiar to be with people I could just be myself with.

Today, I met with my haematologist and yesterday with my hepatologist.

Mum travelled to Dublin with me and last night, in our hotel room, we chatted and had fun. When, at 5 am we woke to hear other guests praying (loudly) on the floor below us, we laughed until we almost cried as we tried to sleep but their murmurings continued for hours.

I had a good consultation today. I feel well – despite my now-worsened hand tremors, painful cramping and occasional palpitations. I am genuinely worried now about work; in so many ways I want to go back but am so terrified of the tough decisions, huge responsibilities and my noticeable zap in energy. Now seems like a good time for new plans but I don't feel as though I have options. I'm just not deemed reliable right now. Dr. Murphy offered to write to my employers and confirm that I am being very closely monitored, we don't know how my energy levels will be and that easing into work one or two days per week may be the most logical solution for everyone - especially me, obviously.

I felt like hugging her; she offered me such support and understanding, empathy and sense. It was like a huge load was lifted from my shoulders.

That feeling of joy from this display of support, understanding and reassurance is just immeasurable!

11th April 2015

Dear James,

Do you hear me calling to you? Are you hearing me asking you for help? Asking that you stay with me and we continue to work as a team for another while? I need you and want you to stay with me. We fought together for over nine years. At first I resented you, you know this, but then I began to live my life with you. I felt I owed you that, I felt that I had to live every single day to the best of my ability to show you that I felt grateful, so grateful to you for your gift. I realised over time that I can only live for myself. I had to be true to myself and listen to my body. That the days I didn't want to get out of bed, couldn't summon the energy to face the day – I had to learn that they weren't wasted days; they weren't dishonourable days to you. I received your liver but, and I still find this difficult to say, I don't owe you anything for it. I mustn't forget that there were no conditions attached – by you at least. The conditions that were attached, the caveats, were that I must live a controlled life with a routine and as long as I maintain the routine, take my medication, avoid infections and 'dangerous' situations, I should live as long as any other person within the normal population.

Unfortunately that little promise I felt I received hasn't been kept. I don't blame anyone, not Diarmaid or the surgeons, not the coordinators or the other nurses – and not me. I did nothing to provoke this fresh attack on my body. And I know that no-one foresaw this. Well, I suppose my haematologist did – or she gave me the option of trying to prevent the new thrombus. So, maybe I just blame me for not agreeing to chemotherapy when she recommended it two years ago. I don't though. If I have to deem anyone or anything responsible I would have to call my evil blood to the stand. It's thick with platelets, large, sticky irregular platelets being pumped out at a ridiculous rate from my bone marrow. I can't control it, even though it's a part of me. I try and visualise it flowing healthily through all my veins, arteries and especially my arterioles. It needs to flow; it must keep bringing oxygenated blood to my liver.

So, today, I am calling out for your help. I need you again. I appreciate this liver; I've become very fond of it and don't want to lose it any day soon. You are part of my life now and I don't want you to leave. I have learned, just in the last few years, to live as a transplant recipient. I have learned that living my own life as happily and as fully as I can is how I'm supposed live. Not by pushing myself to 'enjoy every day' or by keeping lists to ensure each day has been 'productive' and I don't need to feel guilty that I've wasted a day, wasted one of our days. Please help if you can. I want to stay as I am for as long as I can. I'm not venturing into goals or targets. I'm absolutely terrified of asking for years, months or weeks. I'm now living day by day, not making large-scale plans for the future, though some people in my life don't seem to realise this (is it my fault that I haven't made it completely clear that nothing is certain?). I am happy to remain 'stable' and keep my head down, avoiding change for as long as I can. You know me, I don't want a transplant. I didn't want it before and I am so horrifically scared of facing that again, now that I have a statistically significant probability of not making it through.

I've been melancholic and lethargic these last few days. There's little fun in my life. I'm too busy concentrating on being 'healthy' (or maybe I'll go with 'alive') to have fun. I've walked in the woods, I've done some gardening, practised my music and kept the house clean and organised. NOT FUN! I think my nightmares and poor sleep don't help my mood. My immunosuppressant medications have, like all meds, side effects. Kidney issues, diarrhoea, anxiety, heartburn, tremors, headache and hallucinations to name a few. I don't notice any side effects – I never read the list as I

117

guess I worry about psychosomatic effects – but I do experience hallucinations. Biting badgers, men with guns, tall women with large staffs – usually all chasing me and wanting to kill or hurt me. I wake up regularly crying or shouting at shadows in my bedroom, shaking in fear as I try to escape my predators. I see them so clearly – in my bedroom, at my bedside. It would be funny if it wasn't!

5th May 2015

Dear James,

The swallows are back!! I saw them last Thursday at the lake, wheeling and circling over fields and water, so happy to have arrived at their destination. Now I feel safe and secure. Illogical and ridiculous though that sounds, I feel happy and safe during that period when the swallows, swifts and martins are nearby. Their presence, their vigour, energy, freedom, fun-loving ducking and diving seems to assure me that I will be well for a while at least. I can't explain it - this certainty, this complete belief and enthusiasm.

I am usually so afraid to say aloud that I feel well and my optimism and hopefulness is returning – I might jinx the situation. Since October my brain has been muddled, everything has been in shadow except the news that my artery is blocked, muddled with the uncertainty of what's to come and the terrifying fear and horrible hopelessness that there is nothing, nothing I can do about it. Suddenly, very recently, coinciding with the return of my amazing happy birds, I find myself planning for the future (just never too far forward!). I've begun to buy nice things for myself, begun to smile and enjoy good days and even the rain. Before, a few months ago especially, I didn't even notice what was happening around me, new growth, tadpoles, bluebells, daffodils. I was turned inwards, concentrating on the uncontrollable – the functioning of elements of a sick body which I can't even see, let alone help.

I've begun swimming again. I think it's important to stay fit and get as much exercise and oxygen as possible. It seems like the right thing to do – supply rich blood throughout my body – to my heart and also my liver. Maybe more exercise and oxygen will result in better collateral blood flow. It also makes me happy so it must be good for me.

I've thought long and hard about my 'OCD list' today – at last. It was difficult. I judge it very negatively, branding myself obsessive and ridiculous to have a list of things to do every day. It's been there for quite a few years but recently I've become tougher on myself to get through the items daily. If I don't it's like I'm not honouring my liver – or you. If I don't get through the list I beat myself up for not having a 'full day'. I deem the list ridiculous and unnecessary yet I force myself to stick to it; I make myself get through the six items daily, including practising my clarinet, getting in contact with friends and family, maintaining my personal hygiene routine and getting at least 30 minutes of exercise.

My opinion of the list is of distain and negativity; self-criticism and impatience.

After examining it more closely I realised something. All tasks are similar in that they are self-improving, nurturing and caring tasks which enhance my life and demonstrate my love for myself. I want to enjoy my music, exercise, feed and cleanse my body and maintain contact with friends and family. Another element linking my list items is that I have control over how I look after myself and how I protect my body. I lost some of that control in 2006 and again with my October episode, but I'm holding firmly to the elements of my life that I can control. I'm retaining whatever power I can. I imagine rich oxygenated blood feeding my liver, and feel that my music brings me joy and self-satisfaction. While I still feel my judgement on my daily list is quite negative, it looks different and less 'wrong' to me now from another angle. It also demonstrates to me how little control I have over the inner workings of my body and how I've subconsciously taken back as much control as possible. My artery silently clotted, in a few minutes? Hours? Weeks? Who knows? The collaterals formed to take its place. Were they always there or did they just generate when necessary? When did that all happen? In Canada? Before my birthday? After my 40th?

I hate not knowing the details. Pinpointing the exact time and cause (apart from my blood disorder 'ramping up') would somehow give me some peace, something to cling onto.

The only changes I see following my arterial thrombosis are a number of minute tiny red blood vessels weaving their way along the right section of my transplant scar and a matching network of blue veins (not great to look at!) on my right side – mirroring a river valley pattern. Are they good or bad? Necessary or dangerous? I have so many questions for Diarmaid. I don't feel my consultations have been all that useful and assuring of late. I need more. I need more than any human can give to me. Something bad might never happen? Nothing bad might happen? I might be okay for a while? I might avoid a transplant – I want that for as long as is humanly possible.

My friend texted me yesterday with news of her father. He had heart bypass surgery last week but has had a number of strokes since then and yesterday he didn't talk at all; just slept. I've known him all my life – as my friend's father. Yet I've had one adult conversation with him. He spoke to me when I came home from hospital in 2006. I called to visit my friend who came running out and hugged me in the front garden. I looked very sickly then – jaundiced and horribly thin with a protruding abdomen. My teeth were huge in my tiny shrunken face. She told me I looked terrible. We laughed. Her Dad looked at me and sternly instructed me to never scare them again the way I had done. I told him I'd try my very best.

I'm sad he's sick, sad he's not likely to ever be the same again.

It also makes me feel two things.

It brings me back to the morning in St. Andrew's Ward when Diarmaid told me I had a HAT and he didn't look me in the eye. Death seemed so close. The world around me kept moving, sounds remained, voices kept talking, the world outside of me remained happy and 'normal', unconcerned and unaffected.

The world didn't stop, people kept breathing and eating, holidaying, working, washing, cleaning.

My world stopped. It felt like it chugged to slow motion, then stopped. But the hustle and bustle of life continued elsewhere. I wonder is that what death feels like, the final few minutes slow down while the outer world still flies by, shadows racing around, the air still circulating, birds still singing when it all seems so wrong, rude even, that everything else doesn't stop in some solidarity and unity with a dying person. I think too much sometimes…

The second thought I have of my friend's father being very ill is, if he dies before me, that's another person I know who will take the plunge before me and may be there, wherever there is, when it's my turn.

Against all the odds, I'm outliving people even though I was technically dead at 31.

20th May 2015

Dear James,

I met with Diarmaid today; a long, frank, no-punches-pulled consultation.

The day began with the usual routine. Awake at 05:45 quietly eating breakfast after applying my makeup and putting on my nice clothes. I left the car at the train station and took the 07:28 train to Dublin. With my rucksack on my back, I took the Luas. It was late arriving so I missed my connecting DART to Sydney Parade. Following Jennifer's advice I had arranged to speak with Diarmaid (only him) at 11:30. I made Suite 4 at 11:34, panting and breathless from running (jogging/walking fast). I've been pushing myself recently to stay fit; 'feeling the burn' on hills and controlling my breathing to achieve a better, less-sedentary life. So, happily, I didn't hyperventilate for too long when I arrived. . .

Diarmaid saw me at 12. I had a list – my usual inventory of questions and queries. Some people don't feel the need to know about their condition or prognosis. I want to know everything I can. I want to know about my health and how to enhance it, how to improve my life and ensure I take care of myself properly. I get 'advised' about this 'bad habit' from loved ones, friends and medical people. The former groups seem to have the opinion that I take on too much, that I should maybe do as I'm advised. As time has passed, my close family appreciate that mistakes can be (and have been) made and my knowledge and interest is beneficial to my situation – crucial even. Maybe the latter groups believe my medical issues are not entirely my business? I'm certainly not trying to take over my own care and I have no intention of blaming anyone for my blocked artery and ailing body. I'm too thankful for all the work done by my haematology, hepatology and surgery teams to date to consider blaming anything else but sheer bad luck and my JAK2 mutation. I owe my team of 2006, including Prof., Diarmaid, Dr. Murphy and the surgeons everything. They, and you, saved my life.

So today, I met Diarmaid with my list, not to confront or challenge him. I wanted straight answers about me. I needed to hear the truth about what may be in store. I wanted to know what he has been thinking about my future chances.

I asked all my questions – the obvious and most frightening one being am I heading towards a re-transplant?

He looked me in the eye and told me about two cases of HAT he is familiar with, pre-empting his opinion with a caveat; I will not find any useful meaningful statistics on my own, very unorthodox situation.

The majority of HAT occurs within hours or days post-transplant so the rarer ones (like me) that occur years after a liver transplant get lumped in with the early HAT data, as a consequence of the smaller numbers. For the record, most early HAT patients receive emergency re-transplants or die.

One case of a late onset HAT is of a man who was diagnosed over two years ago. He was promptly assessed for transplant and placed on the waiting list. He remains fine and has recently run a marathon.

The second case Diarmaid mentioned is of a person with late onset HAT who subsequently developed a septic liver abscess and died before a transplant could be performed.

Diarmaid doesn't know what the future holds, can't know, but my LFTs now are very stable and that's a great sign. The only diagnosis he can make is how I am, how I feel now. It definitely sounds less scientific and less medical but how I am doing now is the best diagnostic tool he can use, with my LFTs coming second. Despite my lethargy (so frustrating and never-ending) and heaviness, I feel well, excluding my tremors, dizziness, cramping, anxiety, nightmares and right side pain. On a scale of 1 to 10, the pain is a 2-3, so easily managed.

He advised me to get on with my life and to do absolutely everything I want to do. I must not be limited by something that may never happen (or by something that has happened but has now stabilised). The bit he added was a reminder that when asked if I were a good candidate for a re-transplant the surgeons and other medical team members gave a resounding yes. This is based on how I have been post-transplant, how I have cared for my donor organ and maintained my medical routine, attending appointments etc.

I walked out of there, smiling. I phoned my Mum and Dad and sister who were delighted, genuinely thrilled and relieved for me.

I was so happy too; it felt like a huge horrible weight had been lifted from my shoulders. I felt, for the first time in seven months, free and light.

Am I wrong to feel heavy, stressed and worried again, hours later?

26th June 2015

Dear James,

I feel elated. I feel so happy, confident and in control. This is one of the best phases since October 2014 and my HAT diagnosis. The reason? I am free to do and behave as I want. I don't feel the constraints that have prevented me from feeling this way in such a long time. Emotionally, I've always been in control – afraid to let go and just be. Now, following my recent clash with my mortality it's as though things cannot get any worse – so the small things like the discomfort I feel when trying to socialise are just swept aside. Damn the insecurity, (it's still there, don't mistake this 'new me' for a 'complete' new me), damn the "frig, I shouldn't have said that" or "Karol, that wasn't a funny / smart thing to contribute to the conversation". Now, it's fuck it, and fuck anyone who doesn't want to be in my company. It's like I've sweated the small stuff all my life and this new attitude is a revelation. Now that the huge scary dreaded return-to-illness demon has appeared, I see the huge stuff, the wood for the trees and the small stuff really is meaningless.

Since March 2006, I've described my life as being in a grey corridor – I'm not part of the normal living population (the white room) and not yet dead or dying (the black, dark place). My corridor I share with you has become a darker place since October; sad but true.

But recently, my grey world is better. It's still grey, I'm still in-between places, in an uncertain situation, but the corridor can have some colour sometimes, coloured vibrant paintings on the walls, splashes of red and yellows on the floor. This week I splashed the walls with pinks, greens and oranges. It felt good, so very good.

It reminds me that even with a really tough situation or painful diagnosis there are breaks, spells of joy which are more, much more meaningful and stronger than previous moments of joy.

I love medical dramas, always did. And I've learned a lot from them. One episode of a hospital show remained with me since I saw it years ago. A couple was facing a shorter life together when the wife was diagnosed with a cerebral aneurysm. She and her husband received word that a neurosurgeon could offer her an excellent shot at life – aneurysm-free – if she was prepared to undergo pioneering surgery.

She refused, no hesitation.

The doctors were baffled and tried to convince her that though there were risks involved in the surgery, she was practically guaranteed a normal life expectancy post-surgery but without surgery her life could end at any time, should the aneurysm rupture.

She refused and couldn't be convinced.

They asked her to explain.

It was simple. In her eyes, the situation was black and white. She said that since her devastating diagnosis she had learned how to live. She and her husband had never seen blue skies and puffy clouds, never smelled flowers and never heard birdsong. Since she found out she was dying she had fallen in love again, not just with her husband but with the world around her, the beautiful things she had previously not noticed. She now loved her life and was afraid that if she opted for surgery she would return to existing without living, feeling trapped by money, career and material things, and forgetting to appreciate everything around her.

She wanted, if she had the choice, fewer years of intense joy and happiness than a long life of mundane work, deadlines and a life without love – or a life without living. Her mind was made up and she walked away, hand-in-hand with her husband.

I know it was fiction but since my diagnosis the world has become clearer. The scary thing I've dreaded for over eight years (a problem associated with my blood disorder or liver failure / creakiness) has happened. I've been expecting it and now that it's here, it's less scary and there's an unexplainable relief that the 'dreaded' thing I've been looking over my shoulder for has now arrived.

My happiness these days is more intense. My heart flutters and there are butterflies in my tummy (maybe that's the medication causing palpitations and nausea). Simple things bring joy – robins feeding nestlings, bats wheeling over the river, weepie movies and eating my own cupcakes. I know this is probably a happy phase and there will be tougher times but I am so aware of the happier days now – and that's black and white with clarity!

I also have some nice plans – some already undertaken and others brewing. I'm going to a wedding in September so I have begun my search for a dress, shoes, plans for my hair and accessories. We've booked a hotel for two overnights – and the day after the wedding we're driving to Dublin airport for a two-week holiday in the south of France! Yeah! I feel great, I look well and, generally, I am doing well. My HAT is still very much there but my liver is fighting a good fight and I haven't been admitted to hospital since late last year. I obviously still attend outpatients' appointments but everything is quite settled and steady.

Hydroxyurea is agreeing with me. I'm tolerating it once again. I take it three times weekly to lower my blood counts – within reason. With fewer platelets, there's less chance of them clumping and causing clotting. I wear gloves when handling it and take it before bed as it definitely causes drowsiness – but I'm genuinely very accustomed to fatigue so what's a little more? I haven't returned to work on my haematologist's advice but it could be soon. That's good news, in many ways.

oOo

We had a break in Italy last month – taking in Sorrento and Positano and generally just absorbing the west coast of Italy. I tried to take it easy – generally my holidays consist of touring, late nights, early starts and lots of sightseeing. This holiday, I planned to read, lie around, swim a little – and just relax. It didn't quite work out like that; I had to explore. When I'm on holidays, I just can't settle; I've always been happier to keep moving and discovering. So, every morning, I read my book and rested. In the evenings, however, we walked and toured, searched for nice restaurants and planned the following days. The sunshine, the swimming pools, great views and cobbled streets of Sorrento all contributed towards a really refreshing break.

I'm living – trying to keep on moving!

17th July 2015

Dear James,

Well, I have returned to the workplace after nine months. I meant to write the day I returned but I was too tired! That day went well; everyone was so kind, some were unbelievably curious or just damned nosy. "I'm doing better" was my truthful, unexpanded, undetailed response to most queries. It was a phrase that told a story without detail I didn't want or need to give. Nothing much has changed for me. I have an inoperable blood clot in my hepatic artery; I may need a re-transplant but that's something my consultant isn't advising right now. I am taking more drugs than ever before, including hydroxyurea, which wipes me out and seems to result in a deep right side back pain. It also makes my stomach upset and causes severe dehydration (I'm definitely drinking more fluids these days!). However, that's it – apparently that means it's agreeing with me and I've no dramatic reactions to it.

In the meantime, I'm trying to focus on other, happier things and live life without analysing and worrying too much. I am literally excited about the prospect of an upcoming day out for me. I've signed up for a 'playday' in a music college in Galway – something like a summer camp for adult musicians. There are likely to be at least 20 amateur musicians there – all wind instruments – and we're to launch the beginning of a wind instrument band, a group that will eventually play at concerts and compete against other groups. I'm so excited that this opportunity will make me feel like a real musician. In addition to meeting with this group every month in Galway, I also intend to gain even more experience by joining the Mayo Concert Orchestra. I love playing my clarinet but, from my few short experiences, playing with others is such a huge joy. When I play in harmony (some of the time) with other musicians, nothing else matters. It's an escape, a break from life that makes me so happy. Music awakens my spirit (if that doesn't sound too naff!) and the pride in my ability also gives me a boost – to know that after a few short years I can actually read music and play along with more experienced people is amazing for my confidence as a person. The rewards from my music have been more than I ever could have imagined.

I also, at last, put my bat detector to good use recently. I persuaded a friend to join me in a bat detection course where we signed up for some voluntary bat surveying work in east Mayo. The course itself was enlightening; examining different species of bats and learning a little more about their habitat and diet preferences. My favourite bat has always been the tiny pipistrelle bat, but the survey was undertaken to quantify Daubenton's bats – another cutie. We walked the length of a river, stopping at intervals to identify and count the natterers species in the dusk. Such an enjoyable evening! Not many people would share my enthusiasm but there was something fun and entertaining about chasing bats in the dark.

A few days ago, I arranged a catch up with a friend I worked with in the EPA. Yes, I still maintain contact with some friends from my past – I spent eight years in total in the Environmental Protection Agency – but I had a particular and very personal motive for meeting up with this guy. Ray, a fellow scientist, described symptoms to me a few years ago that sounded very familiar. He was constantly fatigued and had been observed by his GP as having a very high platelet count. Maybe there were more symptoms but I was not hugely surprised when he shared with me, after meeting with a haematologist, that he too has essential thrombocythaemia. I wanted to meet with Ray to hear about his experiences with ET – I literally don't know anyone else in my life who has this disease, yes, I've made some contacts through the MPN Voice website, but this is an actual person I can talk directly to, discuss symptoms and treatments with and hear about his personal story. The isolation is crippling sometimes – as though I'm the only person with this frustrating blood disease. Meeting Ray was a breath of fresh air. While he's less hands-on and has an attitude to let the experts do their thing – in that we differ enormously – he was full of new information, suggestions and inspiring ideas and in that I really benefitted from chatting with him. He's well, has never experienced clotting episodes and is on treatment to reduce his platelet count. Sometimes one can feel so alone and isolated in the world of illness – just one friend to share it with can certainly lighten the load.

10th August 2015

Dear James,

I had what I can only describe as a meltdown yesterday. After one week of injecting myself with clexane, my abdomen is horribly bruised and tender. I should explain what clexane is and my hate for it. Clinically, clexane is an anti-coagulant or a medicine that thins the blood. It works like warfarin, in that it keeps one's blood running smoothly and should prevent clotting – my ultimate fear. But, unlike warfarin which is a simple tablet (or number of them) taken once-a-day, clexane is dispensed by injection. Its advantage over warfarin is its prompt reversal should blood become too thin or should I bleed too readily – externally or internally! The disadvantage of clexane, though, is that it's simply a painful injection. In my experience, injecting has four nasty stages. After finding and pinching a spot on my abdomen, I insert the needle (nasty step 1), inject the required amount with stingy liquid (nasty step 2), pull the needle out, trying to ensure the tummy fat doesn't get pulled up with the obstinate needle (nasty step 3) and wait for the sting (nasty step 4). Clexane hurts like hell, like no other needle or injection I've ever had AND, I've had to do this twice a day for the last week as I was preparing for a bone marrow biopsy.

But my issues with clexane are not the only problems. I just felt as if, all of a sudden, all of this, my life, its complications, the uncertainties, the pain, the side effects from medication and my absence of life's choices, they just seemed all too much to bear.

I try and live my life as I should, as everyone should. Without limits or without the fear that, at any time, with little warning, my collateral flow might stop and I'll have no blood supply to my liver. Then, I know or suspect that I will be placed on the transplant list but only as a token gesture. I don't think my body will accept another liver with the already convoluted blood supply draining my liver. Now, I have no hepatic artery – and I know the difference between the anatomy of arteries and veins, capillaries and other blood vessels. I try not to think about it too much – its torturous – and surrounding myself with work and 'normal life' and people helps so much. At times, though, it doesn't help. It makes me feel even more isolated – and unlucky.

Yesterday was a day when I was feeling nauseous from reducing my tacrolimus, my principal immunosuppressant. It happened exactly like that over a year ago. My dose was reduced from 2 mg b.d to 1.5 mg to 1 mg. With each reduction I felt sick and experienced the side effects one feels when starting on tacrolimus – good to know! I asked consultants about that before but they didn't think that should be the case. I'm a guinea pig they should listen to – I pay close attention to my body and am constantly monitoring myself. So, the reduction in tacrolimus was nice news; also Diarmaid reduced my water tablets as there doesn't seem to be any ascites or accumulating fluid in my abdomen! That, for me, is great news. Added to the fact that my LFTs are great gave me a boost, but with the ubiquitous voice advising me not to get too cocky – it's always one day at a time.

So, back to my bone marrow biopsy! Four days ago I had the second bone marrow biopsy of my life. The first was in 2001 when I was initially diagnosed with ET so I knew what to expect - and it was indeed horrible. It was necessary, however, to procure a baseline sample of marrow to compare it to future samples, and also to note changes since I've begun on hydroxyurea. I felt that the anaesthetic was just beginning to take effect when the procedure began. The registrar took what I now know was an aspiration or a liquid sample of marrow. That didn't hurt too much – not pleasant but pretty manageable. The second was a core from my marrow – using a hollow needle, a quite wide needle. It was going pretty well, painful but manageable, when she pushed that bit further and I felt as though the needle was coming out through my pelvis – at the front. On top of that, a nerve in my right leg twinged and I shouted that I had had enough.

"I'm done now, that's enough, I can't take it anymore" I heard myself saying. I think that explains how difficult it was. I was also aware that she had begun to tell me how great I was doing and that she was almost done – a sign to me that she was only half way there and still needed to continue.

It ended, finally. I felt my back was wet from blood oozing from the incision – and, though that didn't bother me, I worried would the clexane make me bleed uncontrollably. When I stopped bleeding and was bandaged up I worried that I wasn't bleeding enough — that my blood was too thick and sticky and might spell trouble for my liver.

The appointment afterwards was quick and painless. The registrar advised me to come to St. Vincent's daily to manage my warfarin dosage. That, in itself, caused complications as it was a Thursday, so it was decided that I would stay off warfarin until my GP was back after the weekend. It also meant I would have to inject daily until then...

Mum came with me to my appointment and we stayed in a hotel as always. I like her company but sometimes I miss the independence of travelling alone and getting things done without explaining all my medical business to my family. On the one hand, I appreciate that they're always there but I don't want to worry them and don't want to make their lives more stressful because of my health concerns. It's a vicious circle...

oOo

After my trip to Dublin, after my hepatology appointments, after my biopsy and haematology appointment, after buying a nice dress and seeing that my abdomen is a little too large to fit into clothes that fit me only a few months ago, after counting out pills day after day, after having my blood monitored to make sure it stays flowing, after feeling nauseous from medication and after injection after bloody injection into an area which is already so black, brown and blue with bruises that I've run out of places to stick a needle, after everything that's been flung at me since March 2006 and again since October I cried. I locked myself in the bathroom where I broke down and sobbed and weeped and bawled my eyes out until I couldn't cry anymore. Then I stopped.

When I came out of the room I felt so afraid, so worried, so terrified to feel safe and to feel as if everything will be okay because it mightn't. I try to fit in, try to act normally and live life as I should but at times, it's so difficult to feel isolated and so alone in my world of uncertainty.

Where do I go from here?

oOo

My friend's father died last week. He had been left paralysed after his stroke and confused at times. Apparently, he acquired a serious infection too, and just died peacefully in a hospice section of the hospital. I went to his funeral, looked at his body and tried to say something, murmur a prayer or ask him for something. My mind went blank and all I could do was look at him and feel upset. I hugged the girls and their mother, feeling sad and maybe a little too empathetic.

I left there and had my usual feeling following seeing someone's corpse laid out. It's not our business to stare and comment on how he looks. He was a private man and here he was, in a room open to the public and open to any sort of comments, uttered or otherwise. It seems unfair that we present our dead and put them on display, not allowing them the privacy they may have wanted when alive. It's as though the living have the final say, the final control, all choices completely taken away from their loved one. I'm not sure it's fair – or what I would want. Maybe that's because I always yearn control – especially over my own life. It makes me realise that I should maybe arrange my own funeral – the way I would want it.

I will write again soon.

31st October 2015

Dear James,

It's beginning to become an ingrained habit; how everything revolves - or I seem to make everything revolve - around my health, current and past issues and current trials.

I am continuously scanning my body for how it is and if there are any changes as a consequence of new medication or my MPN. I'm always tired – that's now a given. It's a fatigue that few people understand yet most people feel they can relate to. I am tired after waking up from a night's sleep. I look forward to going to bed; sometimes feeling as though I haven't slept in nights. I'm obviously very aware I don't have the monopoly on fatigue but it pains me when old people (in their seventies and eighties) ask how I am and respond to my claim of tiredness with a "sure, we're all tired". I feel like screaming "you're old!", "you should be tired!". Nurses, too, surprise me with the retort that "everyone's tired". I don't complain but when asked how I am, it's easier to provide one relatable symptom than a raft of technical and specific ailments. I realise that, most of the time, when people ask how one is, they truly don't want to know the truthful answer – they hope for "I'm fine, thanks" which is now the go-to phrase I'm slowly getting into the habit of using.

I hate my night sweats! With a vengeance. Since I was a pubescent teenager, I've dreaded the menopause. I wouldn't dwell on it, or fear it, but I just hated the thought of 'the change' and the possibility of feeling hormonal much of the time, losing my mind and breaking my bones on a regular basis. So much of the symptoms are apparently preventable – I know that now – but one aspect of menopause which I really feared and dreaded were the night sweats. I've always been a sweat-phobe – I'm certain that's not a word – but sweating in bed, uncontrollably, drenching me, my night clothes, the bedclothes, and my hair is the equivalent of my worst nightmare...one of them Waking up, drowning in my own body excretions was something I've placed at the back of my mind, imagining I wouldn't have to experience the whole thing until at least 45.

I'm 41 now. I'm 41, not menopausal and I have nasty night sweats. They're a symptom of ET, or probably most MPNs and I resent this symptom – with a vengeance. I hate waking up wet and uncomfortable, unfresh and in need of a shower at 3am, 4am, 5am. It's like yet another betrayal of my body; it's showing its control, its reminder that I haven't all the choices or all the cards.

I suppose I now know that my ET 'volume' has indeed turned up a notch or two. My tiredness is now very difficult. I hate wakening up drenched in sweat and seeing how dark my urine is (probably related!). I'm always thirsty but at least now I've realised that I have to drink so much more.

I am now concerned about my severely-reduced platelets though; I reckon that hydroxyurea could be suspended or reduced the next time I'm in clinic. Thankfully that will be next Thursday so I won't over-worry until then.

I want to keep going, keep minding myself with my head down, feeling unnoticed by fate – or whatever. I want a long life, whatever management and sacrifices I have to do and make. I want to live, sort of with my head in the sand, not dwelling too much on the past or present or the potentially scary future and the 'what-ifs'. I'll continue like this as long as I possibly can. As long as I can enjoy most of the things I enjoy (and maybe my abdomen might become a little flatter, please).

Today I woke to two little birds outside my window. The two little wagtails brought with them a sunny warm day and a desire in me to play music – and to experience a flat abdomen. That's a really good start to my day.

10th November 2015

Dear James,

I feel afraid and so full of questions. Questions that I've asked – and I'm not sure I trust the answers. I saw a haematology registrar last week in St. Vincent's. I asked about my platelet and white cell counts and she reassured me that the white cells were just on the lower side of normal and my platelets are still fine (and safe) so long as they're over 50,000 (they increased to 135,000 last Thursday).

As always, she explained that managing my case is such a delicate balance for them, between keeping me safe from infections and 'safe' for surgeries / injuries.

My mention of breathlessness, night sweats and itching made her a little concerned. She picked up her handset immediately and requested a film – to confirm my ET hasn't progressed to MF (myelofibrosis), a possibility. MF is another MPN in which the body's bone marrow becomes significantly scarred and the production of normal blood cells is impaired. But they ruled that out by the bone marrow biopsy in August, didn't they?

I feel the need to be so alert, so careful and in touch with my own management that it is literally taking over my life. I am also determined, despite the tiny tiny chance, to pinpoint exactly when I was exposed to the mutagen that caused a gene of my ninth chromosome to mutate and led to my ET development. It wouldn't make any difference if I knew where this all began – what caused the mutation - but it would give me some form of closure; identifying the episode when I went from 'normal' to having a mutation with quite a lot of power to change my life. Was it my fault? Was I careless with my own personal care – during my twenty-something years?

o0o

Today I am off work – my head is full of questions and my heart is challenged; I am breathless and have regular palpitations. I am a little itchy and am still waking up drenched in sweat. I am on a huge cocktail of meds now; some with nasty side effects and others with basic ones like hair loss and weight gain (yes, I am being sarcastic!)

I feel unsupported and sometimes a little isolated. If I take iron supplements that my body craves (breathlessness, tiredness and palpitations) it will fuel the production of more blood cells – I don't need any more clotting platelets. If I don't get my iron I barely get through the day. Not only are my muscles weak and tired but my brain and my concentration are affected. I'm not as sharp as I was; I feel more 'woolly'.

A doctor recently told me, cheerily, to 'stay interesting'. I initially felt proud, important – and interesting – as a case. I am a young woman with a blood clotting disorder which I acquired from who-knows-where. I developed a deep vein thrombosis which killed my liver and then it all settled down. In the last year, I developed a hepatic artery thrombosis and my MPN is possibly progressing. So I'm interesting – an interesting case. Then, after her words sank in, I felt angry. First and foremost I am a person, a human with a blood disorder, not a medical case with a person attached. Yes, I'm asked to remain a challenge for them. My case is interesting, but, again and again, I just want to be me and not feel like a 'case'. I want to stop taking all of these meds I take and leave the artificial pharmaceutical crap far behind. I just want to be the joyous and carefree Karol that I was in Canada, fun and free; not weighed down by all of these worrying challenges. I was asked to 'stay interesting'; I just bloody well want to 'stay'.

Are there others who feel like I feel – fear, rage, frustration, uncertainty, lack of control. Did I say fear? I felt so afraid at the weekend. I felt scared, terrified to my core – of death, or going into that end stage liver disease of confusion and loss of my faculties. I don't want to die, but I'm not sure what my compromise is, a messy complicated second liver transplant? The loss of my walk that was predicted in 2006? A bleeding episode in my brain? A clotting episode somewhere else? It's horribly scary – and I need other people who understand. I know there's no miracle cure, no new meds I haven't heard of, no other treatments or procedures I can try. The words 'hopelessness' and 'despair' are parts of my 'case' today.

17th November 2015

Dear James,

I have spent the last few days feeling very sad and a little sorry for myself. While my last appointment was quite positive I was advised since, on phoning my haematology nurse, that it's not a good time to take iron. I'm slightly anaemic but not enough to warrant it – and fueling the production of more blood cells. Everything is such a delicate balance, I know this. Too many platelets = clotting, too few platelets = bleeding, too high an INR = bleeding / stroke, too low an INR = clotting, too much iron = promotion of blood cell over-production, too little iron = anaemia, dizziness, palpitations and fatigue. . .it's balance, balance, balance.

I seem to be working very hard at this balancing and a lot of the time I feel so isolated and alone, managing and contacting my consultants, doing my research on diet, exercise, what to avoid, what to expect...and the truth is that no-one really knows. This is a disease that seems, for me, to be at a new phase. Also, the JAK2 mutation was just discovered in 2005; just a mere 10 years ago. In the medical world, that's just like a few minutes.

24th November 2015

Dear James,

Do you know that its only when I consciously ask myself how I am – and listen to the answer – that I really can understand and explain what's going on for me, how I really am?

I am, probably like most of us, in a situation where I say "I'm fine" or "I'm doing well" or "I'm good, thanks", when I'm asked and depending on who asks me. For people at work it's the generic "I'm fine, thanks", for some family members and friends it's "great, thanks, how are you?" and, thankfully, with my close family it's mostly honest, with a little false optimism thrown in, whenever necessary. My consultants should get the truest response, the free don't-hold-anything-back response but, and this is becoming more common, I don't generally give them the true response. With myself, it's difficult to be true because I am still learning how to examine all of my body's elements and am only beginning to understand that while parts of my physical health may not be as good as I would like or hope, there are a number of parts of my entire body that are actually "fine". I've tended to overlook that until quite recently, judging my health as the parts that have gone wrong and ignoring or forgetting about the perfect parts that are working away as they should. I'm now concentrating on 'how I'm feeling now', as opposed to how I feel with the knowledge of my horrible diagnosis in October 2014 and its associated worries, fears and pains.

Today I woke up, like most days, with my mind whirring like a windmill. As soon as I waken, my list of items begin to float around in my mind, demanding my attention, reminding me of what my day will entail, what errands I must do, what aspects of my clarinet practice I must focus on, what Christmas presents I can add to my list (and can buy before my next payday since my extended sick leave has seriously reduced my bank balance).

I get stressed when the windmill rotates, but recently I've been putting more and more items on it – and have been putting increasing pressure on myself to get through the list, tick off all the items as done. It's as though I want to be prepared for whatever comes my way in the future. I want things to be organised, want my list to be clear.

Today I feel well. I notice some pains in my bones and lower back, I have a headcold which is a minor inconvenience and the severe diarrhoea that I had last weekend has passed (no pun intended!). I am, as usual, tired, and my shoulders feel tense, but I feel well, with no liver pain, or anything else of note. I do notice the continuing appearance of more and more blue blood vessels under my skin. They are at their most concentrated around my OLT (orthotopic liver transplant) scar but now they've also made their presence known under my chin, beside my left eye and along both sides of my torso. I look at them with a little fear, since my pride in my body is all but gone. If I / should I / when I (let's go with 'if') do need a re-transplant how will it be possible to remove this current liver from me? It's so well settled into place – being securely held where it should be by a vast array of blood vessels, a huge network of muscles, refusing to let it go, shackling it to me so tightly.

I notice some new tingling of my baby finger on my left hand; it's not numb but there is a different sensation in this finger than my others. It's not quite itself anymore. And, right now I have a big blue left foot where a blood vessel has burst and spread blood over the top of my entire foot – and down one toe. I bled a little from my bowels at the weekend, but I won't say anything to a doctor or consultant just yet – it wasn't very much.

But I feel well, in general, for three or four reasons – Christmas, my still-ongoing correspondence with other MPN friends from the MPN Voice website and the feeling of being less alone and isolated, the deep love and support from my family and friends and the feeling of being loved truly as a normal woman and capable of a perfectly happy and fulfilling relationships. Right now I am enjoying life and trying really hard to focus less on the 'what-ifs' and the possibilities of what may lie ahead. Today I am living for today and in the past year I have really learned how to take one day at a time.

I am at transplant clinic in St. Vincent's tomorrow and want to discuss attending appointments less. I want my health issues to take a back seat. I need them to be less in control of my life and want to be freer to live my life and to enjoy what I enjoy. For you I am listing the things that I love / enjoy just to give you a better insight into 'me' as Karol, not as the recipient of your liver.

Reading (especially historical fiction and biographies), my clarinet, good music, challenging myself, working on projects / plans in progress (like this diary to you), gardening, birdsong, drawing (mainly with pencils), beach walks, cooking (a new one for me!), travelling, buying gifts for people and pretty things. There is an endless list – this is a snapshot of me right now.

25th November 2015

Dear James,

Well, I felt reassured and lighter leaving my transplant clinic today than I have in quite a long time. I need to be reassured and know that I am being cared for and monitored closely. I just cannot do this all on my own.

I sat in the Outpatients Clinic today and looked around me, in disdain. I didn't want to be there; I've grown so sick and tired of transplant stories and hate wasting my precious time and money just to meet young junior doctors who ask me questions such as why I had a transplant. I am not there for their training purposes anymore – I am there for me. As I looked around I thought that all of us in the waiting room are striving to feel better, to live a little longer, to undergo a transplant, to improve the function of the current one or awaiting a re-transplant, knowing the horror of the process and more than terrified that it may be necessary to go through all of the pain and fear again.

One thing that came into my head as I sat there today was that, when I was diagnosed with my artery thrombosis in October, the words 'gradual' and 'not like before' were used to describe what would be ahead for me. The 'good' news is that, next time, my liver will deteriorate gradually and, unlike the emergency and shock diagnosis of 2006, the exact reason will be perfectly clear – it will not be provided with enough oxygenated blood. I will be monitored, my progress will be known and I will meet surgeons to ask any questions I may have before the surgery. There won't be drama, no rushed investigations revealing horrible nightmarish unexpected diagnoses. I've been there, I did it the dramatic way so if it happens again that I'm back on a transplant list, it will be on my terms and with my consent (insofar as possible). I'll retain as much control as possible. This time I get to experience the whole process in slow motion – and this time I get to give my consent. . .

Today I was informed that my spleen is a quite enlarged and acting like a huge sponge for old blood cells. This is yet another symptom of my ET. While ascites continues to haunt me and make me sad when my abdomen enlarges, there is a need to know why this is still occurring for me. Generally, ascites occurs when there is a blockage in the outflow from the liver – this isn't the case for me so it's a mystery why it occurs at all. Even though I'm responding to the diuretics that I take to regulate my body's water and salt concentrations, it's vital that we understand why it continues to happen. My LFTs are excellent, apart from GGT which, for me, is always the liver enzyme outside of its normal range.

Christmas is coming and I was advised, strongly, to leave my case up to the experts and enjoy the holidays. I'm looking forward to the break, some nice presents, relaxing, spending time walking with family on the beach and in the forest and to good sleeps.

Today I am beginning again and intend, not for a second, to worry or imagine what the future will bring. I might stay unnoticed, concealed and get to escape that chapter of my life. Maybe one transplant is all I'll ever have, just the one.

I want to stop the bargaining that I've begun to notice myself doing – subconsciously but quite a lot. I look at raindrops on a window or on the shower screen and tell myself if two drops join within five seconds, I'll be fine. If a starling, not my robin, appears in the garden to eat some seeds I've just thrown out, that's a bad omen. If a clock changes within 10 seconds of my looking at it, that's a positive sign for me. I know this sounds so crazy. Now that I've written it down it makes me feel very embarrassed that this is the bargaining I'm undertaking – with inanimate objects that have no correlation whatsoever with my health.

I would like to try and break this cycle – before I completely lose the plot!

2nd December 2015

Dear James,

I am excited and very happy today. Having contacted various people through the MPN website with my various concerns and offering others advice from my experiences, I really feel a part of something. I no longer feel completely alone with this mysterious disorder that very few people have actually heard of. I now 'know' tens of people who, not alone, have essential thrombocythaemia but are also being treated with hydroxyurea to reduce symptoms. It's been a revelation. I feel the same; no better and no worse, but now with that human connection I don't feel like the only person in the world with this disorder. There are, as I expected, quite a few people who like to moan and revel in their own issues, but in general, most online participants are upbeat and trying to get on with things. We discuss bone marrow biopsies, the aches and pains from hydroxyurea, the chronic fatigue that comes with ET and how we're wondering about the future and the possibility of an amazing, life-saving JAK2 inhibitor. I know I've explained before about the JAK2 mutation and how many of us with ET also have the mutation. With a JAK2 inhibitor, the gene controlling platelet production (or in my case over-production) would be switched off or turned down a notch or two to allow platelet and other blood cell numbers return to normal. The 'slot machine' I described would just spit out the right number of cells, instead of the bucket-loads it wants to spit out.

Recently, I have been analysing how I am and how I am 'tolerating' my various medications. Right now, and pretty much since my diagnosis in October 2014 I am taking a total of eight types of tablets. I hate when people ask me how many I take (they actually do!) because some of my tablets are 1 mg in concentration while others are 500mg, so the number of tablets is not really relevant. But, just for my own interest, I counted them all up and I was a little sad at the number and type of pharmaceutical artificial stuff I'm ingesting (I refused to take tablets for anything when I was growing up – not even painkillers!).

I take tacrolimus as my immunosuppressant to ensure I don't reject my liver, warfarin to maintain my INR at 2.5 to 4, diuretics to manage my ascites / fluid retention, aspirin as an anti-platelet agent, hydroxyurea to reduce my blood cell count and keep ET 'under control', calcium to maintain bone health, beta blockers to reduce my portal hypertension (high blood pressure in my hepatic system) and pantoflux to prevent ulcers from all the other meds. And many of these are taken twice daily!

I am tolerating them all well, I think. Who's to say? I'm now 41 so the fatigue I experience could be due to age, the pains and aches I notice may be from age and my lack of 'sportiness'. Something new and a little sad that I am noticing are my unmanageable breathlessness and now-spontaneous palpitations. Also my muscles ache when I exert myself a little (climbing a flight of stairs). But I am certain this is still due to my iron deficiency so am hopeful that eventually I will be able to tolerate a little iron which should help my body with its oxygenation of muscles. I also think that a little more exercise, gentle exercise, would be a better idea than what I've been doing recently – pushing myself to fast-walk uphill and run upstairs when I just really am not up to that right now.

I took another step following my joining the MPN network. I actually emailed one of the country's leading haematologists directly and asked to be considered for a patient study on MPNs.

I'm not quite sure why, because I know it won't help me or cure my disorder but when she said I would be considered for the study I felt so useful and proud to be possibly involved in the research into MPNs. I guess it's the same feeling as donating my body to medical science – no I won't be donating any parts of my body – but I'll be 'donating' my experience and medical history. To be involved in any small way in the research of MPNs would be such an honour and a joy for me. I feel useful and hope that I can provide help or some assistance towards the study.

I'm still struggling to change an old habit of mine - my daily listing and my need to 'tick off' the items on a continual basis – sometimes ruminating over them to ensure I've done all I set to do with my day. I realise now that this need to list and document my days is to somehow prove that I am living my life completely, following my transplant. I feel it shows that I am as busy and productive as a 'normal' person and also serves to fill my days, and not for a second waste one single one. However, there's also another reason for this obsessive and now, almost dangerous habit. I feel that by living every day to the full and following my list will somehow honour you and prove that I am eternally grateful for your liver, your gift to me. This is not working for me. I am torturing myself daily to finalise my lists to the point where I am not 'living'; I am working through a list that I begin when I get up and only complete when I go to bed. It's wearing me out, making me feel stressed and anxious and is definitely not proving to be the way I demonstrate my gratitude to you.

It has to stop. I am consciously, but gently, easing myself off the listing and trying to help myself to realise two things; I don't have to live my life for anyone but me and that, should I chose to honour you in some way by 'living my life' it should be by enjoying my life without constraints and lists.

Shouldn't it be by spontaneous actions not listed on a piece of paper or in a diary, but by the sheer enjoyment of an unplanned and unexpected happy day of sunshine, spring showers, a walk in a meadow or a paddle in the sea?

A few years ago, struggling to accept the changes to my body from my transplant and dramatic weight loss, I was dared to go for a swim in the sea wearing a swimsuit. I swam previously but either wore a wetsuit or consciously folded my arms over my larger-than-I'd–like abdomen and pulled at my swimsuit to cover up my withered legs with draggy skin – as a consequence of the sudden loss of fluid from my poor legs post-transplant. One week my legs were like tree trunks, bloated with retained fluid but following a few days of leaking nasty stuff onto my hospital bed, they had returned to near normal (weeks later, they were as thin as a child's legs). When someone dares me to do something, I mull it over, think about it, consider the pros and cons and generally overthink it to bits. This dare was different as it included the word 'brave'. It was suggested to me that I had been through mush more than the embarrassment imposed on me by a few strangers, I had tackled illness and adversity head-on and a mere walk on the beach in a swimsuit was hardly required the bravery that I had needed to get through my transplant and recovery. That decided me! I was brave and knew in my heart that I had what it took to walk, almost naked (in contrast to my normal clothes), on a crowded beach in Mayo while anyone present was free to see my legs wobble and the size of my rounded abdomen.

I did it! On a sunny day in July 2013 I drove to Mulranny and made myself walk the length of a beach wearing only a swimsuit. Afterwards, I swam in the warm ocean and had, literally, one of the best days of my life. I felt free, invigorated, happy, excited – and I felt alive. I think it's necessary to have more days like that one to prove to myself that I am living my life! No need to put it in my diary or plan the next dip in the sea but just to admit that seizing the day and allowing myself the freedom to escape from my list or my regular day is living. That's what made me feel alive and so happy to be me! That day still is one of my most proudest and treasured memories – a trip to the beach. A break from the list. . .

That day I felt that I was living for me; I thought of you and thanked you, but I felt that, after everything, I bloody well earned my right to life!

I now demand freedom and want to give that to myself. But it's up to me.

29th January 2016

Dear James,

It was just over two weeks ago, at my haematology appointment, that it was confirmed I was indeed severely anaemic. I'd had all the symptoms - I was ridiculously breathless, couldn't walk much at all, had aching limbs, palpitations and the sound of blood rushing through my ears. It was time to go back on a low dose of iron – and possibly face the associated cramps. At least this explained my new and unfathomable exhaustion. I was blaming my sleeping pattern – or lack thereof. You see, I've become a very light sleeper - after 40+ years of 'dead-to-the-world sleep'. These nights I wake at least three times sometimes I hear a noise, other times it's my night sweats or there may be no reason at all. I'm just less settled than I used to once be. After doing some research about anxiety and insomnia, I've begun to keep a notebook by my bedside to record my 'anxieties'. Apparently, worries seem so much worse at night, so the technique apparently proves that those worries at night don't appear as important in the daylight hours. Also, once someone has written down their worries and fears, they can relax more into sleep – feeling that the worries have been 'voiced' and therefore 'taken care of'.

During my sleepless nights, I think about and am terrified of dying – am I on a journey which will end in my demise?

But we're all dying; we all have one final outcome. Even I don't know when or how I will actually die. The stubborn part of me insists on waiting as long as possible (obviously, in defiance.) This isn't just for me, but to see how this blood disorder progresses. I'm curious. I would feel cheated not to be given a life-and-death fight where I must put up a struggle and try to win. I would feel cheated if I died due to a completely unrelated issue like a particularly nasty infection or a car crash. All my work and research wouldn't prepare me. I'd feel lost in a war against an unknown enemy. My enemies / companions are my liver complications and my myeloproliferative blood disorder. They have become familiar, close to me now; I know their strategies and I am learning, insofar as possible, to fight them, while keeping them very close. I feel like I know their moves and I might not always be a step ahead but I'm never too many steps behind.

Two weeks ago threw me. I had noticed my symptoms, obviously, but never thought my haemoglobin would drop so low. Dr. Murphy was quite concerned and the main fear was that I was bleeding internally. I hadn't noticed any bleeding recently, no blood in the toilet bowl or from my gums or nose. I'm constantly vigilant, though one would be rather stupid not to notice bleeding from one's body, so I really can't take any credit for my care and observation. She wanted my liver team to know and to try and figure it out. Her discipline necessitates a hands-off role; as a doctor she's generally more concerned with patient biochemistry than the immediate physical presentation of a patient. And, as a medical professional, she obviously never becomes too familiar or close to patients. So, I knew she was quite concerned when she repeatedly touched my arm and shoulders with reassurance and sympathy. I was prescribed stomach-unsettling iron yet again – with the knowledge that while my haemoglobin will rise, so too will my body's yearning to create more unnecessary blood cells – I'll need very close monitoring.

Yesterday, I returned to clinic to meet Dr. Murphy. My haemoglobin is on the rise and so are my protein-grabbing pacman-like cells – eager to create more and more blood cells. This is what ET does – signals my body to create more and more platelets. With added energy from iron, more platelets can be produced. No huge surprise then in my blood results which highlighted increased blood counts, but no other option is available to me as I still need iron. I've been feeling so much better – no palpitations or severe breathlessness. I'm still very tired but I am accepting that that's a given…

I came away from clinic happy but warned. I will be back to see her – and my liver team – in five weeks.

I also came away with a haunting phrase in my head. On discussing our next move in this battle, Dr. Murphy described my transferring from hydroxyurea to pegylated interferon (a cytokine drug), apparently the drug of choice in 2013 that I chose not to take. So, this is our 2016 plan. I think we both admitted (inwardly) that when I began to take hydroxyurea, the older persons' drug, no-one knew how long I would last with my broken liver and limited blood supply. Not that I'm still 'around', the safer, more preferred cytoreductive agent for a 'younger' woman is pegylated interferon.

I'm okay with that; I think it's a weekly injection. I'll do what I have to do.

I'm not okay with the words I took home with me.

"You're too sick to change your medication now, it's better to wait a few months".

She told me I was 'sick'. I reeled at the word and wanted to disagree, to shrug off the 'too sick' label and insist that I'm 'fine'.

I know I had a transplant, I have a blood disorder, I am dealing with a number of health issues, I have some struggling to do for the sake of my health but I don't consider myself 'sick'.

Does that sound crazy? That resilient denial that I am not sick? I have some disorders and illnesses. I have a blocked artery and I take a decent amount of medication to keep me alive and generally well but I'm not sick.

Today I am planning a nice sunny holiday – I'll go in a few months. I also want to look at dresses for the coming year's three weddings and my niece's confirmation.

I'm not planning on going anywhere I don't want to go today or in the near future. That's a too-unfamiliar move.

Imitation of Life

Dear James,

In October 2014, I received devastating news. Just days past my 40th birthday I was told that I had an inoperable blood clot in my hepatic artery. The news was filtered to me over a few days as a series of diagnostic tests were carried out. I grasped at the 'not-so-disastrous' concept of a narrowing of my artery or a tiny clot (a ball of hardened blood that would 'move along' and somehow be removed from my body, leaving my artery to run properly as it should. The final, the conclusive diagnosis was a clotting of my entire hepatic artery, from root to tip (don't know why I used that term!). It wasn't a removable ball that could be dissolved or disappeared from my life; it was an extensive clot, a long scab of tough, unrelenting platelets that hardened my artery completely, blocking any blood flow. It wasn't a partial blockage; my body and I don't do things by halves. The artery is essentially useless now.

I got over the initial horrible shock, after going through stages of horrendous fear, gasping episodes of crying, anger, shock and a little else. Now I'm left to get on with my life and keep on picking up pieces that continue to tumble down. Nineteen months later, I'm 'doing well' and my liver continues to receive oxygenated blood from collaterals; it's in a good state.

The episodic incidents of ascites seem to have stopped, the very severe fatigue has downgraded to fatigue and my night sweats have lessened. Since I discovered an iron supplement that, in general, agrees with me (and my insides!), I can take my much-needed oral iron without too much fuss. I'm doing well.

But I'm not, not really. Two months after my diagnosis, I went on a fabulous, magical trip to Iceland. At that time, I had moderate ascites so, in hindsight I'm proud that I, apart from a number of iron-induced cramping episodes, had a wondrous holiday. It was magical; snow, frozen waterfalls, geysers, Northern lights and thermal spas under the stars (at -11°). I kept my cramping and distended abdomen to myself insofar as possible. It was a fabulous trip, a romantic adventure - but now, in hindsight, it's as though part of me wasn't even there. You see, that's how life has been for me. I am not depressed or dwelling on my diagnosis but it's such a heavy weight to carry that, for the most part, it preoccupies much of my waking (and sleeping) life.

Today I am happy. It's a sunny May day, I have a great family who I know cherish me; I feel their love and I hope I show them that I love them deeply, and am thankful every day (every hour) for their love and huge support. I have two wonderful, caring sisters who still treat me as a younger sister, the one who needs a little extra support and time. I love them for that. I have cherished nieces and great brothers-in-law. My friends, too, are more than I ever could have imagined. They make me laugh, distract me and are there to listen and care. I feel so blessed. In one way, having a nasty diagnosis such as mine has reinforced my sense of luck and good fortune to have come into the world loved and to have met and shared my life with so many special and good people.

The tenth anniversary of my transplant has passed. Like last year's anniversary, it was a little bittersweet. I have survived, I have lived 10 years post horrible, scary, levelling, torturous liver transplant. I tried hard to celebrate. I tried to write to you, to thank you. I wanted to write to your wife and let her know that, 10 years on, I am still thinking of her and her wonderful, altruistic, amazing decision. I just didn't know what to write, I'm sorry. Maybe it would upset her, hearing from me, 10 years on. Maybe it might be too painful now.

On another happy note, I did something for me on our anniversary, for our anniversary. Months before I reached 10 years post-transplant I decided to treat myself, to give myself something that I felt I deserved, something special to say "well done" to me for coming so far, for surviving against the odds and for being brave all those years ago. I tried to think of something I really wanted - for me. I realised that for as long as I can remember I have wanted a dog. As a child I tried to adopt cats and always had my eye out for tadpoles and caterpillars that I could use as pets (yes, I'm now completely aware that removal of frogspawn / tadpoles from the wild without a permit is illegal!). I had a terrapin for a few months, but it was as lifeless and boring as a goldfish (I had them too). I coaxed stray dog after stray dog into our garden as a child, hoping that one would realise its luck and want to stay with me and my family forever. It never happened. Dogs would eat the food I stole from the kitchen cupboards (tins of fish and bread) but in the morning, time and again, they'd have moved on. I was 14 when I was promised a dog if I would work hard in school (I was going through a particularly dreamy phase). I promised; got 10 honours in my Group Certificate (1989) but never saw my promised dog. Now, a few weeks ago, after months of searching and research, I found a beautiful maltichon – a maltese / bichon frise mix – a bundle of white softness, mischief, cuteness - and love. I've named him Scamper Beau and already he's breaking my heart with biting, nipping, licking and eating my flowers. I wouldn't have it any other way. When I'm peeling vegetables at the kitchen sink, he lies on my slippered-feet and sleeps. When I eat my dinner, he crawls onto my crossed legs for a warm snooze. His big brown eyes make me forgive every piece of furniture he chews, every piece of paper he shreds and every puddle or other accident on the kitchen floor. I love the mornings with him when I take him out from his crate and into the garden (house training is exhausting but he's smart). We sit in the garden at 6:30, he on my lap as I sit on the porch step. The sun rises and the world feels still asleep. He's a handful, but adorable – and a great choice of gifts to me. I feel like he's my dream come true!

o0o

Since February, however, I've noticed a severe pain in my right leg, a throbbing, darting shooting pain from my buttocks to my foot. The day begins okay; I play with Scamper and make sure he's fed and exercised. I go to work and work hard. By midday, the pain is tolerable but by end of my working day I need to lie down and get some relief. On my anniversary and yours, I planned to go to the beach and walk (in or out of the water). I only managed a three-minute drive to the lake and a 15-minute walk to the bridge from the carpark. I threw in that rotten Lindt bunny that sat on my bedside locker during my time in Brigid's Ward in 2006. He needed to go so I threw him into the water. My plan was to watch as he slowly became overcome by the water, leaving me to reflect on the passing of one bad chapter and the advancement of the beginning of another 'who-knows-what's-next' chapter. I expected to see the sun shine on the golden foil of that bunny as he became submerged by the water, one piece at a time until there was no gold left (for once I put my own needs before those of the environment and hoped I wouldn't get a litter fine). My plan backfired. The bunny floated (I should have expected that!). I saw him bob up and down as he hit the water, then float on down towards the river. As I walked the path alongside the lake, he floated along with me – damn it!! So much for forward planning!

So now, here I am. I don't know what's next and I think I'd rather not know. All could be well and my blood disorder will settle and absent itself from my life for a long while (apart from regular appointments and a huge collection of anti-platelet and anti-coagulant pills). I hope and I pray.

In the intervening time, I can't be entirely happy. There are times when I'm happy and I appreciate more and more those moments of joy. However, there's always that invisible weight on my shoulders or that grey cloud over my head. It's like grief, I'm sure. I receive numerous reasons to be happy and elated but the possibility (probability) of my health deteriorating further at some time is always there; hanging around and tied to me like a bag of rotting vegetables. I expect bad news, I expect to hear more almost-devastating news that I must face. In some strange, unfathomable way, I welcome bad news, as its better than the unknown. It's tangible, it's real, it's something I can challenge and fight, something I can bat back and work to keep at bay. These days, though, it's an ongoing match and I'm becoming tired. I don't have the strength to keep myself living to fight the horrible.

I feel at present that I'm flying away, hiding my head, burying my worries and not completely facing them. I'd like to fly away and try to leave baggage behind, that rotting bag. It seems to always come with me. But how do I lose it?

When your day is night alone,
If you feel like letting go,
If you think you've had too much of this life,
Well, hang on 'cause everybody hurts'
REM, Everybody Hurts

5th June 2016

Dear James,

What a day. What I have just discovered over the last few days has left me reeling. It has been revealed by the World Health Organisation (WHO) that ET, my blood disorder, is now classified as a cancer. It has been described as a sister disease of an array of blood cancers such as polycythaemia vera, primary myelofibrosis and chronic eosinophilic leukaemia. I've heard of the first two diseases described as MPNs – the first an overproduction of red blood cells for sufferers who are mostly JAK2 positive and mostly men and women over 60. The second is a blood disease which is characterised by the cessation of the production of normal blood cells and the subsequent scarring of one's bone marrow… But, now, they are all, including my essential thrombocythaemia, classified as blood cancers. I have a blood cancer – a sister disease of chronic myeloid leukaemia. There, I needed to write that down, to say it aloud, to spell it out. I have a rare form of blood cancer. OK, I need to deal with this! I can panic and become stressed by that word 'cancer'. I can smugly admit that I actually wanted a more manageable disease like cancer years ago when fumbling along with my then unmanageable and rare blood disorder. I can be dramatic or a hypochondriac and tell people, with drama and some form of a theatrical performance, that I have the rotten luck of living with a cancer since I was

26. I'm not a hypochondriac, I hate fuss and I am deeply private so dealing with this will necessitate some logic and common sense. I still have the same blood disease that I've had for 15 years. Yes, it has wreaked havoc and it's caused pain and such suffering during my life as a blood disorder. A new name or classification changes nothing. To a newly-diagnosed person, a 'cancer' will surely sound ominous, horrific, terrifying but to me, living with this for many years, there's nothing new in a name. No need for drama or upset. Like I've always done, I will just get on with it.

Unfortunately 'getting on with it' these days isn't proving very simple. I have been off work (again!) since mid-May – a day I admitted to my boss that I was in excruciating pain and really needed to go home. I am now literally confined to bed for most of the time. My leg pain has worsened significantly and now I find it almost impossible to sit, walk, stand – or actively engage in anything. I can get some relief in lying down, but moving in bed becomes a tough chore.

What happened? Nothing new except the pain just increased in intensity. I drove to work and, generally, felt some ease in the early mornings. I sat most of the day at a comfortable desk. On other days, I drove to do some site investigations and cherished the thought of reaching my bed to get some ease after the drive. Driving definitely wasn't helpful. After a day's work, I'd walk slowly to my car, the contact with my right foot on the footpath causing searing pain up my entire leg with every slow step. I walked like a very old woman, slow and carefully, wincing with every step. I would get to my car and sit in, gradually. Then, the pain would just escalate to a state which was almost unbearable. I would sit and cry aloud in pain for a few minutes until I could move my legs enough to drive safely. What was the solution to this pain? I've had regular physiotherapy sessions and have been taking a painkiller daily.

After trying to work and take regular breaks to walk and stretch my back – I even tried to write reports standing up – I had to leave and go home to bed. I explained to my boss that my pain was unbearable and I couldn't stand it any longer. I don't think he realised how much I had been suffering – in silence except for the confines of my car and own home. I left on a Friday afternoon and went straight to bed – leaving Scamper in his crate as he thought I was still at work.

The days have passed since I stopped working just over two weeks ago and Mum has come to live with me and help me with Scamper, as well as everything else that I can't do – shop, cook, clean the house, drive…the list goes on. My boyfriend works long hours, leaving the house at 7:30 and generally not home before 8pm. If he chances to finish work earlier than 8pm or 9pm, he'll go to the gym or a cycle with his cycling club. Therefore I need Mum, or someone who can help me out and – I hate to say it – take care of me. We've been getting along fine, yet I'm not great company and I know Mum would like to be in her own home with Dad. Dad visits regularly and we have dinner; me standing to eat at my breakfast bar.

Last week was our scheduled holiday and I didn't go. We were due to go to Venice and Verona for a few days and I was so looking forward to the break. I booked it almost two months ago when my back was fine and there were no issues about flying, driving - or walking. It was a break for the two of us; a week in the sun with some new experiences, interesting scenery and nice food. Scamper was to go on his holidays to Mum and Dad's. But it wasn't meant to be. I knew days before we were to fly out that I wouldn't be able for the trip. Even if the flight and subsequent days in the sun were calm and relaxed, I didn't even know if I would be able for a drive to Dublin, a hassled walk in the airport, let alone haul a 10kg suitcase. So, disappointingly, I had to postpone my uninsured trip and squander €800. I had been to both Venice and Verona on day trips previously so missing out on those particular cities wasn't a huge deal – the disappointment was about my precious lost money and missing of a trip away. So, my boyfriend went alone. He decided that, though he wouldn't enjoy it as much without me, he would go – he had booked annual leave from work and had been looking forward to it as much as I had. He went; I made him promise to buy me a gift from every place he visited (there were two scheduled tours included in the trip itinerary).

A few weeks ago I had an MRI on my back, a copy of which was sent to a neurosurgeon in the Mater Private Hospital. Then I was advised by his nurse to discuss my haematological management with Dr. Murphy. I knew because of my blood disorder that, if back surgery was necessary, it would have to be carefully approached so as not to result in additional bleeding or blood clotting risks. This bothered me; I was possibly facing back surgery and my blood disorder was given a reason to cause trouble. It felt like ET affected practically every aspect of my life!

Now, however, there is a plan in place. Within days of him seeing my scan I heard from the surgeon's secretary who informed me I was scheduled for back surgery on 16th June. It feels like ages away! I asked if I could be fitted in sooner – that my days were just about lying in bed with no ease at all, but she explained that I was scheduled for as soon as he could fit me in. I have two desiccated discs in my back (L4/L5 and L5/S1) with a prominent bulge on the lower one – that is probably pressing continuously on my sciatic nerve, causing the now-familiar and so-severe shooting pain up and down my leg. The plan is in place so now I just have to wait. He intends on doing a discectomy and disc decompression – I need relief now; I really don't care what the surgeon's plans are, so long as this pain is taken away.

Dr. Murphy has sent me a lovely letter, detailing her advice for my haematological management. As I expected, it makes reference to (twice daily!) injections of the dreaded clexane, instead of my warfarin. It's my understanding that warfarin and aspirin, while excellent anti-platelet and anti-coagulation drugs, are difficult to manage; this is a huge disadvantage from a surgical viewpoint. So, I find myself with a plan to stop my aspirin and warfarin switch to clexane before being admitted to hospital where I will begin an IV infusion of heparin – another anti-coagulant drug. I'm even boring myself with this jargon so that's where I'll leave our conversation today. I am in pain but I am so looking forward to the 16th June where I really believe

I can put this pain behind me and move on. Move on to playing with Scamper again, taking responsibility for him and all my other life's routines, including work and - just living.

Now, I'm in bed (as usual) but hopeful and happy to see some light at the end of this tunnel. Really, I'm not managing too well and with pain every minute of my day, I really can't write any more to you today.

> *'All my lovers were there with me*
> *All my past and futures*
> *And we all went to heaven in a little row boat*
> *There was nothing to fear and nothing to doubt'*
>
> *Radiohead, Pyramid Song*

28th July 2016

Dear James,

Today I realised that the last few weeks have been so intense that there are aspects I have been able to deal with – and some places I haven't been able to visit. Now, I'll give it a try.

My back surgery, so long awaited and yearned for, was a complete success. I'm still taking painkillers but I can walk, bend, sit, stand – all of those basic experiences I had lost. The Mater Private Hospital experience was like a holiday. I ate good food, met some very nice people and felt very well taken care of. My neurosurgeon and his nurse were so great and competent. I faced the surgery and wasn't overly worried – just impatient to have it over with and get 'fixed' so I could walk - and function - again. The pain was probably like nothing I had ever experienced and my life was completely on hold. I was helpless and just existing to eat and lie down all day. I was losing weight too, likely from the pain and the stress of it all. I remember little of the surgery process; I was wheeled down after saying goodbye to Mum and Dad. They were anxious and tearful; I hate to cause them stress. After the surgery, I was put on IV heparin – as per my haematological plan. I remember the relief, sheer blissful relief from pain as soon as I came around and found myself in a hospital bed. I was on painkillers but I could move my legs and back very well. The back pain from the surgery site was minor in contrast to what I had been experiencing for weeks prior to my surgery. I was ecstatic. The pain was gone and, with physiotherapy, I began to walk normally and do my back-strengthening exercises. The days went by and it was almost time for me to go home. I guess the management of my blood thinners was the reason I stayed a little longer than most patients. I watched people leave on crutches following hip replacements or women and men swagger off dragging bags following discectomies. My neurosurgeon visited and advised that I would be going home very shortly. I 'enjoyed' hospital – I was feeling well and surrounded by caring, attentive people.

Six days after my surgery, however, the day before my discharge, while I waited for a bout of constipation to pass (no pun intended), I had a pretty standard Wednesday. My back, with two discs, one recently decompressed and the other partially removed, was feeling great. In the late evening, a cough developed – a phlegm-type cough which I couldn't quite clear. It persisted and, subconsciously, I coughed the phlegm into a tissue. My heart leapt when I saw a star of fresh blood. Within minutes, I was coughing quite violently and struggling to catch my breath. The cough was 'wet' and, after alerting my nurse, I was whisked away to a room where three doctors stood over me with serious expressions on each face. I began to panic and asked, demanded even, through coughing, to be intubated; I needed to feel the relief of being unconscious - not this drowning fear that every new cough brought. My family was called – I asked the nurse not to alarm my mother – she would panic at receiving a call from a Dublin hospital after 11pm.

My cough continued to bring up more and more fresh blood. I looked at Martin, the fun Canadian doctor; his expression was so grim. I was so afraid. . .

My coughing became relentless and I just remember liquid flooding my throat, this inability to take breaths, the fear as I struggled to breathe and the panic as I really felt I was failing. I remember calling "please intubate me"; demanding they put me out of this misery and help me to breathe, help me to lose this panicky, horrific, cruel, torturous feeling of loss of control. I needed to relax and breathe easily but it wasn't working. "Please intubate me, please"…

oOo

I held hands in mine and heard calm voices. I squeezed like mad. "I'm here". "Don't go". Later, who knows how much later, I opened my eyes and drops were put in both eyes.

Pain, absolutely everywhere. My whole body, once I was aware of it, ached. There wasn't one part that didn't hurt, but my chest and right arm were so sensitive to any touch. I felt bruised, flattened, in such pain that I couldn't describe. What had happened? Had I been hit by a car? I felt immoveable and weak but so, so sore.

I was in ICU – again. I was seriously ill – again. I thought to myself, "No, I can't do this again".

I was confused about how I had ended up there. Later, much later, I was told that I had been dangerously ill. The blood that, days ago, flooded my throat had originated from varices or enlarged blood vessels in my oesophagus (remnants from my portal hypertension or high blood pressure in my hepatic system pre-transplant) which had spontaneously ruptured; I had aspirated the blood, causing my lungs to flood. I had thought I was swallowing it, but instead of ingesting or vomiting it, like most people subconsciously do, I had taken huge amounts of blood down my trachea and into my lungs, where it promptly clotted and severely compromised my lung function. What I had experienced in aspirating blood into my lungs felt something like drowning. I had been very dangerously ill and very lucky to have survived. What I begged the doctors for – intubation – they succeeded in doing, but only after a very fraught number of minutes as the clocks ticked and my life was beginning to ebb away. My sister and her husband arrived in time to see me saturated with my own blood, but desperately begging someone to help me to breathe. The doctors helped me and saved me, against the odds.

For days after I came around, consultants and doctors came to see me with proud, happy smiles on their faces, admitting that they were delighted to hear me speak and to see me conscious – no-one said 'alive' but it was insinuated. For days, I had been the most unwell person in ICU, and was transferred to the unit only when doctors were very certain I would survive the move. The clot that had developed in my right lung had to be surgically removed – a very delicate procedure which my family was advised was necessary but extremely high-risk and complex. My parents were informed that, while my life was in danger by facing such a difficult procedure, my life would come to a certain end without it. They signed the consent for a surgeon to remove the clot, hoping and praying that it would work. The odds weren't great.

After I came around and faced the ICU nurses I still felt so helpless and completely dependent on them to do everything for me, though they were all so kind and cheerful. It was like a horrible recurring dream; feeding tube, urinary catheter, heart rate monitors, BP cuff, commode. . .it brought me right back to my transplant recovery in 2006. I vaguely remember having a tube in my right side pulled out – my ICU nurse explained this tube was in my lung and she turned up my morphine dose to help with the pain. It came out – sore but not impossibly painful. I was accustomed to pain and fear – my pain threshold was obviously high.

ICU became HDU after a few days and following my move and the happy realisation that I was alive and doing extremely well, physiotherapy began. It was difficult. Because I had aspirated so much blood into my right lung and they had only been able to remove a certain amount, I had to avail of physio to bring up the rest of the blood from the bottom of my lung. First I practised the 'huff' but, just like 10 years ago, it evaded me. The 'huff' sound came out more like a 'haaa', complete with 'old man cough' noise. Then, I was brought, with difficulty, to my feet for marching the spot. It wore me out.

I struggled through HDU, seeing every single minute on the clock and trying so hard to breathe. Generally, a nebuliser and oxygen mask covered my face, making me feel hot and uncomfortable. This time, however, unlike 10 years ago, I was less concerned about bed baths and toilet issues. I didn't have the energy to care about my dignity or to feel embarrassed. I felt ill and lethargic and knew I needed help.

After a few more days, I could do three laps of the HDU. I was moved back to the Mater Private Hospital where I met the staff I had left so abruptly. They were so genuinely happy to see me and chat about that night and how shocked they all had been when I haemorrhaged. It was such a happy experience to feel their genuine joy at seeing me well. After a few days, a gastroenterologist came to see me and to explain again what had happened. He admitted that my parents and sisters were told it was a very difficult procedure and not to be too hopeful. Now, I feel so scared and alone when I imagine the alternative, had the procedure not gone well. I can only comfort myself with the thought that, had things not been successful, I would never have known. . .

When sufficiently stable, I began to undergo treatment to rid me of the remaining varices which endured following the rupture. Basically, I had a number of oesophago-gastroduodenoscopies (OGD) and banding. An OGD is basically an endoscopy, the examination of one's oesophagus, stomach and duodenum with a tiny camera to identify any issues. Banding is done concurrently with the camera used to aid a physician's task. Banding or endoscopy band ligation is the placing of tiny elastic bands around enlarged veins in the oesophagus to tie them off so they wouldn't bleed. The banded varices are sloughed after a few days and this considerably reduces the risk of bleeding within the oesophagus after it's healed.

Banding was fine – I was sedated and woke up with a minor sore throat and no other issues.

I saw a liver registrar also as my abdomen had begun to take on its familiar 'dome' appearance, indicating some ascites or unwelcome free fluid.

The registrar, Clifford, assured me that my liver was quite stable despite my increased abdomen. My LFTs were very good and I had no jaundice or confusion. That made me very happy.

After a few days in the Mater Private Hospital, I was transferred to St. Vincent's – an ambulance ride took me back, once again, to the National Liver Unit.

Within hours, I met Diarmaid and the new liver team who recently began at St. Vincent's; Clifford was one of them and I was happy to see his familiar face.

'Don't give in, don't you dare quit so easy
Give all that you got on the soul'

Snow Patrol, Don't Give In

1st August 2016

Dear James,

Well, from a fraught time in the Mater following my back surgery and associated, unplanned complications and near-death experiences, I somehow, ridiculously, imagined life here in the Liver Unit would be somewhat calm and uncomplicated. I expected that, after some more observation, I would be declared stable and allowed home within days. My liver is now described as stable and I am feeling very well, despite everything I have undergone. I know, deep-down, that my stable liver won't always be that way, but I anticipated making my escape from here a few short days after I arrived. For me, this isn't the time to discuss a re-transplant. I'm certainly not ready for that conversation now. I want to go home before the discussions begin. I really miss Scamper so much – I was only due to be away from him for less than one week. Now, I've been gone for over six!

But, life in St. Brigid's has proven to be a continuation of stress and fear. They've begun to discuss a re-transplant with more fervour than ever before, despite my disinterest. I'm not even certain why, but I can only imagine that the rupture of my varices and subsequent banding has demonstrated that there is a build-up of pressure – portal hypertension – in my hepatic system. It's nothing I can see or feel (I do suffer from a little heartburn but nothing significant) but it's something that I imagine Diarmaid observes when he undertakes my now-regular banding. The last few weeks have left me reeling and very stressed, fearful, yet again, for my future.

Today, my head isn't reeling anymore, it's become very still and calm. Initially, I planned, organised, made lists and envisaged the two outcomes when they discussed, ever more certainly, a re-transplant. Now, I just can't go there. There'll be enough time to discuss it, to feel 'on the list' if that will be the case. On Thursday morning, a group of hepatologists, haematologists, surgeons, anaesthetists, radiographers will gather and discuss me. On Thursday, I will know more – more to cram into the already overflowing box in my brain – the one with the tight-fitting lid.

I do want a transplant and I don't. I read the stupid hospital book that the coordinator gave me; the one with the silly cartoons and illustrations of livers and the assessment process for 'the list'. It really didn't help me much, having gone through the process before and still living through 'failing liver' difficulties. I want a transplant, need it, so my portal hypertension will be resolved and there'll be no more pressure on my hepatic system – or my oesophageal varices, which I'm having so carefully banded. I don't want the ongoing cloud of worry that never goes away – the worry my varices will rupture again like they did following my back surgery, or that my collaterals will just give up and my liver will be completely oxygen-deprived. I yearn to feel normal and to be able to just 'move on'. Since my HAT diagnosis I've been living in deep fear – it's as simple as that. This must end, before I crack up.

I don't want to go through another transplant. Obvious reasons! Fear, pain, worry that it won't go well or that the procedure that the surgeons are eager to undertake will leave me with a poor quality liver, or one that I'll reject – or one that will be perfect but my body's blood vessels won't support. That's the concern of the medical team; the blood vessels so necessary to support a donor liver won't cooperate. There's also the literally petrifying fear of the recovery phase. . .can't even discuss that now. I'll wait – with concern, apprehension, fear, worry and anxiety. I'll await the outcome. I'll await a result that will determine the course of my life – at 41.

Days here are, in general, fine. We, the inpatients of St. Brigid's, spend the days getting to know one another. Some people want to discuss themselves much of the time – I'm happy with that; I don't particularly want to discuss my business with some of these mere strangers. I'm actually quite careful not to mention that I've had a transplant previously – it may scare or rattle some of the newer members of the transplant group. In 2006, if I had known the chances of necessitating a second transplant were actually quite high, it would have bothered me – another worry to add to my increasing pile. Apparently, there are quite a lot of 're-dos' in the transplant world. As if once wasn't enough of the ordeal of a lifetime!

My roommates are all at various stages of recovery. One is two weeks post-transplant but finds her energy levels devastating. She sleeps much of the day and turns her nose up at every meal. I enjoy few meals – but I'm sometimes hungry! Another lady had her transplant one week ago but is struggling with confusion. There's a possibility that her immunosuppressants are causing her to remain in her own little, hazy, confused world. On the corridor, an upbeat jaundiced lady walks with Joanne, the physiotherapist. Her pink dressing gown flashes by the door at least four times a day. She's got a determined air about her – this surgery and its associated recovery is not about to phase her.

And so it goes on. My days are filled with visitors and reading. I walk as much as possible, noticing that my abdomen appears to be filling out more than in recent weeks. Is this more advanced ascites? (I know it is – there's nothing else it could be; my weight is climbing a little and hospital food is not responsible for that). In between reading and keeping myself occupied, I have regular banding appointments on Tuesdays. They are continuing to wheel me down to Endoscopy for my OGDs and banding. The routine is the same every time. I may have a light breakfast before 6am and then fast until late afternoon when Brendan, the porter, wheels me down to an older part of the hospital where my bed is parked in one of the appointment rooms. Diarmaid, huge smile and wearing scrubs, greets me while a nurse pops (always very efficiently!) a tiny cannula into my arm. By now I know that a small cannula is fine for administering a sedative while the cannula for a CT is a larger, green one. The nurse positions a blood pressure cuff and a mouthpiece while Diarmaid sprays the noxious banana-flavoured local anaesthetic at the back of my throat and administers sedation into the small cannula in my arm. For me, I know little else of the procedure.

Brendan, while I'm sleeping off the sedative, wheels me back to Brigid's where I come around, feeling groggy and hungry, and with a raw throat. Generally – it's becoming quite a habit - I request rice krispies and a yogurt following the procedure.

I feel like I'm rambling on a little – but really there's little else going on right now. I am waiting to be discharged and will likely continue with my banding programme, while continuing on my twice-daily clexane injections, for a number of months until all the varices have been treated. This part of the plan is fine – fortnightly banding sounds like a reasonable plan – but there is quite a substantial hitch. Due to the danger of bleeding associated with banding – particularly because I am on blood anticoagulants – it is strongly recommended by a number of consultants that I should stay in Dublin until my banding is finished. It's predicted to continue until at least October. This now horrifies, scares and stresses me so much. From my internet search of houses and apartments in the South Dublin area, I know for certain that I could never afford to live in Dublin while paying a mortgage on my house in Mayo. It's a huge decision – and a risk to take. There are just two options; to try to afford a place in Dublin on my limited illness benefit or risk my life by having banding in Dublin and travelling to Mayo afterwards. Never in my life have I wished I had settled in or near Dublin, rather than staying so close to where I was born and raised. Is this the time to sell my house and move east? Or am I being dramatic now? Is this a life-changing decision – or just a number of doctors who are being very, very cautious? I already had a rupture and know it had been only with a lot of luck and skilful surgeons and doctors that I had survived that one. Is it possible, could I be so unlucky that my varices might rupture once again?

Now, so very regularly, I find myself mulling over the difficult decision related to my living arrangements, the thought of staying on here while I'm treated. There's no possibility of my staying in Brigid's – there are no spare beds and technically I don't need a hospital bed for this programme. I just need to be within a short distance of the hospital...of the people who know the risks and know my predicament. Years ago, when I was critically ill in the months following my transplant, my family stayed at a hospital-provided house. It provided comfortable ensuite rooms with clean beds and compact bathrooms. It was a perfect base for families who needed to live close to the hospital. Now, 10 years later, that house has been demolished for St. Vincent's Private Hospital. There's nowhere for me to stay – within my limits.

While here, I have also sorted out another issue from my hospital bed. I'm not well-off, and even less so with my measly salary and illness benefit but I wanted to update my will. There are items on it which I am not happy about. So, I had a consultation with my solicitor in the dayroom of St. Brigid's Ward...and updated my will.

Jesus, that's a very 'getting your affairs in order' type of move. But I now find myself mulling over health issues most of the time and subconsciously 'getting organised'. Little else occupies my mind. I did the transplant thing 10 years ago – the confusion, the pain, cannulas, x-rays (sitting up in bed against a hard vertical board for vital chest X-rays), the feeding tube, severe diarrhoea, trying to eat and learning to walk. It is a place I don't want to re-visit. I used to occasionally re-visit those days, especially in the first few years. It somehow gave me a sense of comfort, maybe because I could measure how far I'd come; walking, working, holidaying, playing my clarinet and socialising.

Simple things still bring me right back there though — smells of alcohol wipes and certain shower gels and perfumes, the sight of chocolate *Lindt* bunnies or the strong smell of plastic (plastic prongs bringing oxygen into my nostrils). Then I stopped going back. I began to allow myself to move forward; allowed myself the luxury of feeling more confident and self-assured about my prognosis and my 'chances'. But, the complete clotting of my hepatic artery changed me. I felt sad since then — never completely free. . .still stuck here and having flashbacks of the past.

So now, I so want to just go home where I can try and escape these worries. I miss Scamper like crazy. He was really only a puppy when I left him and now I'm certain he'll have grown up so much and maybe even forgotten about me. I had so many plans for his training — I read so many books on training and rearing a puppy and how to give him a good life. Now, he's spent weeks in a lonely kennel with my vet as his carer. I know he'll be walked daily and fed well and taken care of, but he won't have my love, the love I promised his little face the day I brought him home. I promised I'd train him to sit and roll over on command, shake paws and be a well-mannered little guy. Now, I'm not even there for his first few months of life. It's such a horrible loss of control — my little bundle of joy taken away from me. I hope he's doing okay but I completely ban thoughts of him from my mind — it just hurts too much not seeing him or being close by.

'Every time I try to fly I fall
Without my wings
I feel so small'

Britney Spears, Everytime

23rd August 2016

Dear James,

I'm home! I'm in my own house with Scamper (who has grown exponentially since I left him in June). He is no longer an innocent little puppy but a confident intelligent adolescent dog. I missed two whole months of his young life, missed the training I intended to do with him, the daily brushing, the moulding of this delightful soft puppy into my much-yearned for dog. But God, any fears that Scamper had forgotten me in two months were completely cast aside by his glorious emotional welcome. He wagged his tail to bits, cried and barked, ran under my legs and licked my hands as I tried to pat him. He's so beautiful but he has grown so much from the baby I left behind.

So I'm home; Mum has moved in and Dad visits regularly. I've had my hair cut, bought some clothes (my abdomen is now quite distended), shaved my legs and had the garden fence painted. I've had a new shower installed and have begun to clear out the wardrobes of old-fashioned skirts and dresses. I've finally watched the last two episodes of the latest season of *Game of Thrones,* seen the last three of *Homeland*; shows I thought I'd possibly never get to see..., read more books, did some drawing and bought new running shoes. But I still feel flat, deflated and lost.

I'm home following the rollercoaster re-transplant discussions, the strongly-urged and stressed (and nervously ignored by me) advice to base myself in Dublin for three months of variceal banding, and the sometimes head-wrecking differing opinions which affect my life so much but to consultants are only the opinions on Patient 0020492SB.

Now I feel bland and a little lost, impatient and confused. I've no enthusiasm or huge interest in anything. I don't feel afraid, worried or anxious. I'm not apprehensive about a possible future re-transplant and the outcome. I'm not excited that my banding programme is going very well. I'm not angry that this has happened to me, that I was critically ill again. I'm not overly upset that I'm injecting myself with clexane again. I'm not particularly gutted about my severely bruised abdomen from reactions with this anti-coagulant when I hit the 'wrong spot'. I feel very little.

Maybe that's called numbness. I feel numb and a little in shock. I'm floating again – in a big balloon, depending on the wind direction to determine where I'll go. That, and maybe the clotting of my blood. I feel so little right now. I don't have the energy or enthusiasm to feel anything.

'Only in the darkness can you see the stars'
Martin Luther King Jnr

28ᵗʰ September 2016

Dear James,

Recently, I've felt completely lost. It's like I'm sitting in a boat and bailing out water; over and over and over. But it keeps flooding back in. I'm drowning; I'm either going to capsize and tumble into the water or it'll saturate me in the boat. My options are limited. I'm tired of bailing; wrecked with fighting and trying to stay alive. Last week the option to go on the transplant list was put to me. Scary. Not to go on the list. Scary. I'm damned either way. I'm sick of fighting. I want to stay in bed with the bedclothes over my head.

For the last few days I've felt quite unwell and fluey. I can't eat and am continuously sitting on the toilet with diarrhoea. I'm drinking lots but when do I decide to contact St. Vincent's? I'm neck-deep in hospital now; I feel like I'm fading. Sad, grim faces of my hospital doctors; do they think I'm fading too?

I have a beautiful dog that I can't even look after on my own. I don't have the strength or energy for him. Mum still lives with me; she's so dedicated to my care but I feel my independence is gone. I want to feel free. I want to be single again. A relationship is too hard – I don't have the energy and feel anxious about how I've changed. I know that I can't really truly let someone love me. Not properly. I'm sick; I have a potentially tough time ahead of me and I don't look the way I want to look anymore. I have a distended abdomen punctured with needle marks (sore and so bruised now after months of injections) and I have a figure which really isn't attractive. All that I have to offer is just me, as I am right now. My boyfriend doesn't seem to want that – I feel that he wants us to be just normal again but for me, everything has changed now. I'm anxious, preoccupied and dreadfully sad.

'Great minds discuss ideas, average minds discuss events, small minds discuss people'
Eleanor Roosevelt

17th October 2016

Dear James,

After a busy, eventful and even painful time, emotionally and physically, I realise that I must admit there is the possibility that you and I will go our separate ways. My abdomen is now uncomfortably large and though my ankles are no longer swollen, I am retaining large volumes of fluid, making me feel heavier and making me find dressing in anything other than tracksuits or flowing dresses very difficult. That makes me sad. I am petite everywhere else but am displaying a belly which makes me look six or seven months pregnant.

Last week, I had my liver transplant assessment. While I say those words, write that sentence, it sounds like a milestone event, a life-changing episode of my 42-year-old life. It actually wasn't in any way as dramatic as it sounds. It was four days of attending appointments and seeing various consultants, relaying my history and discussing my future. . .the unknown bit that no-one can really foresee with any certainty or true confidence. It's not a matter of lack of knowledge or expertise – no, it's just that, as is always being relayed to me, I'm a complicated case. But, as is always the case when I'm in St. Vincent's, I felt safe and 'cushioned' surrounded by the consultants determined to do their best to fix me. I hate to admit this, but it almost feels okay to die there too…I'm not sure how to explain or process that admission.

Anyway, my week began with my, now-routine, OGD and banding. Diarmaid admitted that the varices were being successfully banded, causing them to slough and become, hopefully, harmless. The six days post-banding are quite tricky, as bleeding generally occurs during this period. I remember that when my banding first began I was strongly advised to live near the hospital, as returning home after the procedure was very risky, considering my bleeding risk, my previous variceal rupture and the urgent nature of a variceal bleed. I'm still commuting to Dublin for banding and travelling home to Mayo the following day - taking my chances (fingers crossed).

I was struck by Diarmaid's empathy at my distended abdomen and his acknowledgement that we will soon have to make a 'plan'.

Wednesday was a frantic day from hell. While my first appointment was scheduled for 9am, I saw my liver surgeon at 11:30am. She and the other senior surgeons had been poring over my previous scans, trying to reach a general consensus over how to proceed when the time comes to transplant me. With so many useless blood vessels and a previous unorthodox transplant, she explained that the many typical routes to attach a healthy new liver would not be possible in my case. I listened and just waited for her to say "but"… Eventually, there was a "but"! Their plan(!) centred round using one of the few remaining and possible blood vessels – my renal vein. I conjured up an image of the surgery consisting of cutting off various veins and arteries and looping my kidney blood supply around my liver.

Generally, I like to be part of my health management plan. I need to know what to expect, how the experts propose to help me to survive, despite my nasty odds. I need to feel in control – and knowledge is control. On this occasion, I took another attitude and chose to bury my head in the proverbial sand. It was too much. I needed her to tell me there was a possibility to fit in a healthy liver and to attach it, ensuring some semblance of blood supply and blood drainage. I like my surgeon and have always tried to engage in surgical conversations with her; on this occasion it was just a little too much.

The day continued with a pulmonary function test; a two-part assessment of my lung health. Surprisingly, despite my June episode, my lung function was excellent. Thankfully, I still attempted to remain as fit as possible – it paid off. I then had a consultation with an anaesthetist – a funky lady from Australia who was optimistic and yet realistic about my surgical future. I learned lots about my fate – a plan for a line in my neck, lines in my arms and groin, veno-venous bypass, possible need for kidney dialysis post-surgery and ventilator during surgery. I knew that in 2006 my kidneys failed for a small while but apparently a second transplant has the potential to cause further, long-term damage to one's kidneys. Why had my poor kidneys to suffer? Christ, I had compromised so much in losing a previously-healthy liver from a rotten blood disorder, had pulled my lungs together after a huge ordeal after my back surgery. Was no part of my body sacred? This brought home to me that no part of me was really 'safe'. My heart had to be strong as it, too, would be put under tremendous pressure during my transplant surgery. . .an ECG (electrocardiogram) confirmed my heart was behaving as it should. The body is such a wonderful complex entity, but everything is interconnected, and the health and strength of one organ or system is completely dependent on another. While preparing for a liver transplant, a one-organ-replacement, my whole body needed to be ready for this new invasion. This both scared me and amazed me – scared me because I realised how much was at stake and how complex my road ahead was, and amazed me that the surgeons, anaesthetists and other physicians were pretty confident and discussing a plan which they hoped would be successful, given all the possible risks. I wasn't quite so sure, but I knew I had to trust them and leave the 'what-ifs' to them; as much as I possibly could.

The day continued with a consultation with Diarmaid and his SHO. That was a typical appointment; he's happy I'm being assessed this week as there will be a time in the future when I will be on the liver transplant waiting list (nothing I didn't really know, but something I didn't want to hear). I had numerous bloods taken for analysis and met with Dr. Murphy for a haematology consultation.

Then I was assigned my first MELD score – measure of end stage liver disease. It's a 14; falling between 6 and 49, with <6 a healthy liver and >40 a very unhealthy organ. My MELD is based on bilirubin (yellow pigment which gives us a jaundiced complexion), INR (international normalised ratio for blood clotting) and kidney function (mine is much improved but was critically high last week).

oOo

We, he and I, went on a 'holiday' three weeks ago – in Ireland. I was so very tired then and still am, needing to rest twice daily. We decided to go to Clifden for two nights before moving east to Dun Laoghaire. Some of my family find issues with some decisions I make and things that I do; in this instance they were right in that the trip was just too much for me.

I developed severe diarrhoea, a fever and was completely nauseous for much of the first week. It seemed to clear but when I had my bloods analysed in hospital (as scheduled) my kidney function was very poor – my creatinine concentration was extremely high. I had my bloods repeated a few days later - on my birthday. Instead of a nice hotel overlooking the sea as planned, we stayed in a hotel within driving distance of the hospital. I felt safer and secure, even though I didn't feel as though I had a break at all. No escape.

So, for all my passiveness and indifference about my liver transplant assessment week, today is the first time since all of this that I felt real despair. I am so afraid that, should I be forced to undergo a re-transplant (I tell myself it's my choice) it may not be a success. Fundamentally I might not make it through. So, while I'm not living my life to the full now, it may be a much better alternative to a failed re-transplant. The surgeons claim to have a vested interest in me – my case – so I have to trust that they will work their damnedest to make it a success – for their reputations as much as for my life. Now, it just has to be one day at a time. I couldn't possibly analyse the 'what-ifs' of surgery or pre-surgery or post-surgery complications. I know the odds are stacked against me. I find myself wondering about life after death and what's on offer. . .

The more I delve into the re-transplant world, the further I am pulled, yanked even, from the 'normal world'. It's okay to be sick in a hospital where people know the whys and the hows. It's so much more difficult to be ill in my own world – outside of the hospital environment, on my own path, alone.

I struggle to be a kind, happy daughter; instead I lash out as I feel suffocated and fussed over.

I've become an impatient sister; I've never asked for advice before on how to live my life yet they insist on showing how much they care by offering endless pieces of advice.

I just can't seem to cope with being a regular friend or girlfriend; there just seems too much of an effort involved in being communicative – and I don't seem to need any human contact anymore.

Right now I am struggling but am at a loss to find the way to make all of this work.

I need to find the light but the tunnel is too long and dark right now. I need to have a goal to work towards but maybe my goal is in the here and now, maybe a re-transplant is too risky a goal. Being in the now is safer than then.

One clinic I attended last week still makes me sad and stands out from all the others; my haematology clinic. Dr. Murphy admitted that my chart breaks her heart as it demonstrates the horrific outcome of a myeloproliferative blood neoplasm (MPN) and how even though people feel relieved after diagnosis they have no clue what havoc ET can wreak.

Her heart is broken for me to have this incurable cancer – I thanked her for telling me that. For some reason I felt that the medical world and my own world blended into one for a while and I could cry and not pretend to be brave or knowledgeable about my health; I could just feel free to be me for a while – and let the walls down. I could escape from the mechanical discussion of health issues and just be 'sick me'.

'Don't worry, about a thing, 'cause every little thing's gonna to be all right'

Bob Marley, Three Little Birds

9th November 2016

Dear James,

Liver transplant clinic today was good but also sad. My banding – and soo painful and anxiety-inducing clexane injections could be almost done! I'm afraid to celebrate yet but no OGD until February – yeah! I'd be so happy if I didn't feel so ill and uncomfortable. My abdomen is huge (largest in years) but Diarmaid says there are only pockets of fluid. There is air, but I can't seem to get rid of this terrible indigestion pain.

I'd also be happier if Diarmaid hadn't told me of his transplant plan. While at the MDT (multi-disciplinary meeting of hepatologists, surgeons, radiologists and coordinators) four weeks ago, my case was discussed and a number of people of various disciplines planned my life. The consensus from the surgeons was that I'm too well now – and too young. I felt relieved. I can wait. I can push out nasty, scary thoughts to a year or more away. Diarmaid said he'll be back to them, convinced that a re-transplant is the best course of action for me. It's too risky a surgery to leave me waiting too long. The sooner (but not very soon) the better. I must be fit and healthy to undergo the surgery, but not so well that I'll be last place on the waiting list for a long time, or alternatively, 'taking' the liver of someone who's less well than I am. I'm scared, worried and literally preventing the thought of transplant from entering into my already stressed head. I fear I might die – or end up losing my faculties or my ability to remain independent. I can get through the surgery and the recovery again if that's what it takes. I don't want to die though; I'm not ready. I also can't bear the thought of more than one re-transplant. That sounds too rocky a road.

So now I struggle with my huge ugly abdomen which today is not only bruised and ugly but really uncomfortable, making it a struggle to move about. Some days I yearn to escape life for a while; just me and Scamper.

When I find myself in times of trouble, Mother Mary comes to me, speaking words of wisdom "Let It Be"

And in my hour of darkness she is standing right in front of me, speaking words of wisdom "Let It Be"'

The Beatles, Let It Be

22nd November 2016

Dear James,

Well, this has to be as honest an account of now, as honest an account as I can describe.

I've just spent six nights in hospital. I'm waiting to burst, to explode, to scream, to break some glass windows or shout and scream! Nothing is happening. I'm calm. I'm ridiculously calm. I'm annoyingly, boringly, head-wreckingly calm.

Dr. Murphy took my hand on Friday morning last as I lay in bed (in 8.5/10 pain) and asked me (sadly), "how do you do this?" She said that it's okay not to be brave all the time. Her words penetrated my armour a little and I felt my face prepare to cry. It stopped almost as abruptly as it tried to begin. I'm fine. If I started I might never stop.

So, my abdomen stayed inflated. If it was full of wind and fluid at last clinic on Wednesday, it was even fuller two days later. It became horrifically inflated and, though this sounds terrible and so un-PC I looked like a starving undernourished child. Comfortable clothes became past tense. Sleep evaded me completely – it was just too uncomfortable to lie down.

Lying on my sides, the abdominal dome would just fall sideways and pull on my muscles, making me feel incredibly tender. Darts pierced my sides while my back moaned with the heaviness of the extra kilos pressing on my spine. I sat up to attempt sleep. No joy. I propped my abdomen on a pillow while the rest of my body lay on the poor mattress. No joy. I walked to get some ease. No joy. I knelt while propped against two vertical pillows. No joy. I just waited until the morning, trying to 'lose myself' in a book. I never got lost.

My head was starving but my body just wasn't accepting food. After a glass of milk it would protest its fullness. No more. I craved nice food – pasta, toasted sandwiches, steak. I managed yogurts and custards.

Clexane injections continued. The advantage of having a huge abdomen is that the needle plunges in a little easier. It's only after time passes that clexane shoots out its nasty, darting, and piercing pain. I began my warfarin too; anticipating the time when I could bid a farewell to twice daily self-inflicted stabbing.

Monday came and I went off to my GP to get my bloods analysed. I struggled in the car, nervously anticipating Mum's attempted avoidance of potholes and speedbumps. My doctor examined me and advised me to phone St. Vincent's – I had definite pockets of fluid in my abdomen. Later she called to advise that my creatinine concentration was extremely high at 195 (my baseline is typically 90-100).

Things moved – it was, bizarrely, a relief for me to actually have a tangible 'result' instead of ascites or fluid build-up in my peritoneum. I could envision this kidney function test ensuring a plan would be made for me. . .

I made my way to clinic on Wednesday last with Mum. We travelled by train; me, wearing baggy tracksuit bottoms and a t-shirt that wouldn't go beyond my naval. So sad. I covered the multitude with a baggy jacket and scarf. (I really miss my nice clothes and my 'own body'.) I said goodbye to Scamper and Dad; Scamper enjoyed his very early morning tickles and hugs.

Within hours of clinic I was in a cubicle in A&E, with blown blood vessels where a young doctor had attempted two lines in my arms. Then, I had two needles inserted into my sides to obtain an ascitic fluid sample. Both ran bloody. Pain, pain and more pain. Physical and emotional. Still no comfort in my abdomen but more pain from a 'short scratch'. Instead of an anticipated few days on a trolley in A&E, the blood find elevated me to the Medical Observation Unit; St. Patrick's Ward. I had severe pain. I didn't sleep.

CT next morning. Like a hippo moving from my bed. Pain reached a 9.5 that night. Panadol didn't work but tramadol did. Wow, wow, wow. First near-normal sleep in weeks. That stuff is amazing. Why did I never do drugs to experience that cosy blanket-high, numbing my pain, numbing my brain. . .

Now, I'm in St. Brigid's. Reading over what I've just written I think its best I continue my ramblings later – it's all over the place. I'll continue after a rest.

o0o

On Friday morning, a consultant radiologist inserted a drain into my side – a long narrow-ish plastic tube. Like everything in this medical world, it struck me as so fundamental – a tube draining fluid by gravity, into a graduated plastic bag. Over a few hours they collected over seven litres of blood, old blood. It was a little shocking to see, though I looked forward to a flatter, more manoeuvrable body. As the blood came out, they transfused fresh stuff back in – four units. I also received IV fluids. Sleep returned when I went back to St. Brigid's. Familiar, happy nurses, familiar procedures, secure in the knowledge that they know liver disease.

The scariest moment of all of this (obviously it tends to be difficult to rank these days) was the injection I received to completely reverse my anticoagulation. It felt like my safety blanket of 10 years was slipped away. I felt so open and vulnerable to blood clotting. I prayed as the nurse injected it into the line in my left arm. I prayed as if, within seconds, my blood would clump and coagulate and result in little thromboses – in my brain, lungs, legs, hepatic system. My work of 10 years of anticoagulation, avoiding vitamin K, cranberries, rhubarb, mayonnaise, coleslaw. . .all vanished with that one injection. As the nurse plunged the antidote so slowly (apparently it must be done slowly) I literally felt as though I was praying for my life at that exact time. I closed my eyes and hoped. I obviously stayed alive.

The days have passed, somewhat boringly – but that's not a complaint. My abdomen is softer, but still very large (personally I feel it filling up again – fluid or blood?)

I'll take boring. I've read, walked a little, had Mum, Dad, my sister Paula and my boyfriend visit. I've crocheted, listened to music - and ate. I feel as if this ward is where the gladiators are being fattened up. We are actively encouraged to eat desserts, high calorie muffins and rice puddings, cheese, biscuits and crackers. Apparently I need to increase my BMI – to have some fat in reserve for when I need it. I was never fat – I don't need or want a double chin or a wobbly size 14 ass. I certainly don't want muscly shoulders or huge dipping bingo wings. It's not my choice though, apparently. A lot of things are no longer my choice, no longer under my control.

I am waiting to hear if I will be listed for re-transplant. I didn't want it the first time, I've shared that with you already. After 10 years, I've settled with my 2006-liver and have grown very dependent on it, protecting it with everything I've got, in every single way I can. Now, I'm faced with the possibility of doing it all again – if the high-risk transplant is a success.

It's tough, easier in hospital with similar people, but still so tough facing an ordeal that's as big as one can get.

> '…Not sure I understand
> this role I've been given,
> I sit and talk to God
> And He just laughs at my plans,
> my head speaks a language
> I don't understand'
>
> Robbie Williams, Feel

29th November 2016

Dear James,

I'm still in St. Brigid's Ward. Today I came off my IV anti-coagulant heparin and now I'm back on injectable clexane. I wonder will I be injecting myself right up until my transplant?

I was officially placed on the liver transplant waiting list four days ago. Jennifer and Shauna told me and I cried, even though I knew it was ahead. I knew what to expect but the words cut right through me; sounding so dramatic and scary, so 'not my life'.

You and I are going to be parting company – possibly next year. I won't be able to talk to you anymore, share my stuff with you and moan about my worries. I'm so very sad about that. But now at least I have a plan, a goal to work towards. I haven't thought about the actual transplant process too much – I have subconsciously, but consciously I'm putting it in a compartment in my brain, parking it. I know it's there, I know what's inside the compartment but I don't need to look and analyse until I'm ready.

So my plan now is to take on a 'stepping stone lifestyle'. From now until the big day (must name the transplant day more appropriately – T2!) I am going to strive to enjoy myself as much as possible. The stepping stone concept will be like this; I will look forward to something nice and hop from one good experience to another until I receive that phonecall summoning me to the operating theatre. I have no intention of just sitting around and setting lots of goals for post-surgery – that honestly might not happen and I must face this. My first stepping stone is Christmas. I want to have fun, get a Christmas Day walk on the beach with Mum, Dad and Scamper, eat nice food watching fun TV and spend time with Mum and Dad – who will hopefully understand that Christmas is fun, happy and precious time.

Though I'm not certain of my next stepping stone, hair appointments, clothes shopping (albeit for larger-waisted flowing clothes), nail appointments, concerts, theatre visits and afternoon teas will all happen.

Christmas is first. That will feel safe. I really don't envisage getting a call for my new liver during 2016. And I'm not ready yet.

'Blackbird singing in the dead of night
Take these broken wings and learn to fly
All your life
You were only waiting for this moment to arise'

The Beatles, Blackbird

8th December 2016

Dear James,

Its 04:09 and I've just woken up with cramps. They're not too severe; I took my iron supplement late in the evening and with little food. The cramps will pass and I'll be fine in the morning.

I'm doing fine. I'm keeping busy. My Christmas 'stepping stone' is keeping me fully occupied with shopping, making lists and planning the last few gifts.

I'm also getting my suitcases organised for when I receive 'the call'. I'll be happier when I've fully packed though I mightn't need those bags for months. I'm in St. Vincent's next week for a breast ultrasound and also a quick dash to transplant clinic for blood analyses. I feel okay. I feel pretty okay for what's going on in my life. Physically I am very itchy and my abdomen, while not as bad as two weeks ago, is still quite 'pudgy'. My appetite is normal but my hair is coming out in clumps (steroids?)

I feel stressed but this is really because I am living at home with Mum and Dad and feel like I've so little of my independence left. My own house is empty and I'm stressed that it's not as I'd like it. There are no Christmas decorations up and it's likely not looking very festive…yes, I am aware these are very, very small concerns but they all contribute to the 'lack of control' feeling I have so much these days.

If getting the call meant successful (yet painful) liver transplant, a repaired hepatic artery and a delayed return to what I had pre-October 2014, I would be so excited and completely happy. I just fear that might not happen. I worry so much about a poor quality liver which might not be as healthy as yours. I worry about bleeding or clotting and I worry about stuff I can't even imagine going wrong. . . My abdomen is so much more lined with blood vessels and collaterals. It's so ugly, but I love myself no matter what. I'm brave and strong and determined and that's better than beautiful.

On a happier note, Scamper got groomed today and smells of blueberries. He looks like a three-month-old puppy and has the shortest coat with his big brown melting-chocolate eyes even more adorable than before. My heart bursts with love for him and he is such a distraction for me, and Mum and Dad, these days. He's full of fun and so smart. For a while I wondered if having him made life more complicated and difficult – and his care contributed to my tiredness and my parents' workload. He makes it all worthwhile though. It was a good choice to get him and I know I'm lucky to have him for company these days.

> *'A woman is like a tea bag; you can't tell how strong she is until you put her in hot water'*
>
> *Irish proverb, circa 1860*

28th December 2016

Dear James,

It's almost five weeks since my name reached the transplant list. I meant to write but couldn't summon the enthusiasm or motivation.

I'm still far from enthused today but I feel guilty about not putting my thoughts to paper. Physically, I am falling apart before my own eyes. Emotionally, I'm like a can of pasta characters. I'm fine, angry, afraid, grumpy, emotional, okay – the seven dwarves of emotions! I've now realised that this is a shocking situation to be in. I am waiting for a call – to take my (almost-packed) bags to Dublin where, within hours I'll go to surgery (if everything proceeds). I don't know who'll drive, have absolutely no idea when this will be or who will come with me. What about Scamper? I've asked everyone to give me Christmas. I wanted to leave all of these decisions and plan-making until after the holidays so at least it will feel as though I've had a 'normal' Christmas. I didn't really. I tried. My head is full and I tried so hard to 'enjoy' myself that I got lost along the way and came out like a grumpy, angry, terrified, preoccupied twit. I feel like I'm suffocating. I don't feel free and as though I'm enjoying my life before transplant. I get up at 7:30am, take pills, eat before 8am, inject myself with blood-thinning clexane at 9am, sleep until 10:30am when I take more pills. Then I rest until 12pm. I generally try and exercise but after that, the day just passes in an unstructured haze of unfocussed nothingness. I'm certain I'm making Mum and Dad's lives miserable. I don't want visitors and yet some people insist on visiting. I hate being the 'sick one' and anyway, I have no further news to offer bar transplant news and little else outside of the confines of that topic. They don't understand; they talk of work and small stuff; there's a chasm between us right now.

And the other thing. . .my abdomen is growing again – presumably fluid and not blood, and I am ashamed of how I look and uncomfortable that I look so large. I don't look or feel like myself. I have no control over how I look but I can control who looks at me!

I don't want sympathy or pity. I'm losing my hair and I am certain I have a moonface – steroid side effects.

This week has brought an interesting new challenge for me though. It's almost humorous! I had a breast biopsy on Monday 19th. Yes, it was painful and uncomfortable – as expected. I held my clexane as advised but went back on it as quickly as possible afterwards to prevent clotting. Now, I have a right boob shaped like a dolphin's head! I am so serious! Well, maybe a porpoise?! There's a purple and brown large bruise, right in the middle of which is a large lump, about 5cm in diameter which hurts and throbs like hell. I think it's a haematoma and might need to be lanced. That, or it's an infection which needs antibiotics. I refuse to act on it this week. I want my Christmas break free of surgeons, hospitals and consultants. I don't think that's too much to ask. This isn't getting any better though – and it really hurts. But 2017 is likely to have lots of pain so I better be ready. I feel a little less 'fighter' and more 'runner' these days. I need a good focus but there are so many uncertainties… If I had a guarantee that I would undergo a successful transplant with a good healthy graft, work hard and have a pretty uncomplicated recovery to receive a great outcome, I would be so delighted – ecstatic even. But I'm fearful of a myriad issues arising, not least bleeding and / or clotting or a new liver which just doesn't work well. I wonder is it too much to ask for a good, happy outcome? Yes, it's asking – begging – a lot. How long do I want to live for? How many more scares and complications can I face and how much more pain and fear can I endure? A lot – is really the answer. For the proper outcome. . .

> *'You never know how strong you are, until being strong is your only choice'*
> *Bob Marley*

3rd February 2017

Dear James,

Where do I begin? I'm here - almost at my destination. I'm in St. Vincent's for over two weeks now and it seems likely that I'll be here until my transplant. I get butterflies just writing that sentence down. I'm so frightened, really terrified. I fear all the things that can go wrong, the issues that may arise, the unexpected. I obviously fear the pain, the nausea, the incision to my abdomen, the cannulas in my arms, groin, shoulders. The main fear is that it won't be successful and I don't make it through. Or that it seems successful, I begin my recovery but something goes wrong and I have to go through the whole process again. (I don't think I can do it again – I'm set for this time, this push, this 'deep-digging' fight – but I don't feel as if I have more than one 'push' inside me). I have to do what I can so I can stay alive, the injections (I now let the nurses inject my clexane – I'm taking a break!), the discomfort, sleepless nights, cramps, hair loss... I'm sacrificing absolutely everything about my body to stay alive. I look okay but really have very little control over my appearance, my weight or my diet, my fat face or my thin ass. I should explain what brought me here this time. . .

Two weeks and three days ago, I had an ovarian scan. I convinced Mum that I could travel alone. I needed to prove that I could – to myself and Mum and Dad. The journey by train was tough. My abdomen was taut and larger for a few days. I'd had diarrhoea but that wasn't the worst thing. I also had a burning, searing pain throughout my entire pelvis. It was as though my ovaries, bladder, kidneys and some growth were hugely inflamed and so heavy in my body. I know (or felt) I was carrying some fluid so I wasn't certain if this was putting pressure on my organs by pushing down on them. I had a heartburn pain too, but the pain in my lower quadrant was almost unbearable. It didn't help that poor Scamper had been furiously itching his ears for a few days. I knew he needed to see the vet. . .

The day before my scan I got out of bed and immediately needed to go back. I decided to contact St. Vincent's and request kidney function tests to be done when in hospital for my scan. That off my list, Mum and I went off with Scamper to the vet. The poor pet had the beginning of a mite infestation so he went on a course of ear drops.

On Tuesday I took the train again to Dublin, cursing the train driver and Iarnrod Eireann for the uncomfortable dirty train and the whizzing around corners at speed.

I struggled with public transport to the hospital but within an hour found myself sitting in the ladies with cramps and diarrhoea (so much for a full bladder for my scan!).

Eventually, I was having the scan, narrated by a concerned radiographer and doctor. Apparently, I was actively bleeding from my left ovary – or a left ovarian cyst. It seemed like another issue for my list.

It never ceases to amaze me that, with an ever-deteriorating hepatic system, issues like breast cancer and ovarian dysfunction fade a little into oblivion (don't sweat the small stuff – though I'm completely aware they're not small). I left the hospital and made my way back to Mayo, presumably still bleeding.

First thing next morning, Diarmaid phoned and asked me to make my way to St. Vincent's. There were no beds but I needed treatment; my kidney function was way off. My creatinine, normally less than 100 had more than doubled - again. Also my haemoglobin was low; the breathlessness and extreme fatigue made sense.

He suggested that I travel the next day but phoned within a few hours letting me know there was a bed available in St. Brigid's and I needed to grab it while it was available.

Bloody hell. . .this is boring reading. . .I'm going to cut to the chase!

After night time blood tests (I had arrived with Mum at 10pm) and a day of sample taking (another large needle into the abdomen) and monitoring, I found out I had a critically low haemoglobin concentration of 5.6 (apparently I was coping 'remarkably well'!) and my creatinine was 288 – not good at all. . .essentially I was bleeding internally leading to my drop in haemoglobin. The sample to examine the fluid in my abdomen revealed fresh blood. A tube was inserted and attached to a glass bottle. Apparently, the bottle was full of blood in minutes, emptied and full again minutes later. I don't know how many 5-litre bottles were filled but there was no stopping the flow once it began. No one could definitively determine its origin but I didn't feel very worried. The reason was that, though I didn't realise it at the time, I was very drowsy and exhausted from the blood loss. The blurry days passed by with a mix of blood transfusions, IV fluids and bottles of albumin (to try to rectify my kidneys).

I really couldn't wash; too tiring and uncomfortable to stand in the shower so I washed myself at the bathroom sink…never feeling fresh. After days of blood and albumin I was put on IV heparin – my blood thinner or anti-coagulation therapy. The 'joy' with heparin, unlike clexane and warfarin, is that it is reversible should I bleed again. In hindsight, the IV heparin and the wheeling around of a drip-stand were so inconvenient but gave me a much-needed break from injecting clexane.

My internal bleed was just like November – a diffuse bleed into my peritoneum. The horrible irony this time – and the truth that makes me worry more about my rotten blood disorder – is that the blood has now clotted and cannot be removed. A syringe would block up – I joked that they'd need a bigger bore - like a hose, but this would probably kill me!

The discussions, pondering and studying of research papers led to no suitable resolution. Surgery would be the only option to remove it...but that would bring huge risks to my liver.

In two days, I was hit with three pieces of information that turned my life on his head – well, at least two of the three.

One – Prof. MacNicholas decided that the best course of action for a bleeder-clotter like me was to keep me as a resident right up until my transplant...

Two – Anthony the surgeon told me it may be quite a wise option to remove my ovaries during the transplant – while my abdomen is open. They have determined that the bleed is likely an ovarian cyst (I queried the menopause and whether I'd go straight into it. He looked at me directly, almost amused, and reminded me of my three life-threatening bleeds, insinuating that the menopause for me would be quite 'manageable').

Three – I will have a large abdomen, inflated with a large blood clot until my transplant surgery. Until then, I will look heavily pregnant, weigh an abnormal amount and drag this heavy load under a stretched nightdress. It may get bigger and the ascites might even become worse.

Limited space brought me to a room with an old lady begging God to take her, begging the nurses to 'knock her out'. She cried, screamed, begged, pood. I cried with sympathy and sadness. She was moved to another room as she deteriorated – her family needed privacy in her last hours. She died, never making it to a transplant.

Today I cried again. I am so anxious and scared. There are just too many things that can go wrong – the ones I know and those issues I can't even begin to imagine. Most of all I worry frantically that the liver they give me will be a poor quality one which will be a stop gap to free up a bed. The 'really good' liver I was promised in November might now be gone forever from my grasp. I worry about the surgery, after the surgery if I make it through, clotting or bleeding, losing my colon or having a dreadfully complicated recovery.

I find it very difficult to imagine an uncomplicated, successful transplant surgery with a typical recovery. Now I'm making myself visualise just that – and I pray that it might happen for me. I never ever imagined how lucky and uncomplicated my eight years post-transplant were. I was bloody fine – in hospital only two or three times. . . I never knew and, while grateful, probably wasn't quite grateful enough. Now, I feel this path might be rockier. If I survive the surgery will I become a more frequent visitor to St. Brigid's?

I avoid a certain lady on this ward. She's small-minded, melodramatic and just plain annoying. I say hello but avoid conversation. This morning, at the lockers, I felt I had better make an effort and initiate an 'infrequent' conversation. Within seconds, she told me that a hospital acquaintance of mine; a fun, smart and optimistic lady, is back on the transplant waiting list – her third time. I'm sad – for her and for me. She worked hard to get through two transplants within two months of each other. Now she has to go again – with weaker blood vessels and a knowledge of the pain.

I didn't want – or need - to know this sad news. I put a stop to my polite conversation with that annoying cow.

After the 'altercation' and my anger, I wandered down to the church for a visit. It's a peaceful place where I feel some semblance of escape from my current 'lifestyle'. But, my brain, my mind never switches off from where I am and why I'm here. So I prayed a bit. I have some favourite prayers that I like to say – nothing too holy or long-winded but just some calming and reassuring petitions. I also lit some candles before I meditated a little.

My sister Noranne and my nieces are coming later. I've put on makeup, new nightdress and feel excited. I hope I can be happy and enjoy their visit. I feel sad today, maybe more anxious and worried than sad – but I'll try to not think. I'll go shopping online again – three dresses and a book so far this week!

'A time to be born, a time to die
A time to plant, a time to reap
A time to kill, a time to heal
A time to laugh, a time to weep
To everything - turn, turn, turn
There is a season - turn, turn, turn
And a time to every purpose under heaven'
The Byrds, Turn! Turn! Turn! (to Everything There is a Season)

7th February 2017

Dear James,

This is definitely a place for thinking. . .

Thinking pensively and ruminating. What's going on outside these hospital walls? What is my family up to? What are they all thinking about? How many women gave birth today? How many people died today, learned of a terrible diagnosis, passed an exam, got engaged, celebrated a birthday, hit a partner for the first time, fell in love, decided to emigrate, decided to retire, got divorced, picked a wedding venue, picked a flower, saw a beautiful tree, asked someone on a date, broke a bone, had a most-important-life-changing interview, had good sex, had bad sex, shared a first kiss...? Somewhere, today, all of those events – and so many more – happened. It's strange, wonderful and awful, all at once, that life is going on, the world is still spinning, traffic is still moving and clocks are still ticking when my life is out of step with the world. I have my own timeline, my own 'events', my own pace of life that is so detached from the world of others. Or so it seems. It just feels as though my life has been derailed and it never really got back on its normal track since my HAT diagnosis. How can things have been right since then? Getting that diagnosis was like a death sentence, or at least a promise of very bad things to come.

Receiving that diagnosis led me to gather my thoughts and contemplate MY LIFE. What has it actually been about? What difference have I made? What has been my point? No, this isn't me being hard on myself (as I generally am) and conclude that my life has been a waste and I didn't conquer Everest or cure a devastating disease. This isn't me asking a huge question which begs a response similar to the one George Bailey received from Clarence the angel (*It's a Wonderful Life* and James Stewart make my every Christmas!). This is just me asking myself the simple question – what has my 42-year-old life entailed? Is my greatest achievement, my biggest accolade to be my battling illness for many of my years? Will my most cherished accomplishment be living to 45?

My hair colour has influenced my life; I really believe that. I was a child who felt different, an outlier, dissimilar from the other girls who shared my all-girls convent schools. Now, of course, I see this as ridiculous – it was just a colour but at a young age, told regularly how different it was, that no dye could copy *my colour*, I couldn't help but wonder if the admiration was actually criticism or hidden disgust. Now, I know the reaction was more likely indifference or just mere disinterest – something adults just commented on (better than pointing out my large teeth or face stained with freckles). But the hated red hair set the scene for years of self-criticism and feelings of inferiority. Shyness too, didn't help my cause so I settled for inferior younger sister by over two years, the one who didn't necessarily speak up and offer opinions, the one who quietly observed lots but said very little. I loved our weekend visits to our cousins where I would regularly sit on my uncle's knee for most of the day, sucking my then-wizened right thumb and listening to the chitchat by my aunt and mother, two sisters so alike and so different.

My teachers were mostly nuns in primary school, so my experiences in school were mostly negative – lots of enforced praying, strict rules about chattering and, I have to admit, three nervous, tense years of terror by one nun who was, in hindsight, mentally ill and highly unsuitable for teaching seven to nine year olds. I found myself, at that young age, nervous about shuffling in class, moving my feet or any body part or, horror of horrors, looking around, should I receive a slap or a spray of her saliva as she shouted and shouted until she was purple with rage.

Primary school ended with the most kind, caring, interesting, intelligent, clever, inspirational nun of all times. Sr. Finbarr was a tiny little thing who loved all things history and nature and she loved her pupils, her 'little women'. The two years with her were the complete antithesis of all that had gone before. Never did I feel so confident, so interested and interesting, so inspired and enthused by the world around me than I did in those two years with her as my guide. Those were the happiest days of my entire school life.

Now, I'm digressing. . .

Who am I now?

I've had love – the sparkly, tingly, butterfly kind that keeps you awake all night, bans all appetite and takes over your entire life. The love you want to last forever, the love that lets you see you and him grow old together, see your house and your future life. The love that literally awakens your senses and makes memories from his scent, the feel of his hand in yours, his kiss, his laugh and voice. The love that, when it ends, causes pain so real that it physically hurts. The love that you want to find again, the love you hope is possible with someone else but you fear, so fiercely, that you won't ever find again. It's no huge surprise that so many songs are penned about love, losing it, heartbreak, new love, whatever. It's a universal sentiment, an often-felt emotion, but when it's your emotion, it feels so exclusively yours.

I have no problem in admitting that, in my twenties, I saw my life pan out as my parents did. I would be married in my mid-twenties and have some children. We'd have some issues and problems, typical family stuff but I'd rear clever, musical and confident children and encourage them in their decisions, careers and try not to project my choices into them by turning out doctors or nurses. I'd have a meaningful career and my husband, too, would be equally successful. Maybe he'd be an accountant or a lawyer or doctor, we'd have similar values and opinions, or at least we'd compromise on our stronger opinions. I never imagined that the family life I envisaged wouldn't happen for me. I assumed the man 'of my dreams' would just materialise and I'd 'just know'. There would be no doubt we would find each other and no doubt we would just have children. Maybe I spent too much time watching TV when I was a child but I firmly believed that meeting 'the one' would eventually happen. There would be bad relationships, inappropriate boyfriends (believe me, I have a bunch of those in my past!), incompatible men, but then the important one would arrive and banish all thoughts and references of those who had gone before. He would be tiresome, have quirky habits and unusual hair or teeth but I'd love him and he would love me, imperfections included. So, it didn't happen. I have lived with my parents for many months now and my current relationship feels derailed, or is it? Am I imagining that it's been fractured, that we've needed to talk through and discuss a lot of things recently, but neither of us have said this aloud? I'm not feeling overwhelming, blanketing love from my boyfriend recently, but is that because we've not had the time and space for a real, normal relationship? These days, it feels like I only have the (beautiful) memories of love from men - but right now, I don't feel that I'm deeply in love.

But, lying here, stuck, I am having regrets that I wasted so much of my time. Why, why did I engage in stupid and wrong relationships with unsuitable men? Yes, many were nice but there was a bunch of 'outliers' I'd prefer to fiercely erase from my life. Now, I'm not sure why my bar was quite so low, but my gut instinct is that it was self-preservation. Nobody wants their heart broken, so if one is the relationship controller (the one ending the relationships), a sad, inevitable, devastating, breakup is completely avoided. I don't know – maybe I'm waffling but if there was the possibility of turning back time, I would skip the stupid, timewasters and take a chance with the one or two nice, kind men who I managed to let escape.

Post-2006, selecting a boyfriend who 'ticked boxes' involved a more precautionary tactic. Among the list of traits – generous, handsome, clever, witty and kind – would be included 'must like scars'. Ok, I jest; what I really subconsciously included on a list was – must not be put off by scars, floppy skin and the idea of dating a 'physically broken' female. Who wants to see a man recoil at the sight of my abdominal scars, or become impatient by my cumbersome-yet-not-unsurmountable routine of daily fasting and routine blood testing? I don't consciously feel broken – time and again I've described myself as proud of my body, as it documents exactly what I've achieved, it's like a map of my struggles and winning battles. I generally overlook my 'war injuries' but, in a relationship setting or situation, I still feel dreadfully self-conscious and embarrassed about my body appearance.

I'm completely aware that my mood is quite low so on days like today everything seems a little negative. I think I can pinpoint the reason and I'm a little flabbergasted by it. I am here until my transplant. I have to accept that and try to just be patient and hope that will be very soon (or not soon if it means certain death. I mean that as a joke but there's some truth in it too…). I do not want to be here and I think the majority of people would not choose to live their lives in such a controlled, routine, monotonous environment. I feel like I'm merely existing but I have hope that it will be worth it – in the end. Today, however, a member of staff called in and we spoke about what is ahead for me. I am quite stable now but not sufficiently enough to travel home. I was advised in January that I will be here until my transplant so now, these days, I have to work on being fit (I am cycling circa 10km most days on the ward stationary bike!) and on eating high calorie and protein foods – that's manageable when I enhance my nasty hospital food with protein supplements. We spoke about my current condition, LFTs are stable if not great, my ascites is increasing and my energy levels are depleted (yes, I cycle daily but it leaves me exhausted and needing a long nap). Then she said something I am still gutted by, as well as confused and bemused as to why it was actually said at all. It was definitely not something that I needed to acknowledge, it is something I am, and have been, acutely aware of, but the speaking of it aloud by a qualified health professional was just astounding. We talked and laughed at the food I was eating (trying to eat). We discussed my current accommodation – a one-bed hospital en-suite room. Then she / we discussed my pending surgery and talked a little about the surgeons' plan – as cryptic and enigmatic as it is proposed to be. She then imparted these words of wisdom to the already-anxious me. She told me that my surgery is classified as high-risk but wanted me to know that sometimes high risk surgeries have good outcomes – and some have 'bad outcomes'. In between the lines, was she telling me not to get my hopes up that I would survive? Was she preparing me for the worst? Was she filling in the gaps that my consultant and surgeons had failed to disclose? I'm not sure – I just felt numb when she left me alone. What exactly was the point in telling me that, basically, the surgeons had their work cut out for them and may fail to undertake my high-risk surgery in full (a partial transplant is, admittedly, pointless). I know the risks and I worry every single hour of every single day that the outcome might not be positive. But, what will I know if it's not? I'll know nothing. I'll just remain asleep and drift away, oblivious to the surgeons' failure to complete the high-risk surgery. If I think or focus on the eventuality of not making it through, then what on earth am I doing here? If I am of the opinion that this will fail, the outcome will be negative, then I should just hop on the next plane to the Caribbean. What's the purpose of being here if not to be hopeful and positive about my outcome? Literally, she needs a good kick up the arse!

Then she left me to my own devices… At times like this, and other times along the last few months, I've really felt the need to discuss my thought processes with a professional. A counsellor or a psychotherapist? There is no-one to bounce these very real, very much relevant and, let's face it, very much expected fears with. The coordinators, qualified nurses, are about from time to time, but they're overworked, busy and have their hands full with numerous patients. I'm just me, in insulated isolation. I need help to handle this, to tackle and cope with all of these convoluted, terrified feelings – but I feel so alone.

'Come away, O human child!
To the waters and the wild
With a faery, hand in hand,
For the world's more full of weeping than you can understand'
William Butler Yeats, The Stolen Child

13th March 2017

Dear James,

I've thought a lot about death, of course I have mulled and ruminated upon it time and again. I know I've faced death head-on at least five times. Am I to be like a cat – meaning I've three or four left to wrestle with. Fundamentally, because of my Catholic upbringing and quite-religious parents, it has been ingrained into me that if one is 'good' and kind to others, caring, selfless and honest (though not humble and meek as some nuns insisted on translating altruism!) one will be rewarded with a happy 'afterlife' and secured entry into heaven. I, even as a 42-year-old scientist cannot shake this belief so embedded into my brain, though, I've always half-thought that heaven cannot possibly exist. As I've claimed before, it's too impossible to imagine a 'place' housing my grandparents, aunties, David Bowie and Anne Frank...

I'd love to have a firm, strong, unwavering belief in an afterlife. I need to hope that the suffering, pain, fear and worry I've been subjected to and living with (at least since my thirties) have to be for a reason. They have to count towards something; some exchange of terrible times for future good ones, pain for future painless days, fear for relief and joy. It can't all just be random, can it? If it is all random, then, as humans and so advanced in terms of our earthly contemporaries, we are no different from badgers, sheep or mayflies.

I imagine heaven as a feeling or an aura of joy – like the joy and happiness experienced momentarily in everyday things; happy relationships, feelings of being loved, a newly-dressed bed – without the sting of a sad day or the memory of the loss of a loved one. It is happiness with no bounds, joy with no end.

For the nasties, Adolf Hitler, Myra Hindley and Charles Manson – there's nothing. Nothingness, to be precise. They die and that's the end. Like slipping an anaesthetic and just sliding away into nothingness.

I've spoken to people who've 'seen the light' and wanted to go towards it, were drawn to it – not wanting to come back. This scares me; I've never experienced any draw towards anything, never felt a pull away from my life to go to a 'better place'. That makes me fear two things – I'm either a baddy who'll just stop living and end or there truly is nothing after death. Maybe there'll be no afterlife for me. All of my hard life will have been for no reason - except to retain my life – no reward of joy and happiness. That is my fear about death – isn't it everyone's? Will my fate in death be equal to a sex offender, murderer, a rhino or a piece of moss? Just over, lights out, gone.

It's diabolically terrifying though – to really, truly 'face death'. Many of us think about it in passing, after losing a loved one perhaps, but no one ever, ever really thinks and deeply dwells on and becomes consumed with death the way a person with a serious illness does. It becomes a fixation, a waking nightmare, a preoccupying mindful of seriousness that literally can chill, and has chilled me.

Bizarrely (and horribly) though, having faced it and 'entertained' the prospect of death so many times, I now feel half-ready, as though I've travelled some way there already. Death seems like *déjà vu* for me – I can't explain it any better than that.

When diagnosed with my HAT, I imagined it was the end. I imagined just not existing anymore, that it was my turn to go, before my parents, sisters, friends. It was unfair. I was too young, I had so much still to do with my life. But, after days of imagining facing death, of wondering what it would be like, how 'I would end', I almost, almost – albeit very reluctantly and angrily - accepted it. Maybe accepted is too strong a word? I felt if there really really was no other choice, no other option or treatment to save my life, I would just have to go.

Since then, during the tough times, I've still felt 'ready', unwilling and angry with it but as ready as someone who doesn't, definitely doesn't want to die, can be. Everyone dies but we continually live in denial, as if we're able to fight this, or as though we have some choice, some power to changes our fates.

I've lost so many good people in my life; two aunts, two uncles, friends and acquaintances that I have to believe I will see them again.

Recently, whenever I hear of the death of someone young or someone I know, I firstly feel for them in the unfairness of it all. I also feel that since 'they've taken the plunge' I can do it too, when my time comes.

> *'…There is no armour against Fate,*
> *Death lays his icy hand on kings,*
> *Sceptre and Crown*
> *Must tumble down,*
> *And in the dust be equal made*
> *With the poor crooked scythe and spade.'*
> James Shirley, Death the Leveller

20th March 2017

Dear James,

Crikey, the weeks are flying but the days just drag. . .

I'm gaining weight from fluid more rapidly now – I am at least 5kg above my typical weight – and it's all on my front. My face is gaunt, arms thin and fragile, and I'm certainly not enjoying the food enough to be 'fat'. Actually, I should be gaining weight all over thanks to the pre-transplant high-fat diet…unfortunately I have less of an appetite for chocolate and croissants and all things tasty and sugary than the transplant dietician would like. Instead and possibly also, she's prescribed a variety of protein 'shots' and shakes – all as nasty and evil-tasting as one would imagine. There's a stack of them in my fridge at home, waiting to be lovingly devoured. They will remain waiting. I guess I've narrowed the best of the worst down to a strawberry flavoured fortisip. I can generally drink three of those daily – as long as they're chilled. Nothing worse than a warm vanilla fortisip directly after breakfast. Nothing worse?! Well, there are a few things.

I have to get on with things. I just have to get on with all of this. There is no choice in any of this for me but to 'enjoy' every day and try to see something positive daily – sunny days, happy nurses, kind visitors, new friends. We all resent the 'time out' from real life and being forced to stay here but moaning about it won't improve the situation one single bit. St. Brigid's Day has passed, St. Patrick's Day has passed. Patients and friends have come and gone. Sandra, my friend who's been here since before December, has gone home for a while. I miss her, but she's stable enough to be discharged from hospital. I'm wondering whether that might happen for me? Will I be discharged and allowed home until my new liver is available? I've already moved rooms three times; at least I'm travelling light. Experience of hospitals teaches one to travel light. No excess baggage or unnecessary nice stuff. Who needs foundation or mascara? Who needs body scrub and hair conditioner with UV protection? I'm inside practically all of the time. Who needs shaving essentials? I can't even see the tops of my legs with my abdominal mound and my underarm hair seems to have come to an unexpected stop.

Other stuff has happened too, difficult and challenging stuff. A lovely man I shared a ward with last year has died. He had ITP, a blood disorder just the opposite of mine, in that his body produced too few platelets. His bleeding couldn't be controlled so he was always in danger of 'bleeding out'. He died and I feel sad.

Just a few weeks ago, I was chatting with Sandra and a second lady I had met in the dayroom. We were giving out about food but otherwise, we were just having a normal everyday, non-medical conversation. That can happen in here sometimes! We were just women being women – except in dressing gowns camouflaging liver disease. I enjoyed the normal conversation and the second lady gave me a pile of magazines as I was popping back to my own room, telling me to call again and she'd give me another bunch. I didn't tell her I hate those tacky gossipy magazines but welcomed her kindness. The following day, she was wheeled away to the operating theatre as a suitable liver had been found for her. It was all quite sudden. I imagined her being brought down, wearing her pink dressing gown, eyes wide and anxious – like the first time I met her. She had been told just a few weeks before that she had a HAT (blocked hepatic artery) just like me. She was startled and so worried that she had to face another transplant over 10 years after her first. I couldn't console her without facing the fear of my own very similar situation. I guess I tried to convince her that our surgeons knew what they were doing and we all had to have faith in them and the surgery. I never saw her again, but Jane, one of the transplant coordinators, called in a few days later to tell me that she didn't survive the surgery. The clotting in her hepatic system was too extensive and the surgeons couldn't find a viable option to connect her new liver to. I cried, Jane cried and we hugged. What an experience for all of us. There was an air of muted sadness in Brigid's for a few days, as everyone thought about what had happened. I had never known anyone not to survive the surgery. As anyone would, I contemplated my own surgery and the 'what ifs'. What if that very thing happens to me? What if my veins and blood vessels are worse than they appear in the scans and it's not possible to surgically attach them to a new healthy liver. I concluded two things that day; I would just pray and hope and trust in the surgeons, my body and God that that wouldn't happen to me and two, should that happen – and I knew how high risk my proposed surgery was – I wouldn't know. Let's be honest, I wouldn't be wakening up from my anaesthetic to find out that I wasn't going to make it. I would never know. From my experiences of anaesthesia, I have to admit I really enjoy the 'slipping away' sensation. I love that feeling of closing my eyes and just – succumbing. It's so peaceful. So, though it's a strange thing to admit, I had to acknowledge that should I pass during my surgery, it would be painless, easy and relaxed – and I would be fearless, ignorant - and completely unaware. I don't want to die, all I want is to get through this and go home 'fixed'. It's funny how, when one is in this position (knee-deep in this position) one will bargain absolutely anything just for a shot at life. I want what all of those people – at work, on holidays, unemployed, homeless – have. I just want to be alive. Once I'm allowed to live for another while, I won't demand another thing. I don't need an expensive house, a huge car, jewellery or anything along those lines. I just want to live. Already, I've compromised so much for this promised holy grail. I've been forced to give up my real life and wait here in a hospital where everything I do is controlled and monitored. I have no freedom. I have had to give that up completely, along with my physical appearance. I can't look the way I want but am forced to carry around an abdomen-full of fluid and blood, wear a grey-brown face with black bags and new wrinkles. Makeup doesn't help me to look any healthier. I can't travel abroad since going on the transplant list in November and I really had to take a step back from my career a few years ago when I had to opt for a three-day week. The absence of these basic choices and human rights has reduced me somewhat. I feel levelled; my basic confidence has been bashed and practically erased. I have trouble loving this new me, this weak, frail being with a failing body. I'm proud of my bravery but I sometimes feel it's all I have left. From a physical viewpoint, I have been brought down as though some greater being has decided I was 'too big for my boots' or I became 'too cocky'. I've been 'taken down a peg or two' just in case I become too sure of myself or too sure about how strong and well I have been. I'm not cocky. I'm not sure of myself. I'm still as self-deprecating as I was as a Stephen King-reading and REM-loving teenager and 20-something. I didn't need this reminder to level me. I've spent all of my years since my 2006 transplant looking behind me, waiting for the day when things would fall apart or I'd be back waiting for a new liver. I've never been cocky or ungrateful yet here I am, levelled.

So many times when I look around, I think that, here, we're all exactly the same – all equal when we turn to dust; our achievements aren't even real once that day comes. I guess I've been thinking that, as a transplant recipient-to-be, I'm the exact same as the young man down the corridor who drank his liver to its demise, or the old lady who's liver failed without warning, forcing her to undergo an emergency transplant, very reluctantly. We're all just here, willing ourselves on so we can be fit enough for the proposed surgery and give it our best shot. We're all the exact same, behind the smokescreen of academic achievements, wealth, success and beauty. I'm no longer feeling attractive or sexy in any way – I'm just an ill woman waiting for a life-saving transplant. We're all just heading towards what we hope will be a shot at life.

I've settled into a routine, I guess. While I'm always looking over my shoulder for someone to tell me "it's time!", I'm really not expecting my surgery very soon. Initially, I thought it would all be over by the summer. One of my surgeons will be leaving in July and she expects it to happen before then. That gives me two and a half months to 'relax'. It's funny – I want to hear that it's soon, and yet I don't. For now, a good day is one with little physical suffering – bar the twice-daily clexane injections. In the meantime, I have lots of visitors. It's interesting for me to notice how I behave around different visitors. It's not intentional but I don't act the same with everyone. For some, I'm the fun, sarcastic, everything-is-fine, 'normal' Karol while for others I can just be myself. With Mum and Dad I can be myself. I can have good days when I tell them my news – doctors' advice, blood test updates – and there'll also be bad days when I'm tired and moany because I'm still stuck here and not with Scamper. I really miss him and it saddens me so much that the little dog I have wished for my whole life isn't with me. Mum and Dad take care of him but it hurts when they tell me stories about what he's been up to. It hurts because I'm not there to see him. I suppose I feel jealous that they're enjoying his little antics and I'm missing them. I'm missing his early years and I don't even know if he'll recognise me when I get home. He might think I left him on purpose and I don't care about him anymore. I feel so sad that I have to banish thoughts of Scamper from my head – yet Mum is always there with a story to remind me that he's getting on fine without me, his Karol. She means well – that Scamper is well and happy – but that upsets me.

My friends try to understand. Two of my closest friends have been here a few times and visit me as 'the sick one'. I resent that. For over 20 years, the three of us were very similar; shared a house in college, partied together, supported each other, chatted about everything, began work the same year and have taken holidays together. We are very alike in our outlook on life, in our values – and generally, we share similar opinions on many things. There is such a close bond between us and I literally cherish them, like sisters. Now, though, I feel a distance between them and me. I am the one who's in hospital for months, who had a transplant 11 years ago and now faces it all over again. I'm the one who almost died then and a few times since. I'm the weak one, the one with the dodgy liver, 'the sick one'. I always feel angry and resentful in their company because they arrive to visit me, looking great, wearing nice clothes and full of energy. I think it's the only time when I ask myself those often-quoted words "why me?" I hate being the ugly, unattractive one of our little group – with straggly, greying hair, discoloured teeth (from medication and illness), huge out-of-control figure and agonising fatigue. They visit me while I lie in bed, yellowing – attempting to look 'good' in my favourite fresh nightdress. They claim they don't care that I look a wreck (my words, not theirs) but I care! I'm not the independent, energetic, holidaying Karol they've known for years. . .now I'm reduced to just being a sick woman…and very little else.

My boyfriend's visits are different again. He arrives on a Saturday afternoon, usually after a morning game of golf. When he arrives, I'm allowed time out so we've been going for lunch, usually followed by the cinema. It's all very normal and – just normal. I'm dressed, makeup applied, hair done and I behave as though I'm not living in a hospital but we're just two people going for lunch or to see a movie. I suspect, in fact I'm certain, that he wants 'normal'. He wants us to be going out like we used to, visiting family, having dinner, going for walks. Now, we go on a date and, looking at us from the outside, we are like a regular couple out for the day – pregnant girlfriend maybe, looking a bit haggard from the pregnancy; that's possibly what people see. But, with him, I feel that there's no room in our day for moaning – or discussing real, true feelings. No room to discuss how scared I am or for him to tell me he's worried or empathising that it must be a horrible situation to find myself in. In his company, it doesn't feel appropriate or ever fitting to tell him how I actually feel. He just strives for normality. He wants me as the energetic, hard-working, money-earning, good-humoured Karol – or so it feels. I'm not sure – he hasn't expressed how he feels about all of this. When I knew the journey I was setting off on in November 2016, I told him I would not think badly of him if he wanted to 'walk away'. I knew; I felt it would be a tough, stressful, difficult road and I gave him the option to not be part of it. I meant it – if he felt unable to go through this with me, I wouldn't think badly of him. I was healthy and well when we met – yes, I was a transplant recipient with dodgy blood – but since then things have changed a lot. I knew the road I was heading on would be tough for me and I would need his support and strength more than ever. He assured me that he was going to be there for me. I'm not feeling it. I'm not feeling that he's supportive. I just feel that he's anxious for me to get fixed and back to 'normal us'. I feel as though he's seeing me as a machine that needs a new part – and once that part is found all will be well. I feel less like a human and more like a broken piece of equipment! Maybe I'm completely wrong but I've found myself reminding him so many times that biology and biological beings are more grey than black and white. Bodies are complicated – I'm not a physics experiment but a part of a biological / medical intervention, nasty and barbaric as it actually still sounds to me. Swapping organs with a dead person? I'm still not happy about it… Also 'normal' is much further away than just a successful transplant. There's more to this than a physical mending of my body – there will be emotional issues too, I know it. Will we get through that? Will he be supportive then, when my emotions are literally not under my control? When my fears for my future manifest themselves as dark moods and nagging? When I cry for no good reason? When I'm happy in the morning but gloomy two hours later? When I shout at him and pick arguments over small things just because I'm frustrated with the bigger things? I hope he will be. There definitely seems to be a gap between us that has widened a little more in recent months. We're living very different lives now, I guess, and I'm not sure how this will affect us in the long term.

I continue to visit the church – on bad days, it's an excuse for a long walk through the hospital and an escape from my routine and the people around me. I've also made friends with one of the hospital chaplains who shares deep, thought-provoking discussions and opinions with me on life and God and what it's all about.

Some days, though, my church visits turn into crying with despair, begging, through my tears, for somebody to listen to me, to hear my prayers, my begging, my pleading, my bargaining. I won't share this with anybody, and feel happy to share it with you how very, very desperate and distressed my imploring voice is. I will do anything, anything, to just hear that my liver is here and that it will all be well. I cry, almost feel the need to lie on the floor and howl with distress and deep fear and pain. Who is listening to me? Who cares for me?

Then I leave and smile at the porters who have now grown familiar with me and my daily walking (no longer slippers, but nightdress, dressing gown and running shoes!), who acknowledge me and say hello. I meet my visitors and smile and chat. This feels like a double life – I feel like a hypocrite and a fake; appearing carefree and happy on the outside, but, internally, a scared emotional wreck. So, in the intervening time, I distract myself with as much non-transplant and non-death stuff as possible. I'm continuing to buy clothes online at a crazy rate – wide dresses, narrow optimistic-that-I'll-eventually-be-thin stripey jumpers and cute jackets. If I buy them I have to be around to wear them. That's my explanation for it.

'The best thing for being sad is to learn something. That is the only thing that never fails. . .That is the only thing which the mind can never exhaust, never alienate, never be tortured by, never fear or distrust, and never dream of regretting'

T.H. White, *The Once and Future King*

17th April 2017

Dear James,

Today is Groundhog Day. Yesterday was Groundhog Day. Tomorrow is Groundhog Day, and the one after that, and after that. I've no frigging idea when 'Groundhog Day' really is – it's not really an appropriate Irish concept, is it? Groundhogs are not indigenous Irish species. I just know that every single fucking day in here is the same as the one before, and the one before. This place is testing my nerves, my patience, my spirit, my tolerance – it's a fake, existing-but-not-living life. I am here on a Monday in hospital. Monday differs from every other day as we're all swabbed for hospital-acquired infections. A swab to the nose, groin and two for the rectum. Is it embarrassing? Is it something to dread as a nurse runs a cotton-tipped stick into my nostrils, groin and rectum? Of course it's embarrassing – painless – but an uncomfortable and humiliating experience. But, like everything else in this forced existence, I have no choice. It's all done in minutes and then Monday is the same as every other day. Same breakfast, same choices for dinner and tea, same snacks for the St. Brigid's inmates who are being force-fed to put on weight in preparation for losing it as our livers eat into our protein and fat stocks.

I spend my days reading – I've read tens upon tens of excellent, good, disappointing and shockingly-poor books. I've finished them all – even the hospital bookshop Roald Dahl offering which was particularly woeful. I've procured scientific papers on marine coastal erosion and climate change – and swallowed them all. I watch all the quizzes I can – keeping my brain active and ensuring that, even though I'm not working or studying, I'm learning every day. *The Chase*, *Tipping Point* and *Pointless* are my daily TV choices – I feel as though I know the presenters personally now. I see them more than my family and friends. And *The Waltons*, of course; their hapless issues, troubles and predicaments sometimes, almost, make my life seem normal.

Am I going crazy? Have I eventually flipped and am I giving up? Am I becoming institutionalised here? Will I survive the outside world – if I ever join it again? I really don't know the answer to that. So I make lists, the collection of stuff I want to do and achieve when I get out of here. They're simple, normal things like eating homemade burgers, a fish pie, homemade potato salad, visiting my favourite cliff walk near Louisburgh, bringing Scamper to the beach, visiting the zoo and having afternoon tea with my friends. It's as though all of this suffering, pain, fear and stressful days are my torture before my reward, my just desserts. If I put up with all of this now, there's more of a chance that I'll be lucky, be able and strong enough for the ordeal that's ahead of me. That's the deal of made in my head – with whom, I've no idea.

And so I go on, hating and resenting every single day – or so it seems like that today. I have to go on, feeling alone facing this dreadful nightmare that is still ahead of me. I think about my friends, at work, facing concerns and worrisome choices on environmental issues. I imagine them at the end of their working days, going home to loved ones, going out to the theatre or cinema maybe. I imagine them getting on with their lives and I am so sad and jealous. I am happy for them, don't get me wrong, but I am sad for me, heartbroken for me, that I don't have that life now, that I am facing something so challenging that normal life is literally light years away. When did this change happen? When did I begin to feel so weak and insecure, almost paranoid and analytical about what other people are up to? When did my skin, my tough, strong skin get stripped away and leave me feeling so bare, so sensitive and frail? I feel so vulnerable now. I feel like I've lost myself, have been stripped of the real me and have been replaced by a weakened version of myself, with less fight and less spark, less energy and courage.

Something struck me recently after spending over three months here in this abnormal life. People, my family, loved ones, friends, expect more from me than before. Like the boy who cried wolf, there's been a 'wolf issue' with me every few days – something to tell people about; a new problem, a newly-planned investigation, some negative news on my condition or my fitness to endure a transplant. Unlike the boy who cried wolf, however, there really is something to shout about, something to share, something difficult to talk about and seek comfort about. I'm not looking for attention or sympathy for no good reason; my condition is really fraught with complications and my transplant is being described regularly as 'high-risk'. But people expect that I'm more accustomed to having issues so I'm more capable of dealing with them. I've become the owner of quite a lot of health complications, so what's one or two more? What's another few litres in the bucket – I can handle it!

Just recently I had a mammogram and will have a biopsy to examine if the calcifications they discovered contain breast cancer cells. Unlike most other women, I don't get to be worried or concerned about this news. I don't get to be gutted and scared and terrified for my life. Now, I get to calmly nod and just distance myself from me and ask, mechanically, what the plan is and what the medical strategy will be should cancer be discovered. In the outside, in the real world, a woman gets to react, to be frightened, to have sleepless nights, to cry and discuss this scary scenario in depth. I feel as though I am expected to simply add this new issue to my heightening pile. I'm sure it will be fine, but if not, I'll embark on some planned approach. . .

I've just been interrupted to reveal if I opened my bowels today – another routine of the day!

The nurses, so friendly and supportive; they're here for all of us. I feel as though they care, but I've also seen people die here and it doesn't change anyone's lives. If I die, will they even be sad? I've known some of these nurses since 2006 – some remember me from my first transplant so I hope and believe they would care if I didn't make it through. For the newer ones, I am nice and friendly, interested in getting to know them better – so they'll be kinder to me when I need them like a baby, post-transplant. I genuinely like the vast majority of them, a lot of nurses really seem like my friends, but I have a fear about the ones I don't know so well – and how caring and good to me they will be in the future. It's like a bizarre hostage-type situation – be nice to your captors and they'll be nice back!

Crikey, I am in a serious, grumpy mood today. I am feeling so sorry for myself. This doesn't help anyone – least of all myself. There's no point ruminating – this place is about getting on with the business of staying well, until my transplant time comes at me.

I've been considering studying while I'm here – that would take my mind off nasty things and hasten the time. Would hastening the time really be a good thing though?

I've realised what I need, what I really would benefit enormously from, is a day off. Yes, I've been off work for over a year, but I need a day off from my head – my mind needs, yearns for escape from what's churning and turning and tossing around inside. This place is nothing but medical issues; transplant, ascites, medication, colonoscopies, CT and MRCP scans, biopsies and blood tests. I need one day 'off', one day to feel free from entrapment, to shake free of all the stuff that's stuck to me, all the worries, fears, dark thoughts and melancholy ruminations. I try to make a choice to live one day for me. It's not possible here. There are always interruptions, necessary but unwelcome interruptions when I'm contemplating on meditation and visualisations. I try to imagine my happy days, visualise times of joy, fun and delight. I think of my family, of being a young and carefree child and teenager. I think of being a girlfriend for the first time; the butterflies, that warm, cosy feeling of being deeply (at that age!) cared for by someone for whom I cared so deeply. I imagine my holidays and exploring woodlands, paddling in the sea, finding frogs and frogspawn in ponds, seeing my younger sister as a baby, meeting my nieces for the first time, swimming in the sea and having young innocent fun in college. I focus on being in a gondola in Venice, a cable car in Grouse Mountain, British Colombia, in cool stillness of the Pantheon, the heat on my face in the Colosseum, setting off in a boat to Capri and wandering the cobbled streets of Sorrento. I see fields of lavender in the south of France, Van Gogh's bedroom in Arles and feel the dampness of Edinburgh Castle. I imagine seals swimming and salmon running in the River Moy, swifts wheeling high above my town, poppy fields and hedgerows. These visualisations help – I am there, happy, laughing, shivering, warm, smiling and free. There are still places I can go to seek joy and freedom. They may not be real journeys but they help a sedentary, lost sad woman – for now.

'Yesterday, all my troubles seemed so far away
Now it looks as though they're here to stay
Oh, I believe in yesterday'

The Beatles, Yesterday

20th April 2017

Dear James,

As I lie here feeling, admittedly, quite sorry for myself, I am a little pensive about all of the things I've had to sacrifice by having ET and essentially losing two livers. I imagine that being on the third one will be like the third life in an arcade game – you're still hanging on but one slip and it's game over. No more chances. I don't know if I have any more chances after liver #3. I don't dare ask. I just see and know all the damage these multiple surgeries and procedures have done and I'm not going to allow myself to ponder too deeply on the future. I also try not to allow myself to complain. I will acknowledge, however, the opportunities and experiences I've had to sacrifice in the place of fighting to stay alive. I'm missing the entire year of the outside world (bar some trips to Dundrum Town Centre). I'm missing experiences at work, nights out, meeting friends, making new ones, weddings, holidays, new classes, work promotions, new adventures... I don't get to have a family of my own, a husband or a normal wedding and marriage. Should I meet the most amazing man I want to spend my life with, he must be willing to take me on with all of these medical 'quirks'; it would be an emotional, sentimental, nostalgic wedding with tears, mixed emotions, references to you, great joy and great unspoken sadness.

My so-called career is now in ruins. What I do is real and complicated and I actually really enjoy my three-day week contribution to the protection of the environment. But I earn pittance – disastrous money that I can barely live on. I can't ask for a raise. I'm not in a position to. I'm unreliable. I haven't been reliable in over four years, missing firstly nine months of work in 2014 and then being absent since May 2016 until now (cringe). My friends discuss their careers with me, criticizing policy, bosses, other colleagues and the general issues work life brings. I am jealous. I don't have the luxury of moaning about work – I'd be happy to be there, head down just getting on with it. OR I'd be happier as an environmental consultant; independent, happy, busy, sometimes stressed but proud of my achievements and the success that a degree and PhD afforded me.

I never asked for much actually. Really, I didn't want to be extremely rich, didn't yearn for astronomical success, didn't plan an extravagant lifestyle. I love holidays, watersports, clothes, reading, nature – and people. I love my house, my car and my dog. I cherish my family and a handful of friends – and that's it!

Please, please, please know that as I write here, I know that your loves, dreams and ambitions were cruelly yanked away from you too. For you, it was forever. For me, I must look past my pendulous tummy which refuses to fit into my flattering clothes and refuses to allow me to have a waist. I must look past my new wrinkles, hard-fought-for lines of pain, grief, terror, anguish – and even more pain, I must look past all those free choices taken from me; the chance to travel freely without fear of blood clotting, the chance to work hard and not suffer horrific unimaginable fatigue, the chance to meet a handsome, kind man for me – without the smudging of his impression of me with scars, bulges, medication – and mysterious disappearances from life to hospital, clinics, doctors, surgeries… Though I feel like I've lost my strength and a lot of my hope, I must be hopeful and grateful. Sometimes I feel gutted, strung up, deflated and half defeated (I probably should say completely defeated but I don't want to admit to that). It seems as though I've lost the strong, independent woman I wanted and strived to be. I just feel as though I've lost myself, and don't know how to get 'me' back but I want to be positive, to stay hopeful and journey on.

As I lie here, I think of Baz Luhrman's 'Sunscreen Song' and of the movie *Dead Poet's Society*. Why do we learn too late that life is so so fucking short, we're not invincible and procrastination is so easy but so dangerous.

I looked young, fresh and happy when I examine my college photographs. I thought I was ugly. In my twenties, I had a good sense of fashion, I smiled a lot and I was smart. I thought I was stupid, too freckly, fat with crooked teeth and a weird face. When I was 30, I was independent, a house-owner, hard-working and youthful for my age. I thought I was old, unattractive and too fat.

At 31 I had a liver transplant which left me scarred and underweight, with floppy skin and the fears of a new liver not functioning properly forever. But, I eventually learned to love myself, to be proud of me and my achievements. What can I say?

I can say I wish I knew then what I realise now. I know it's such an overused cliché but we, as humans trap ourselves with worries about the future and regrets of the past. The truth is, the universal truth, is that it's the small things that make life. Not the accumulation of wealth or the fabulous car with massaging seats, the mansion overlooking the sea, not diamonds or designer handbags... The small things – experiences and adventures, spontaneous fun decisions, impulsive choices, the "fuck it, let's do it" attitudes that equate to living. If I were to advise somebody healthy, someone youthful, on how to live – it's just that; "LIVE, every day". If there are parents with head-wrecking children, I'd say to them "cherish them – they'll soon be adults". There are people who yearn for children of their own, who would give anything, absolutely anything to look into the eyes of their offspring. There are people who would give anything to hold their sick children and hope beyond hope that their diseases aren't terminal. If there are people in unhappy relationships or there are issues between couples, they should be patient and love them – if there's still love between them. They should leave them if it's no longer there – life is too short to spend in an unhappy unfulfilling couple.

It takes a devastating event to focus on living – essentially dying has taught me how to live.

'Emancipate yourselves from mental slavery, none but ourselves can free our mind'
Bob Marley, Redemption Song

17th June 2017

Dear James,

Some of the most beautiful sunrises I've seen in my life have been in Brigid's Ward. Strange and sad as that may sound, one would wonder if I have I ever travelled at all, it's true. On so many mornings; spring, winter summer and autumn I've witnessed a blanketing orange glow of sunrise telling us another day has come, another night has passed. As I mentioned before, one corridor of Brigid's overlooks the sea and Sandymount Strand, the ferries sailing to Wales, the seagulls wheeling over the blue water. But an early morning sunrise lights up the whole corridor in an amber warm glow of comfort. It feels real, that life outside the walls of Brigid's hasn't stood still, the world is still turning, everyday stuff is still happening outside, life is going on, even if the patients in Brigid's aren't part of it, even if we feel like we're outside looking in; we've taken time out of life.

That's what it felt like – those four months in Brigid's, waiting for my time to come, for my life-saving liver to 'fix' me. How the bloody hell did I do it? How did I spend four months in hospital with no 'release date', no freedom to live my life, no true comfort, no escape from the daily hospital routine of injections, blood pressure monitoring, blood tests, rotten food (it has to be said!), scans, scary conversations – and no guarantees that I would get good news any day soon.

I'm living in my parents' house now, having escaped Brigid's at the end of April. I'm in my bedroom I shared with one or other of my sisters, depending on what age we were (I shared with my older sister until she was 14 and with my younger sister until I moved away for college at 17). I am wondering how I kept my sanity for four months – and how I'm still holding it together – at home with a pretty large daily medication allocation and a pretty large abdomen (still inflated with an inoperable-until-my-transplant blood clot). Life is pretty good. I'm enjoying a more relaxed routine, but am finding myself more tired than ever – sleeping until early breakfast (to take medication on empty stomach), bed until next medication portion, sleep until lunchtime and usually a late afternoon sleep that energises me until bedtime a few short hours later. But I'm free! I can play with Scamper, teach him his lessons (sit, stay, give me your paw) and – great news – I've enrolled us in pet obedience classes for six weeks! He's developed some barking habits and isn't the most sociable of dogs with other canines. . .that's all I'll say about his manners. Otherwise it's so great to spend time with him, Mum and Dad. My niece has been with us on holidays and I've been to the cinema, eaten ice-cream and pizzas and taken her to the beach with Scamper. It's almost normal, barring the ordeal ahead of me and that loaded abdomen I have to carry everywhere, looking pregnant and actually smiling when people smile 'knowingly' at my bump, almost winking at their joy of what they think is an expectant mother. But that's okay because I'm free; I've escaped Brigid's and its warped sense of reality.

How did I do it? Even my favourite, smiley-faced-2006-surgeon-now-friend admitted that he could not do it, spend endless weeks, months wandering the corridors of the hospital, robed in nightdress, dressing gown and sketchers – walking (as fast as possible to keep as fit as possible!) the first floor 'running track' daily and playing 'City of Stars' on the abandoned piano that still sits outside Suite 4 of the Outpatients Department.

I now know how I did it – found the resilience to stay, patiently, in hospital. There are a number of reasons, and I'm not sure in what order to place them. So let's go with no particular order. . .

Hope

Every day, every single day I hoped this would be my 'big day'; that a liver transplant coordinator would arrive at my door and tell me my liver was available – a liver that was my perfect size and blood type, a healthy, happy liver that would take the place of my (and your) now-failing ailing organ. I dreaded the day because there were so many, so many things to be afraid of and terrified of, but, for obvious reasons I also hoped that day would come soon. I had to get my shot – I had to face it anyway so the sooner it all began to take off, the better...unless, of course, it wasn't a success. I imagined myself as a healthy woman after the surgery, yes, I knew the pain and the struggles of life post-transplant, the physical pain of my abdomen, of the weakness of trying to sit up (or lie down) in bed, the tough days of walking with weak, heavy legs and the difficult trials involved in even the most simple chores like having a wash. But, I also knew that that phase would be short – and I had gotten through it before. So I had huge hope, every day.

Love

Cue corny part of my meanderings but this is true. I felt loved and I had love in me. My family, especially my Mum and Dad, showed me never-ending, deep strong love and support. I literally planned my days around their visits which were weekly, or even more frequent. Their visits, delivering clean laundry, mint crisps, bottles of water, the *Times* and smiles were essential, collapsing my weeks into more manageable days. One visit would schedule the next so I always had a visit to look forward to. Maybe that sounds like my family is like *The Waltons* – we're not. Some visits were better than others – some of the worse ones left me feeling guilty over my moody, irritable, complaining behaviour, wishing the next visit would be sooner so I could apologise and start again.

I also felt love from those who weren't even with me. I believe the feeling of love one has felt during one's life can still be tapped into by thinking back on the feeling of love shared or felt in the near or distant past. I've been lucky to have many special people in my life and so reminiscing of their love for me still made the feeling seem real and present.

My friends were also so encouraging and supportive, offering words of advice and sympathy, making me laugh and telling me stories of their 'real lives'. We made plans for what we'd do as soon as my health allowed me to do as I'd liked – afternoon tea, spa breaks, shopping, concerts, the list was and is endless.

Prayer

I'm still not sure where I stand on Catholicism. I become angry that women play such a small and unimportant role in the church, I feel priests (women and men) should be allowed to marry and I've never been a huge fan of mass. But, there's nothing like a near-death-on-more-than-one-occasion experience to make one ponder and deeply consider God and the question of an afterlife. I prayed a lot in hospital and while I did go to mass on quite a number of occasions (and as always, found my mind drifting off), I found more closeness to God and Mary in praying, either alone or with a chaplain. I cried with her, prayed and just discussed life's 'bigger issues'. I had to forgive her for interrupting my viewing of *Life of Pi* – the highlight of my February. Prayers gave me strength, made me feel as if I was doing something productive, helping myself somehow when my hands felt tied in most every other part of my life.

Books

I love reading and have a suitcase of books I read in the last few months. Once my weeks of pain and real suffering were reduced to irregular days of twice-a-day clexane injections and daily blood samples, I literally loved nothing more than to delve into a book. They took me, as always, into a world outside of my own, helped me escape the misery of my own life by swallowing me into someone else's life in

India, Australia, Switzerland, Korea, rural Ireland in the 1920s. Ian McEwan, Emma Donoghue, Lucinda Riley, Liane Moriarty. . .the endless list of authors literally saved my life by inventing their fictional ones. I could escape completely; feel absorbed into another place, away from Brigid's and its pain, its scariness and daily routine. Sometimes the lives of the heroines / characters I read about were actually worse than the life I was living – that helped!

My wishlist

I don't know when I decided to write a list of what I'd like to achieve as soon as I left Brigid's for once and for all. It's a simple list of still undone treats and chores I will, soon, achieve. I want to visit Belfast, have afternoon tea with my friends, have my house painted, visit the zoo, go to concerts, walk in the forest, travel so much more, buy a new SUV, write a book, learn something new and challenging – maybe a ukulele, eat a homemade beef burger, cheese-and-pickle sandwich, spring rolls and noodles, caprese salad and crusty bread...the list goes on. It's a simple list for treats to bring me future happiness, just the little things. It also acknowledges a time in the future when I will achieve all of these things – I have to live to carry them through.

St. Brigid's Ward

I've just spend the last while moaning about it and its horribly dull routine, but I had such support from both the staff and inmates of Brigid's that, without them and the mostly cheerful attitudes, I would have become even more sad and sorry for myself. I'm not sure how or why, but I've never met a patient in Brigid's who hadn't a smile or a friendly few words to share. Generally, and this is actually quite an unbelievable statement, the patients in Brigid's were happy and in good spirits; maybe it was fake and disingenuous but it was supportive. I've shared so many laughs with women and men of all ages, people like me who were in pain, recovering post-transplant, preparing for a life-saving transplant or just hospitalised for a liver-related issue. I guess when one pictures a ward with people facing a huge surgery, the first or second time, the view could well be of sad, morbid, grim patients; jaundiced, gaunt and, in many cases, with distended abdomens. This was generally not the case; the grim patients part, that is. We laughed over food, other patients, our appearances, cruel phlebotomists, young doctors' immaturity and inexperience – and our bodily functions! The latter included wind, constipation, diarrhoea and anything else nasty that, as previously-unacquainted people, quickly broke down any barriers that exist in the outside world.

I loved most of the Brigid's nurses. Unfortunately, or maybe happily, as a liver patient you become very familiar with the nurses and other staff, spending longer terms in hospital than with other ailments. They literally become friends, laughing when you laugh, crying when you're down and smiling genuine smiles when you receive good news. I can't say much more than describe one incident that happened in 2006 when, not long post-transplant, I was very confused and delirious. I had been asleep when I heard some nurses chat about their plans for that evening. One was having a birthday party and they were discussing the food and the time the celebrations would start. I opened my eyes and waited for one of them, Marilyn maybe, to invite me to their party. I would have said yes, feeling that, as their friend, I should be asked. My confusion led me to think I was surrounded by friends. While I obviously know now that I wasn't capable of going anywhere and that there was never a chance of being asked to a party, I felt as though these people were my friends, they cared about me as a young woman, not as a patient with a number, or just a sick person in a ward they were working in. I still value that and can say the same about the doctors in Brigid's. While the relationship between the doctors and I is not as close as of the nurses, there is still a familiarity, a closeness that I felt – they really wanted to see me, and others, get well and get on with our lives.

Maybe it's easy for me to discuss how I got through my hospital stay of four months – because now I'm out. The end of my term came – I eventually got a release date to work towards, to look forward to. Now I'm free to sort of enjoy life, such as it is. I still will have to face the prospect of going back but that will be when I receive my phonecall with good news, beckoning me on a journey to Dublin to face my surgery – with my packed bag. I have no intention of moving back into Brigid's Ward before then. I may speak of it with a semblance of fondness now, but it wasn't something I'd describe as an enjoyable experience – even the 'happy' days.

For now, I'm trying my best to enjoy days of living, injecting myself with clexane (becoming so much harder as I struggle to find spare space on my so-bruised-bloodied-abdomen), still having my daily routine. I miss my friends in hospital and I miss the chatter of the staff, the catering staff, the phlebotomists and the physiotherapists. I'm happier away from there though – obviously. Freedom is just too liberating.

'I plead with you! Never, ever give up on hope, never doubt, never tire, and never become discouraged.
Be not afraid'

Giovanni Paolo II / Pope John Paul II

19th July 2017

Dear James,

I'm struggling a little these days, I'm afraid. I'm really afraid now, not of my proposed surgery but of dying. I've had to contemplate death so many times now – what's ahead, what's after death – the big unknown. The thought of just nothingness, just blankness, life over, scares me more than I can even describe. It's literally so much bigger than me. It's strange, I've always had the drive, the strength of mind, the gut feeling that, no matter what, I can fight for my life – and win. The battle for my life is one I'm able for, a challenge I can tackle and succeed in. I'm strong and if I'm determined enough, I'll win and stay alive. Now, that I've faced death on at least five occasions I realise two obvious flaws in my plan – one, that I will have to die sometime and so I will eventually lose one of these battles, and, two, that many other strong-willed determined people with similar drive and strength – and stubbornness – as me did literally not make it through. Just because there's a will, a want, a drive to live does not guarantee a successful outcome. I know this sounds obvious, but it's only as I'm lying here, afraid and anxious, that my hope, trust and determination wane – just a little. I am analysing the 'why' and 'how' stages of my survival. I know the why I want to live – to see many more countries, swim in the sea again, spend so much more happy times with family and friends, see many more spring times, and to see many more of my dreams come true. . .I'm a bit stuck on the how I will live. How to get through, how to survive and stay alive, against all the odds? You see, I'm back in Brigid's again. Earlier in the month, I began to feel suddenly poorly – very exhausted with a very heavy feeling in my lower abdomen. While my ascites (and clot) is still there since January, the feeling of heaviness seemed to have increased somewhat. I felt a 'pull' one day when driving, and afterwards I just felt more uncomfortable, heavier. Dragging myself about became more difficult – my legs weren't used to such a rapidly-growing body. I was also very breathless and noticed palpitations and blood rushing in my ears when I 'exerted myself' which didn't take much.

We, Mum and I, decided it was time to make another trip to St. Vincent's. To make this journey from my bed to a Dublin hospital required a huge effort – and was literally almost impossible. Never did I wish more for a 'beam-me-up' scenario!

Every time I got out of bed, my body just seemed to collapse in on itself. My legs were very weak and I was unfathomably lethargic and fatigued. (I was sleeping around the clock). I had to lie down after a quick (and very demanding) shower. I lay again until just before we got the train, having thrown a few bits into a light suitcase which Mum carried while watching me with a pained expression. I sat in the train, feeling every bump and turn reverberate in my large abdomen. I had no appetite and no desire to drink – I think I hadn't urinated in two days – how stupid was I not to have foreseen a near-emergency?! I guess I had convinced myself that I had just accumulated so much fluid that my stomach couldn't fit any nutrients. I had my head completely in the sand – in hindsight I think my entire body was submerged.

We eventually arrived at A&E where I promptly vomited and felt very faint. Liam, a very kind porter had me sitting in a wheelchair in seconds and I was brought to a curtained cubicle. Diarmaid and his team arrived shortly after, examining me where I lay, feeling very ill and very faint. Bloods were taken – through my foot – which revealed my kidneys were practically non-functioning, with a creatinine of 296, my haemoglobin was 5.6 and my LFTs were more elevated than they had been. After a scan, the memory of which I don't recall, a bleeding ovarian cyst was discovered – probably the source of bleeding in November and January last. A mystery solved but for me, it felt like just more bad news; further complications to add to an already heaped list.

Diarmaid arranged for the cyst to be 'taken care of'. Before I was wheeled away I cried,

"I can't keep bouncing back like this. I can't do this anymore...". I felt so sick that I admitted I wanted to die, to literally escape, there and then. I'd had enough – enough pain, sickness, fretting and fear. This was the first time I had ever felt truly beaten.

"You will feel much better in two days", he promised, "this guy is the best".

'This guy' was a surgeon who explained his plan to kill my cyst. He would inject some tiny particles into a vessel supplying blood to the cyst, which would clump together and essentially cut off its lifeline. There was a chance it wouldn't work and a bleeding risk but I gave my permission to 'plough on'.

At that point, I had no resilience, little fight and no qualms about what this, or any professional, needed to do with me. My body no longer felt like it was mine anymore – it no longer felt as though I had to give permission for strangers to bore holes into me or invade my body with whatever tools were necessary to 'help me'. My consent meant little – it was agree or face failure. I felt as though I had already handed myself over months ago – my entire body had turned into a broken thing to be fixed – it was no longer precious or private, or mine. If holes had to be made in it, so be it. Scars, by then, were just more scars.

Following the procedure, during which I heard myself moaning in pain – I was under conscious sedation – I found myself in ICU with a 'hose' bored into the right side of my neck (for kidney dialysis) and an ABG (arterial blood gas) line in my wrist. ICU – again...like bloody Groundhog Day. I spent a week on dialysis before escaping back to – you guessed it – Brigid's Ward.

My body has grown since then. My abdominal girth is not in fitting with my petite frame, my back hurts and just this morning I photographed my giant 'hobbit feet', swollen with fluid, so painful to walk or even bend. My slippers are bursting at the seams with these new hideous feet. I am weighed daily to monitor the volume of fluid I am accumulating. When my weight reached 10kg above my normal weight, I asked the nurses to stop telling me.

I feel my spirits crashing and my mood is low. I want to be alone for a while, to cry when I want to, or just stay in bed under the covers.

But I must talk with the nurses, doctors, caterers and phlebotomists. I must be communicative and civil or there'll be more issues to deal with, more people asking more questions. I accept the endless 'visits' from medical students – recount my medical history as they frown, nod in sympathy (genuine or otherwise), write furiously and ask if they can examine my abdomen.

"Sure" I think, "work away; it's hardly an invasion of my privacy after all this time!"

I am somewhat saved by Jimmy, the man I am sharing my room with. He's witty and relaxed; we're equally sarcastic about hospital food and the numerous shakes and shots we ingest daily – nasty-tasting vials of protein, masquerading as tasty milkshakes. I must gain muscle for my ordeal ahead; he must gain weight post-transplant. He's emaciated and jaundiced but 'doing well'. We don't talk continuously all day but we have our own space for pondering, planning – or just nothing. He's the best roommate I could have asked for and I'm reminded that the people in this ward never cease to amaze me. With liver disease which is definitely, at times, worse than cancer, we laugh and joke about everything from our diets to donors to death – death is never far from our minds. Maybe we're in denial or avoiding serious nasty conversations but this way helps – a lot.

And so, I'm still waiting, getting bigger and finding days tougher. I'm afraid, dreading what's ahead, terrified of dying but know I have to do what I have to do. But I'm distracted by my roommate – we're 'not allowed' to be grumpy and morbid, we silently conspire. We find fun and some joy in conversations with nurses, doctors, other patients, having a laugh every single day. As he sums up our situation - which consists of days of pain, fear, dread, worry and anxiety - when someone visits or a rare piece of positive news comes our way (he gains weight and I lose a little!). . . "It's the little things, Karol!"

'Our greatest freedom is the freedom to choose our attitude.'
Viktor E. Frankl, Man's Search for Meaning
'Some walks you have to take alone'
Suzanne Collins, The Hunger Games

26th July 2017; 01:45

Dear James,

I'm here. I've had a lopsided type of day which began much like any other...

I had my medication at 6a.m. including clexane jab, my weigh-in, blood pressure monitoring, temperature check and a chat with Mary, my nurse for today. I'm in my own room now – a little lonely and quiet but mostly I'm okay with my own company.

Just before lunch, Suzie, a student nurse (with the extraordinarily long eyelashes and a lovely manner) came in and informed me I was going for an X-ray. We walked to A&E where I had a very rapid (and uneventful) chest X-ray. I felt fine; no raised temperature, no infection, nothing new. Nothing that would warrant an unscheduled X-ray, at any rate. Suzie genuinely didn't know why I needed it when I asked. I guessed just before Yvonne, transplant coordinator, came in with a large folder in her arms. She told me my liver was here…

Actually, she told me that there were two livers, but the first one was for me. I was strangely calm. It's like I've had all my fear, apprehension and nervousness sucked out of me over the last few weeks – all that's left is a calm resignation, a solemn acceptance that I must give it a go…and let the surgeons give it a go. They had already travelled to examine the liver in a Dublin hospital – correct blood type obviously but they must check its suitability <u>for me</u>. I was okay with that – they knew their role.

My attention drifted for a split minute as I noticed a tall, bald man pacing the corridor with a younger man (his son?). He looked tense – and very thin.

Yvonne told me that she would be back later in the evening with an update but it was likely that I would be going for my surgery later in the evening.

Mary came into my room and proceeded to take my blood; filling considerably more vials than my usual daily donation, and then I began to call my family. They were always waiting for this day, even the nurses were waiting for this day, laughing and hugging me as they too received the welcome news. My phonecalls were calm and relaxed; I urged my parents to drive carefully and I would see them very soon.

I packed my bags; knowing that my packed suitcase at home contained my post-transplant stuff – lots of night clothes, face towels, toiletries and underwear – bare essentials; no makeup, hair dryer or anything 'pretty' necessary for after my surgery…

I phoned my two sisters and prepared a generic text for other family members and friends. I didn't send it – I waited to see Yvonne. I felt hungry, not overly so but maybe it was nerves – beginning to flutter around in my tummy. I was also quite worried about my blood and whether the medical people were aware that I had my clexane this morning – if yes, then they would know that my blood would be thinner and a reversal of the anticoagulant would be necessary later. All of these thoughts began to rush around my head; items to tell my family, issues to discuss with Yvonne, with my surgeon, my nurses. . .

Then a handsome smiley face peered in my door. He introduced himself as my anaesthetist's registrar, the man who would be taking care of my unconscious state during surgery. He assured me that my blood could be adjusted if necessary; there was nothing for me to worry about except getting through my transplant. He then queried if I had any loose teeth – I have one wiggly one following my orthodontic treatment – and he said that, although he would be very careful when tubes are inserted into my mouth, it was hardly a huge issue if I lost a tooth, considering my current situation. I agreed outwardly. Inwardly, I winced and felt sad as I realised that this summed up my whole life at this point – above all, the only issue was my fight to stay alive, despite and at the expense of everything, absolutely everything else. My scars, my crap kidney function, the potential loss of my ovaries and spontaneous plunge into menopause, my thinning hair, fluffy face, discoloured teeth. Living was Number One – everything else was secondary and deemed almost unimportant.

When he left, promising to see me later, I waited for Mum and Dad to arrive. The fact I was already in Brigid's, in hospital when my liver became available was a huge blessing. I'm not sure if I would have been able for the likely stressful journey with my parents from Mayo.

I was scheduled to go for surgery at 11pm and they arrived with about thirty minutes to spare, smiling and excited, though nervous and worried too. Caroline, my night nurse, spotted their pale faces and made some tea for them – I was still fasting since breakfast.

We all sat and chatted – now, mere hours later I don't remember what we talked about. My boyfriend also arrived. We haven't really been 'fitting well' recently. It's like we're on completely different, unrelatable tracks now; he's going to work daily, cycling, doing laundry, golfing, travelling, meeting people, eating, washing and sleeping exactly when and where he wants. I'm leading a prolonged abnormal existence where every single day contains suffering, extreme fear, medical news, medical people, death and the complete loss of control over practically everything in my entire life. It's as though he imagines that I'm in this place to wait – and in the meantime everything is fine. I'm here in this prison-of-sorts while others, everyone outside of this building, it seems, is free to live their normal lives. He's living, I'm existing; and it hurts me when he talks about my moods and how I've changed. It just seems insensitive of him but maybe I'm just being sensitive? I don't know anymore. I haven't exactly been having a normal boyfriend-acknowledging-life for the last year.

oOo

My suitcase and belongings sat in the corner, my second 'post-transplant case' safe in my parents' car. The minutes passed and suddenly it was almost midnight. I knew something was wrong before Yvonne came in with a serious expression.

Basically, she explained, it was a false alarm. Many people experience this while they wait for a suitable liver. I was unlucky that the proposed donor liver that the surgeons' viewed was too large for me. The donor wasn't a huge person but the liver was larger than anticipated. If they used it for me, it would put pressure on my lungs, causing long-term breathing difficulties for me. So near and yet so far…

I looked at her and felt angry, frustrated and – empty. I said little. Maybe I was also silently relieved that I didn't have to face all the scary stuff yet. I would stay here for another while, safe in my cosy little room, my safe haven.

But the second liver?

There was a chance it would suit me but no one had been to examine it, Yvonne explained.

Meanwhile, the tall pacing man had gone off to theatre with my first choice.

As is always my food of choice after fasting, I requested rice krispies. I felt like comfort-eating a lot more then cereal! There were tears of frustration in my eyes. We all sat and looked at each other. I told my visitors to find some accommodation for the night – it was almost 1am.

They all promised to see me tomorrow when Yvonne might have further news. I felt as though I'd had enough.

oOo

Now, krispies eaten and in bed, I'm actually not even sure how I feel.

Alone? Certainly

Sad? Not necessarily

Frustrated? Yes

Angry? Yes, actually

Defeated? Yes, yes, yes, fucking yes

I have no huge optimism about this second liver. Maybe it, too, will be the wrong size or there'll be another issue? Maybe I'll be waiting here in another few months? Sandra had her transplant last week and I imagined I would follow soon after. But, later in the morning? I'm not convinced. Everyone made a wasted trip – the journey and nervousness were all for nothing. I hate to be the cause of so much inconvenience for everyone. I've always lived quietly hating drama and stress, shying away from fuss and attention. When will it feel like I am living independently, not inconveniencing anyone, not putting anyone through stress or strain?

It's late; Mum and Dad have found a hotel room and are apparently settled. I must try to sleep; unbrushed teeth, tear-stained face, packed bags still in the corner. Again the waiting....

27th July 2017

Karol Donnelly

28th July 2017

29th July 2017

30th July 2017

Hello, my new friend, my name is Karol. . . I promise I will take the very best care of you.

Walk Unafraid

Dear friend,

Welcome to my world.

Where to begin?

So, shall I describe the events which took me to seven days post-transplant? Shall I talk philosophically or otherwise of the living nightmare yet again, the trip to the theatre on the morning of 26th July, accompanied by a bunch of people including my parents and a number of nurses, the surprisingly awesome view from the theatre, meeting my surgeon Mr. Hoti, signing my ovaries away (I'd already signed my consent for my transplant – a surprisingly-convoluted contract), closing my eyes surrounded by hugely supportive and amazing people until succumbing to peace, silence and stillness. Do I continue with my weak yet palpable joy at opening my eyes - ALIVE - in the ICU? The realisation that I had made it through, the unfathomable disbelief that the waiting, the begging, praying, wishing, yearning to just survive the surgery before my cautious return to real life was actually truly over. That feeling was incomparable to any joy I've ever felt – thank you for that.

Shall I describe my first meeting with Diarmaid whose opening comment, though with a smile, was about the huge volume of blood I had lost during my surgery – more than my body actually contained had been replaced! Will I continue with my descriptions of how weak and sore I was and how little help my painkillers were? Or will I share my experiences of 'washing' myself, before I could stand or sit steadily in a shower, with wipes which made me smell of freshly polished furniture?

I don't have much energy to discuss my post-transplant days. Suffice to say I survived the high risk surgery and the new re-plumbing exercise had been successful. My ovaries are still perfectly intact as the surgeon made the decision to leave them be

– both he and I had had enough during the 8-hour surgery. James is now gone from my life and I feel somehow lost and bereft; something like grief.

But now you're here and we're just new friends. So, shall I tell you the rest? Shall I describe my blood cancer that has hung over much of my life and destroyed my two livers? Shall I share with you the highs and lows or just talk about the last week since you arrived into my life? Shall I talk about the pain, biopsies, ducts and dopplers, commodes, immense pressure on my abdomen from within, extreme and unforgettable back pain from my daily anti-fungal medication, my still-ongoing clexane injections and bruising, my smiling through the pain? Shall I talk about how I feel so bruised and battered, a failure to have come this far and now feeling like I don't have the strength for the final stretch? Shall I admit to feeling jealous or even envious of other recipients who appear to be stronger than I in the first few days post-transplant? Shall I describe the two bags attached to my sides into which fluid, blood, serum and other gunky stuff flows on an hourly basis? Shall I admit that, at first, it made me so queasy to empty this stuff into a measuring jug to monitor the outflow from inside my body? Shall I share with you my first walk post-transplant when one bag overflowed and gushed hot, yellow fluid all over my legs, slippers and the hospital corridor? Shall I admit the feeling of embarrassment and humiliation of inadvertently 'wetting myself' as a 42-year-old? I won't describe it, can't or won't even allow myself one tiny bit of wallowing. This pain, fear and any discomfort is and will be worth it. I have gotten through so very much and I have absolutely no intention of giving into morbid, negative thoughts now. There's no time for self-sympathy or self-indulgent ruminations. I am there. So, even though I am feeling a little hopeless, despairing and sad that, once again, this very unnatural intervention of replacing my liver has been essential and that I can't live without you, I'm not allowed to moan one little bit. While I honestly hate this unavoidable situation I've found myself in, and resent the way it erodes my independence, strips me of my autonomy and opens up my life to surgeons, haematologists, hepatologists, phlebotomists and nurses – and nosy outsiders, I am still so very grateful. While I feel that my life has been taken from my hands, that it's no longer really, truly mine, I understand that it's up to me to work very hard now to get it back – my life, that is. MY LIFE. I will regain my independence and privacy – must reclaim myself back from the experts. I will run and govern my own life once again – I'll compromise on routine clinic visits and a list of medication but beyond that, I want to regain control.

I am Karol. I am a musician, scientist, reader, lover, sister, daughter, friend, dreamer, travel enthusiast, gardener, techno-phobe, introverted and still-too-passive fun-loving woman. I love people but I love my own company. I want a relationship but I won't compromise on anything less than true love. I am curious but not a gossip. I think I'm interesting – as interesting as an introverted, non-impulsive person can be. I am brave but there's a limit. I love the feeling of being in love, but I get rattled very easily in relationships. I have a deep fear of losing myself. I love having a project to work on, I love research, I love learning and educating myself on new things – on anything. I'm impatient and short-tempered when I don't have a routine. I cannot stand wasting time, energy or money. I have strong opinions but voice few - there are enough loud attitudes in the world - on racism, xenophobia, sexism, homophobia, religious differences and social integration....

I have waited eight months for you, but three years of unofficial waiting - and it's been a painful wait – agonising even. For years – and particularly the last two, I have been tortured, inwardly and out, afraid (petrified), extremely anxious and a convoluted mixture of optimism and deep pessimism, all concurrently.

So while I don't really want you, I need you. I need you and I know that in time I will be more accepting and welcoming. But today, I've done enough talking and I am weak and very tired. I will write to you again soon. For now I ask just one thing from you…please stay with me for a very long time…

Karol Donnelly

'Be cheerful. Strive to be happy'
Desiderata, Max Ehrmann

19th August 2017
Dear friend,

So, I'm still alive and feeling really good. It's been a rollercoaster of an experience but if I had to describe 2006 transplant and recovery and my 2017 experience, there's no comparison. I expected to feel horrendously ill and weak – and useless – after my second transplant. I anticipated being washed, undergoing daily physiotherapy to help my lungs, imagined tube-feeding and trying to walk – or move – from bed. What I didn't imagine was tolerable pain (they've taken me off all pain killers now!), complete independence after a few short days, washing myself with no help and walking, albeit slowly, one day post-transplant. I still have no great appetite but there's no danger of my wasting away – I am still 52kg – despite the happy daily loss of weight (ascites is no more!). I was brought for my 'ducts and dopplers' scan one day post-transplant to assess the health of my new liver. My bile ducts were normal and, my greatest fear, all blood vessels were patent and running with blood. No clots, no blockages, no HAT – what greater news could one have after years of a compromised hepatic system? I watched as the radiologist scanned my newly-opened abdomen, looking at the rows of staples under the sterile gauze; my surgeon had kept the incision less aggressive than 11 years ago.

Now, I'm happy. Now I am quietly, peacefully content. As I've watched so many friends undergo their transplants since January – and go home recovered and happy, I've been envious, impatient and afraid. Would my day ever come?

Now, in my little one-bed room, I have my visitors, my friends, parents, my sister, nieces, brother-in-law – and I can talk about the future. I am no longer waiting and apparently, my LFTs are improving every day. What is this amazing, unfamiliar but welcome feeling? There are murmurings about me going home – actually going home and leaving St. Vincent's – complete with my new liver and a – slightly-flatter abdomen. The tubes draining abdominal fluids have been unceremoniously yanked out and while the nasty gushing has at last stopped; small volumes of fluid fills two small plastic hollister bags attached to my sides. My sutures, large metal clips, have been nipped and taken away; first every second one and later the remaining ones. So, my abdomen is no longer stapled closed but is held together by healed tissue and a rapidly-healing scar.

I'm well in the refreshing now and I can look forward and envisage bright days.

'The bump on the road is an opportunity to overcome challenge' Anon

8th September 2017

Dear friend,

Well, things have taken a bit of a nosedive. I knew; I had a gut feeling that something bad would happen. I knew the road was too smooth; I had my tough transplant but following the tough first few days, I began to settle well and my system tolerated all my new medication. My liver liked me – and I was beginning to really like it! But it was too easy. It was too uncomplicated. I was almost ready to be discharged from hospital, almost there, so close to being released, when everything changed.

One month after my transplant surgery, the end of August, I was given permission to leave the hospital. I got dressed in day clothes for the first time in months – a blue oversized dress to accommodate my still-distended abdomen and a long cardigan. I applied makeup, especially to conceal my black rings under my eyes – no sleep is ever enough to keep the fatigue at bay – and threw up my hair. Mum and I had lunch in the restaurant across the road from the hospital. While it was exhausting, it was exhilarating. I looked almost normal, felt almost normal and literally, enjoyed a normal, routine Sunday lunch with Mum. After two hours and a carefully-chosen meal (avoiding foods high in vitamin K and foods with potential pathogens) I, creakily but confidently, walked back to the hospital. It was all a huge contrast to my first outing following my first transplant. This time, I had back pain and was a little unsteady on my weak, spindly legs but I was very capable and confident.

In bed a little later, Ruth took my temperature and blood pressure, as per usual. My temperature was up; I had a fever. That discovery shocked me. I felt completely fine, a little warm but fine. Within hours, my blood was taken for blood cultures – an analysis of my blood for bacterial infections. Nothing was discovered but as the days went on, my appetite disappeared and I felt very lethargic and weak. The assessments began and an abscess was discovered on my pancreas. Was this the source of my infection which was, following a week, was making me feel nauseous and quite downhearted? The surgeons met with me – and a strong dose of antibiotics was recommended.

"OK" I thought, "this is where I put in the hard work, this is when I have to put in a fight, a fight which will make my return home worth it". For some unfathomable reason, the transplant itself didn't feel like enough of a challenge. I felt I had to prove myself worthy of my new liver; I had to prove that I deserved a happy-ever-after. If I put in hard work and a little more pain, then, once home, I would be completely free of any more challenges. I don't understand and can't explain my attitude. Who would have sought more pain? Who would have expected, almost wanted, complications in order to feel that a worthy fight while in hospital would prevent me from future battles? The answer, while crazy and unbelievable, was - I did. Maybe I felt that, in some way, by replicating my tortuous in-hospital battle of 2006, I felt that I would deserve at least eight or nine years of blissful post-transplant 'normality', so long as a fight ensued in the first few weeks and months? I don't know, I can't explain my own subconscious thoughts or logic.

Without intricate details, the days are now passing and my infection is responding to treatment. I was told that my antibiotics were to be delivered intravenously three times daily for over six weeks – I didn't and don't allow myself to ponder on how this may impact on the duration of my hospital stay, not thinking of how I will continue to manage to administer IV antibiotics every day – from my own home. There was a suggestion that I use an *intermate* IV pump to deliver the treatment myself – but the logistics are too complicated; Mayo has few or no medical supports for such a device and is too far from Dublin should anything go wrong. The only option, right now, is to stay put for the duration of my antibiotic treatment.

Now, again, I'm not allowing myself to think negatively – and my doctors help in their positivity and reassurance – but something else has happened in the last few days, something more worrying. I have begun to reject my liver. My LFTs are increasing, particularly one enzyme (GGT) and my bilirubin; I've turned yellow. Following a fast and mostly-painless liver biopsy, acute rejection was diagnosed. This is much better news than chronic rejection, let me tell you. Apparently, chronic rejection is difficult, almost impossible, to resolve. It's never very good news. Acute rejection is different, quite common, quite normal and, generally, an uncomplicated task to reverse – as routine as any treatment in the life of a transplantee. I'm hoping; fingers and toes crossed.

A few days ago, I began the process of pulsing – where a very high dose of steroids is fed into another cannula in my arm. It was administered every day for three days. While my face developed a hamster-like appearance – like I'm storing thousands of nuts – the steroids didn't work. I felt fine; energetic and less nauseous than the days before but still yellow, with increasing LFTs. A second biopsy revealed that I was continuing to reject – a second round of pulsing began three days ago and just finished today. I'm waiting to hear the results. I'm sick with nerves, yellow and have a rounded face which, I'm certain, increased even more overnight. Also thrown into my 'pot of issues'; the very high dose of steroids has increased my blood sugar level – I've become a temporary diabetic, injecting insulin three times daily! And so, the watchful waiting continues…

On another note, my relationship has become very strained and has hit a proverbial speedbump. I'm just not finding it easy to be in his company as he appears to lack understanding and empathy with my whole situation. I'm not talking behind someone's back and I barely know you, so I'll just say that, there is a lack of closeness and support that I feel should be there right now. We don't 'click' like we used to. Maybe things will improve and we'll get back on track. But, honestly, a fragile, brittle relationship and its mending is not my highest priority at the moment. It can't be…I must focus completely on myself right now…

'After the rain, the sun will reappear. There is life. After the pain, the joy will still be here.'

Walt Disney

17th September 2017

Dear friend,

Guess what? I have come home! I am in Mum and Dad's with a plan to return to St. Vincent's next week for clinic and to proceed with weekly clinics until my bloods stabilise and to ensure my incision remains free of infection. But it's over! My spell in St. Brigid's is in the past and I am free.

My acute rejection responded to the second dose of IV steroids. I almost felt it work differently to the first round – with my face taking on the appearance of – a woman on steroids! But, can I complain? No, apparently it will reduce within days. My course of antibiotics has also finished so I'm apparently in the clear from infections and abscesses.

My trip home was bittersweet – leaving the hospital with Mum for Heuston Station was almost miraculous – no loneliness for my 'home of 2017'; none whatsoever. We sat on the train and focused on the journey ahead – with forbidden-due-to-possible-contamination takeaway sandwiches (my much-yearned for ploughman's) and orange juice.

Then we discussed Dad and I asked the questions I hadn't really been getting answers to, while I was undergoing my steroid treatment. Dad is in hospital, and has been for two weeks. He'd been experiencing breathlessness and had a persistent cough the last time he visited me. He promised he'd buy cough syrup and take care of himself. However, after a trip to A&E, a complete lung collapse was diagnosed. Dad! With his healthy diet, walking mania (he would walk for miles), and hatred of smoking…with a collapsed lung! I'm shocked and now feel so very helpless and useless to have been away from my parents, no help or support to them whatsoever, for the last two weeks. Mum has been visiting both him and me in different hospitals – on different sides of the country, dividing herself between us both, having very early starts, sleepless worrisome nights on her own - and generally having a rotten time. She never utters a word of complaint. She never moans, complains or voices a single, cross, impatient word. She is always so cheerful.

I have to tell you that my Mum and Dad are relentless in their need – or desire – to support me. Throughout this entire journey (throughout my entire life, but more so as I've become a 'sick' adult) they have been by my side without question, at every juncture, through good and bad, worse and even worse. I feel protected, secure, so cared for and so cherished. I am also never surprised by their support. What I mean by that is that they've never let me down, never, so I don't expect them to ever stop supporting me. I don't take them for granted though. They're older now and I worry so much about them fretting about me…

Mum continues to listen to every moan I utter, every blood- or pain-filled story I tell – and repeat – every fear I face and every medical issue I discuss or research. She's relentless in her support, unfailing in her responses to my queries, and completely, thoroughly responsive to my unending crises and calamities. I hate worrying her, I hate being so demanding and needy, begging of her energies and piling on stress and worries of which she has adequate volumes. Mum is a role model in supportive parenting and complete offering of herself as a mother. Nothing I can do will ever, ever repay her for her enduring support and love. And she still has energies for others.

Mum and Dad have been literally invincible in their support, encouragement and love that they've given me. I can never do enough. I have taken so much of them, needed them like a child needs young, energetic parents. I really want to stop needing them. I want to let them have their lives back, and to feel free and happy, free of sickness and medical discussions… It's not fair on them…this intense stress of sharing this nasty journey with me.

So, Dad is due to have surgery to re-inflate his lung tomorrow morning and Mum intends to be there. I can't go for various reasons – mustn't go to a hospital for risk of infection, should avoid crowds as much as possible (travelling home by train was unavoidable), my energy levels wouldn't be good enough for a trip to and from Galway and, well, I'm just unable to go. I've already had one drama since coming home – one of my clexane puncture sites leaked overnight but the blood wouldn't stop flowing. When I woke after a night of bleeding, my bed was saturated and it continued to pour down my abdomen and my legs when I stood up. I put on plasters and bandages but they just became saturated with fresh blood. Mum, to the rescue, bought some hollister bags in the local pharmacy to at least gather the blood but a pressure bandage by my GP was necessary after I continued to fill the little bag attached to my side. Who imagines these 'little' issues post-transplant or post-surgery? Who honestly thinks that transplant isn't the cheerful ending to the story? No-one, I think. Most people imagine the transplant is the uncomplicated happy-ever-after.

I digress. I'm very worried about Dad, but his surgeon is very optimistic that this surgery, described as major, will resolve his issue, and further investigations will result in positive news. It's a worry for him and us all. It's a huge burden for Mum who looks haggard and has no time to think or breathe. She's supporting us all, listening to our every ailment and patiently taking care to put us first, once again. I love her for it, but feel so dreadfully guilty and useless. It will be okay and I will make it up to her when this current episode passes.

'Oh, I get by with a little help from my friends
Mm, I get high with a little help from my friends
Mm, gonna try with a little help from my friends'

The Beatles, *With A Little Help from My Friends*

26ᵗʰ October 2017

Dear friend,

Today I attended my haematology clinic where there's nothing new to report on either my ET or any new treatments for MPNs. My blood counts are quite low and I'm a little unstable to consider hydroxyurea or an alternative cytoreductive treatment just yet. On another note, I know that there are numerous clinical trials going on in Ireland and elsewhere – JAK2 inhibitors are coming closer to being available to us but we're not quite there yet. I imagine a world where I'm free of my blood cancer, where my nasty JAK2 mutation is 'switched off' and my bone marrow produces the proper number of platelets and other blood cells. It sounds like a dream...

Yesterday, I attended my liver transplant clinic and, as always, found myself in my best, most-flattering-clothes-for-a-large-abdomen with nice makeup and hair looking as good as possible. I never get tired of being told how well and different I look in contrast in a few short months ago. No, I'm not fishing for compliments but there's so much joy in receiving a truthful comment about looking 'well considering all you've been through'. I am still quite rounded in the middle and my face is like the proverbial full moon but, in time, these issues will pass and I'll look and feel more like myself. My liver clinic was practically problem-free; there are some issues regarding my poor kidneys and there's a chance I will receive dialysis in the future – this is something to ban completely from my mind until it happens...it might never happen! My all-important LFTs are very stable and actually almost within the normal range. How amazing is that? My tacrolimus (immunosuppressant) levels – monitored to quantify its concentration in my system following metabolic breakdown – are within range. This is very important as, if my levels are high, there's a toxicity risk.

Tacrolimus, an amazing immunosuppressant, is also a high tech drug with very serious side effects.

I continue to share a house with Mum, Dad and Scamper – it's too soon to live on my own - I've been given permission to drive just today! I've been enjoying living at home again, meeting family, friends, having coffees with Mum and Dad, bringing Scamper for walks (not alone just yet as he's too strong and might hurt my back or abdomen). We talk, I rest, Dad rests a little more and does his daily physiotherapy following his discharge from hospital and his completely successful surgery.

Scamper is very clingy and rarely leaves my side, his huge brown eyes scanning me whenever I leave or enter the room. He seems afraid I'll leave him again; my aim is never to leave him again. His welcome for me was overwhelming. When I came home initially, he jumped, licked, pawed, wagged his tail so much and cried with such joy and delight – two of us crying and extremely emotional. Since then, he's had to attend one final obedience class so he could graduate. We practiced his 'stay', his sit hand signals, his 'leave it' and his recall and he graduated with a certificate, appearing on the school Facebook page. (His recall command leaves a lot to be desired but we'll work on it).

I've decided to have my house painted and begin to focus on my Christmas shopping. The reasons? My house hasn't been painted since I moved in 13 years ago and needs a serious freshening up. I also need a change, an overhaul, a reclamation of my old life – but with a fresh new look. The Christmas present list? Well, two reasons. Firstly, I am deeply afraid that I will be beckoned back to hospital before Christmas, a gut feeling I cannot shake. And the second reason? I feel useless and very inadequate as I can do very little these days. I can cook, but ironing and other physical work is not allowed – for now. I walk, but not huge distances yet. I read but am impatient to do more! And so, I feel that life is moving so very slowly and practically none of the items on my wishlist have been achieved. I haven't visited the zoo - I'm planning a weekend with afternoon tea at a castle with my friends soon -

but I haven't done my favourite cliff walk near Westport yet, haven't been to the beach or the forest and I haven't been on a weekend break with Mum as we promised we would when I was in St. Brigid's. It's though life is moving so slowly – when I'm so impatient and anxious to live and continue living. I refuse to relax and won't let any day go by without filling it with achievements and more objectives. I imagine this is a side effect of spending too long in a hospital environment, completely controlled and monitored and so restricted in my daily choices. Now, I'm anxious to get started and not to stop until I achieve everything, go everywhere, eat everything – all that I dreamt about and imagined while in hospital. I acknowledge that this isn't ideal, it's not conducive to a healthy, relaxing recovery but I can't stop.

Everything now seems like a race against time. Christ, even getting these words down on paper is a rush, a gasping rush with almost no time for air.

Another 'issue' I've noticed recently is my almost complete intolerance of others. I find it so difficult to relate to people now. I am lonely and need company but when they talk of bad weather I think 'one sunny day less in this world'. They talk of family issues – my family has suffered and has become completely fractured wholly because of me. Some elements of resentment exist now.

Then I receive a text or a phonecall or meet a fellow transplantee and am reminded that I am not alone. My regular friends cannot possibly understand the myriad convoluted thoughts and, sometimes despairing and impatient, feelings I am experiencing but I imagine I am behaving as someone who has spent many months wondering if she would live or die and is now responding, as best as she can, to the almost-unattainable possibility of a new free life. It's taking some adjusting, but, with time, friends and family support, I hope to get there.

'All her would-haves are our opportunities'
Emma Thompson, *Reflections on Anne Frank (Anne Frank Huis, 2006)*

24ᵗʰ January 2018

Dear friend,

So, it's a brand new year. When I discuss my transplant and living in hospital now I have to say 'last year' as though it's becoming a thing of the past, a memory to be erased or forgotten. I wish it could be written off so easily but it was almost an entire year of my life and I think about aspects of it every hour of every day.

On another note, a new year brings change, new calendars, new opportunities and new life. It's a time for new ideas, to organise holidays, plan weekends away and enjoy the newness and freshness of a new year. It's also a time of change – and change scares me. I've always shunned change, different schedules and, consequently, new beginnings. What's wrong with 'old beginnings'? What's wrong with staying in the same year always? Just in case... A new year, the acknowledgement of a fresh 365 days might rock my boat, might upset the applecart, might jinx me and my liver. In 2017, I survived against quite a few odds. I feel as though I want to cling to that year – the one that treated me well and saw me through.

Maybe I'm just talking nonsense or it's the effect of something sad that's recently happened. I promised myself I'm going to be a positive, cheerful, happy and optimistic person, grateful and honourable. But, I'm a little sad that a fellow transplantee, a neighbour of mine from St. Brigid's, lost her fight to cling to her life a few days ago. Although we were never friends, our paths crossed on many occasions and word of her transplant last April came directly to me for a number of personal reasons (I don't know you well enough to share everything with you just yet!). Now she's dead and it seems unbelievable. Very few die, I thought. Now, I'm not sure. I won't ever ask about the statistics. When I heard the news I immediately imagined the very last time I saw her, getting into a car outside the hospital, presumably on her way home to recover post-transplant. I was jealous, very envious and not afraid to admit that, when she was going home in the middle of last year, I wished I was her. She had her transplant over with; she had survived and looked very well. She sat in the reclined seat of the car; dressed in day clothes and looked the eternally-sought-for normal. She was very thin and had the newly-transplanted curled shoulders I've seen so often (we're subconsciously protecting our abdomens by adopting a humped posture!) But she had a healthy colour and – unlike my pendulous abdomen and waddling gait – she had a flattish abdomen and looked elegant. Now she's dead and I wonder, as I did at her funeral, if she knew she was dying or if it was sudden. Maybe she was told the tragic news that her donor liver was rejecting and there was no possibility of a second transplant? Or maybe she was waiting for a second liver hoping, every day, that she'd hear good news? Maybe she knew nothing and suddenly her varices ruptured and, unlike me, she bled out? Maybe she just drifted into a deep coma and knew absolutely nothing but peaceful sleep? I know I'm wrong to torture myself with thoughts like this; it's not healthy and it's not helpful. Maybe attending her funeral was wrong too, but I had to go, almost felt obliged to represent St. Brigid's and her fellow transplant recipients. Now, I'm left with survivor's guilt, wondering, as I regularly do, why some survive and get to live – and others don't.

oOo

On another note, I have had a nice few weeks and am gradually achieving some of my dreams. I had my friends - my constant friends who visited me so often in hospital – come to stay near my family's home. We went to a castle for afternoon tea and chatted all afternoon; as normal young women do. We laughed, shared stories and made some future plans. Though quite self-conscious about my large face and abdomen, I thoroughly enjoyed myself and wore myself out talking about everything and anything. There were no barriers between us, no interruptions to query my bowel habits, no watching the clock for trains home and no feelings of inferiority and discomfort about my situation. We ate dinner later and, the following day, I cooked them a three-course meal before they travelled home. It was a joy, it was fun – it was normality!

Mum and I made our planned trip to Belfast during November, staying three nights in the city, visiting the main sights and treating ourselves to afternoon tea and nice dinners, shopping trips and museum visits. It was fun but quite a tiring and challenging trip. When there, it struck me that my clothes had become a little tighter around the waist than a few weeks previously even with all of my walking and conscious daily exercise – maybe it's the unhealthy cooked breakfasts and desserts!

o0o

My house was completely painted in mid-December. I enjoyed picking new colour schemes, planning accent walls and envisaging a completely new home for myself. I jest – my passion for interior design wanes after I pick up a shade card. I opted for very neutral tones with a 'feature wall' in each bedroom and the kitchen. These are dramatic purples and bright lime greens – it's my house so my choice! With the painting done, I took a holiday and stayed in my own home, on my own, in the week leading up to Christmas. I intended to clean, to de-clutter the cupboards and fridge of expired foods – almost every item in the house was out-of-date! I did tidy, clearing away mountains of dust following the sanding and painting. I disposed of unwanted rubbish, sorted through months of mail and had bulbs replaced and gutters cleaned, path and drive power-hosed and TV connection re-established. I enjoyed the work, gained a huge amount of satisfaction from the work but there was a downside to my 'holiday'. I am embarrassed to admit that I slept very little while in my own bed. I was afraid. I felt scared and so vulnerable, heard every single creak and groan the house made, imagined someone breaking into my house while I was there and somehow hurting me. I was jumpy and anxious. I can't explain it now, other than I've become quite jumpy in the last year. It's as though parts of my confidence and independence have been stripped away during my hospital stay and I am a more nervous, brittle version of my old self.

Real life seems foreign now and it's so hard to return to what's deemed normal and everyday. And so, I am trying to learn how to live without the constant fear and the nervous anxiety. Now, there's no clotted artery, there's no transplant ahead of me and no worries about failure of the surgery and getting through it all! It's over.

Yes, I still have my MPN but now must be confident and have faith in warfarin and aspirin – and my very low platelet count! It's a challenging life – but this is an unexpected obstacle of sorts. I imagined just 'hopping back into life' and getting straight back into it as soon as I was discharged; returning to my previous life that I had created for myself. It's not happening; recovery is a slower process than I remember.

I am very afraid to return to work; I am currently not physically strong enough but afraid that when I return, I'll just settle back into a mundane normal existence, living for work and other pointless human-made problems and stresses. I refuse to let that happen – I fought too hard for my precious life!

So, I'll continue to, patiently, integrate as much as possible into life, knowing, with more clarity than many others, of the tiny gap between living and dying – it's just a short step away.

'It's the end of the world as we know it, and I feel fine'
REM, It's The End Of The World As We Know It (And I Feel Fine)

13th February 2018
Dear friend,

It's another day. I'm living in my own house for a few days. I needed to escape but it's only when I'm here that I realise it's myself that I want or need to escape from. My head is full and is spinning most of the time. I've been having nightmares and night tremors. It snowed heavily this morning but it didn't stick so now it's just wet and cold and miserable. It's pancake Tuesday. Last year, in Brigid's Ward, I had a pancake with tea. One pancake - without maple syrup, or golden syrup, or sugar or lemon or chocolate spread. A miserable pancake to match my likely miserable mood...

I woke this morning and felt thinner. My abdomen felt lighter and I looked down at it in hope. Had my distended abdomen shrunk overnight? Will I now fit into my clothes and banish scary thoughts from my mind of blockages and poor blood flow? Will I continue to shrink and eventually return to my size 8 petite figure? Nothing has changed. My tummy is still large. I'm still holding onto that six-month pregnant look, still forced to wear baggy jumpers and elasticated trousers. I'm still experiencing the nuisance of trying to turn on my side in bed – only to be forced to heave the contents of my tummy with my hands. My abdomen still sounds like it contains a tub of water – or oil. It's disheartening and so worrying.

Over two weeks ago, I was getting on well. While still living with Mum, Dad and Scamper I was exercising every day, eating healthily and feeling my energy levels rise. Christmas was over and I was feeling a little stress and guilt about not working. I knew that a new year would bring new questions about when I'd return to work, how many days I'd work for and when I'd go back to living in my own home permanently.

Sorry, I'm rambling a little. I was beginning to get on top of things. My outpatients appointments were becoming less frequent – going from weekly to six-weekly intervals. Omar, Diarmaid's registrar, has been so very helpful and professional in maintaining my liver health – and my mental health. I've now conceded – and remembered from 2006 – that it's so much easier, right now, to have transplant recipients as friends. There's a bond there, an understanding and a quiet awareness of the battle we've fought to stay alive. We're all aware of the routine of medication and the – sometimes - robot-like existence that is almost necessary to stay strong and sane. I am still feeling a detachment from 'real life', something I experienced in 2006. Instead of just experiencing this and acknowledging it, I fight it, criticise myself for not being 'back to normal' and 'getting on with my life'. But I'm just not there yet – not quite strong enough to face the daily issues associated with normal living or the stresses that work and other stuff bring. As well as being a remarkable hepatologist, Omar seems to possess an admirable aptitude for understanding people. After discussing work and my intentions with him, he hinted that there'll be time in the future when I'm ready for work but staying positive and well now is infinitely more important. The hope and joy I felt in July and even in September is lessening as time passes as I expect more and more from myself, and feel guilty when I don't achieve as much in my daily life as I once did.

Still, over two weeks ago I was well. Then I noticed something. My weight began to climb. I began at 49kg while in hospital and hoped to gain a little more. My ideal weight is 50kg, while my dietician's ideal weight for me was 52kg. Within a few days I gained over a kilogramme. And it just kept climbing - 0.2 kg, 0.3 kg daily... As I watched my weight climb, my heart sank every day and I began to dread my daily weigh-ins. So, I increased my exercise regime and upped my fruit and vegetable intake, even cut down on my beloved bread. Nothing seemed to matter so I eventually tried to accept this weight gain, which I felt wasn't me. I felt as though I was turning from a petite, thin woman into a round-faced, round-bodied, lumpier version of myself. But I still accepted it, eventually. I compromised on so very much in the recent years – poor hair quality, yellowing teeth presumably as a consequence of medication, withered skin - and scars! A new fatter body in return for a functioning liver in a live body? What real choice did I have?

Then, over one weekend, I gained a tummy, a large distended tummy. My abdomen now looks like it did a few months before my transplant. It's protruded, rounded, falls to the side when I lie down and is just unattractive and awkward to look at. It's like my abdomen houses a tub of fluid which moves around with gurgling noises, causes my clothes to stretch (the few that fit!) and makes me feel so huge, unattractive, clumsy and sad. I, once again, have no control over my body and how it looks. How I want to look doesn't seem to matter, once again.

Within days of this happening, my spirits just crashed. I knew exactly what was wrong. It was the same as in 2014 when my hepatic artery clotted; I knew this had happened again. My LFTs were likely to be elevated. I was facing another transplant. There was no other reason for this significant change in my appearance. It's not natural to just develop a large rounded tummy over a few days, while eating healthily and exercising lots. I was dying, I knew I was. I, once again, began to think about my funeral and getting my affairs in order. I was so hugely disappointed that, after everything I had been through, I was back to where I had been in 2014. Except now, unlike 2014, this had happened with a liver that was only mine for a matter of months. Now, what are my options? Apart from facing wearing smocks and maternity jeans, baggy jumpers and tight coats again…did I have any surgery options?

That was a very painful number of days, almost a week. Waking up was a return to my daily nightmare. I wanted to stay in bed, needed to cover my head with the duvet and just curl up, thinking of absolutely nothing. I didn't want to talk, read, exercise - or live. Ironically, I woke up wanting to die, to escape this daily nightmare – the nightmare of dying of liver failure. I never felt so dismal, hopeless, sad and scared. When it happened before, I had the hope (once the surgeons agreed to a surgical plan!) of a transplant to fix everything, a piece of hope to cling to, a chance. This new issue had happened too soon after my transplant, too soon after my chance to rid myself of a blocked artery, too soon after the surgeons had decided on a plan of action to alter my body's circulatory system to support a new liver, cut blood vessels and created new pathways for my blood to flow as normally as possible, despite my significant reduction in healthy, unclotted veins and arteries. They created a monster body, a Frankenstein's monster of a body, but it worked.

After over a week of this waking nightmare, I contacted St. Vincent's and got an urgent appointment. Last week I was in clinic. I expected Omar to diagnose ascites and tell me that my LFTs were high. I expected him to admit me for tests and I expected the tests to reveal a blockage, a clot, an area where blood was no longer flowing properly. I expected very bad news. Nothing like that happened. He examined me after discussing my great LFTs, good kidney function and my pretty-ok blood biochemistry (low white cell count, low platelets and haemoglobin – what's new?). He did the percussion test I've become so very familiar with. It sounded like wind. No fluid, no blood, nothing liquid churning around in my abdomen where it doesn't belong. I felt some form of relief but also remaining anxiety as I still had no idea what is wrong, why I suddenly had become rounded and large again. He scheduled an ultrasound for three weeks and so I wait. When this happened I believed I was dying again. Now, I'm not sure where I am – playing a waiting game until the results of my ultrasound. In the meantime, I'm scared and unsure, large and sad. I have size 8 and 10 clothes which I'm so scared to try on, sticking to the baggy tracksuit bottoms and elastic-waisted jeans, wide skirts and flowing tops. I refuse to go for the wide smock dresses I've worn for almost two years. They literally make me feel sick.

Today I'm a little less anxious and afraid. I am waiting, impatiently, for the ultrasound. Time is passing slowly but I'm learning to put stuff out of my mind. Well, I'm learning to compartmentalise worries – into boxes in my mind. They're there, waiting, but I don't need to open them just now.

After this latest scare and all of the associated thoughts and fears, of two things I am now certain. One, I am not going back to Brigid's Ward, and two, I am not going back on a liver transplant waiting list.

'I have a dream, a song to sing to help me cope with anything, If you see the wonder of a fairy tale you can take the future even if you fail, I believe in angels Something good in everything I see, I believe in angels'

ABBA, I Have A Dream

3rd March 2018

Dear friend,

After my stress and worry, I eventually received word of two ultrasounds for two days ago - at 12pm and 12:30pm (the first with full bladder and the second on an empty stomach, with empty bladder hopefully!). I planned to take the morning train from Mayo, be in Dublin by 10:30am and make my way to the hospital by 11:30am. I would check in for first scan and plan the second with the staff.

Then the weather reports began! The 'beast from the east', an arctic air mass moving towards Ireland from the east, was predicted, dropping snow - a lot of it - in its path. I don't panic about weather – as long as I have a hat and my hair doesn't become fuzzy - weather doesn't ever bother me. I still planned my one-day trip to Dublin, planned to have my scheduled scans and get home. The weather forecasts continued to predict worse weather, including winds from Storm Emma from the south. As is generally the case, Mum became stressed (she worries about frost, ice, snow and flooding. I don't think she's ever worried about droughts or sunstroke.) My older sister, too, became involved and suggested that both Mum and I travel to Dublin a day earlier so we would travel in daylight and be nearer to the hospital before the snow arrived. I just wanted to take my chances and depend on a bit of luck, positive thinking - and public transport. In the end, I yielded to all the strong opinions around and booked one of three hotels near to the hospital, or at least the one with good public transport available should the weather deteriorate. Two of the three hotels are along the DART line and the third has a bus stop directly outside. The third hotel is a dreadful option. Because of its proximity to St. Vincent's, it's always the hotel recommended for patients and families, should they need to stay nearby. It's a horrible, grimy building with decrepit, old furniture and a dining room from the seventies. The food is poor and the bedrooms are cold, rundown and not altogether pristine. I hate that hotel – for obvious reasons just explained, but also for the memories it evokes. I've stopped staying there, even if it is ten minutes from the hospital and the sea view is fabulous (much the same as that from Brigid's). The second hotel is one I've used for over ten years, enjoying its regularity, professionalism and comfort. The food isn't particularly good, but on many occasions I just eat in the hospital, having breakfast of cereal and toast in the hotel.

It's grand, bland and I've become a little sick of it. Recently, I decided to break away from my routine and try another hotel. I settled for a cheaper-priced one with a train station less than five minute's walk from its impressive exterior. I like this hotel; it's nothing special but it's in a residential area within viewing distance of the Aviva Stadium, which is in itself a little exciting, I guess. And change is good! I haven't had a holiday since 2015(!) so maybe I'm using my hotel stays as something of a number of midweek breaks.

Sorry, I digress – I booked the second best hotel, while also replacing my one-day-return train ticket with a weekly return option – that's where my money goes these days!

The morning we were due to go, the weather was forecast to be at its worst on the Thursday of my appointments, and so Mum again began to worry about the danger of travelling. I had phoned the Radiology Suite and was advised the staff would definitely be there. We took the train and, in the midlands, the snow began. It was heavy, but when we arrived in Dublin, we took a taxi to our hotel and all was fine. Until I received a text. . .the text advising me that all outpatients appointments were cancelled and would be rescheduled shortly. A wasted trip! All of my energy wasted for nothing. And now, my long-awaited and much anticipated 'ducts and dopplers' ultrasound to determine if my blood and bile flow are good will have to wait for another few weeks at least. My God, I've been going out of my mind with worry, fearing the worst but happy to eventually be coming closer to my scan which will reveal all – whether I'm safe and my liver is doing well, or whether I need to start worrying again, and face worse issues.

Here we were, ten minutes from the hospital, literally walking distance (in snow boots) from an ultrasound machine – and it was not going to happen. I frustratingly emailed the transplant coordinators, knowing that, really, there was nothing they could have done to help me. The hospital was essentially closing for two days –

clearly I wasn't so important as to warrant any kind of special treatment or rule-breaking. I was gutted...

'And I think to myself what a wonderful world'

Louis Armstrong, What a Wonderful World

14th March 2018

Dear friend,

Today, I had my scans. The first - examining my ovaries - was fine, nothing abnormal detected. The second, my sought-after liver-and-abdomen-and-wherever-else-they-want-to-look scan was initially scary – and then an enormous relief.

I will explain. The radiologist began when I had emptied my startled-and-ready-to-burst bladder! She thoroughly scanned my liver, spleen, bowel, blood vessels and whatever else dwells there within my abdomen. She commented, as they generally do, on my large spleen or splenomegaly – a symptom of ET. I nodded, knowingly. It's big to my ignorant touch, so no doubt it looks massive on a screen and feels large when examined by an expert. Then she glided the transducer over my upper right quadrant, where my liver sits. She spent many minutes there, peering at her screen, looking at differing angles and concentrating quite hard. My heart raced; I examined and analysed her face and looked, when I could, at the screen. Eventually, she spoke, explaining that, with the amount of fluid in my abdomen, she wouldn't be happy - or authorised – to let me leave the hospital without seeing my hepatologist. My heart sank; the ascites was back, the large abdomen and the feeling of fullness was an indication of fluid, once again, filling up in my peritoneum. Here was the proof – a scan showing fluid. I, sadly, made my way to the Liver Outpatient's Clinic. I couldn't do all this again – even if I had the choice!

Within minutes of seeing Diarmaid, my world changed again. He admitted there were pockets of fluid, different from other, non-transplant people, but – and this is a big but – this is all normal, post-transplant. It is normal, a normal collection of small, tiny even, pockets of fluid, where my body is still settling, still becoming accustomed to a new liver, new circulation, new medication and – following the blood clot sitting in my abdomen for over six months – all of the crap, shock, disruption and torture my body had been through. My digestive system isn't back to normal yet, and I shouldn't expect it to be. My bowels were moved, muscle and tissue was cut and all of my 'insides' were muddled about and shoved aside. I breathed a huge, long sigh of unimaginable relief. My heart soared and I smiled. It isn't ascites, I am not rejecting my liver, I won't be back on the liver transplant list and I – am - fine. OK, my abdomen won't be fabulously thin ever, but, in time, it should become much more normal-sized and less rounded. I need patience! Just a little more patience! I am so unbelievably relieved…

o0o

I am so very happy. After the discussion, I met some transplantees at clinic and a nurse I hadn't seen in months. We chatted and discussed very familiar feelings and attitudes – I never feel alone in clinic and realise I had been worrying and fretting alone. I found out that I can now swim again and there's no reason why I shouldn't look forward to travelling to maybe Bath or Cornwall. Amsterdam one-year post-transplant sounds like a good idea to me right now! My life isn't over and I don't have to be sedentary!

Birds sang today, as every day over the last few weeks – but I heard them! I had lost myself a little, still felt stuck in a world of damaged circulatory systems and medical issues but there is more out there. There are friends and supporting staff, ways to treat myself without feeling guilty or unsure if it's safe? I will try to keep this feeling as long as I can – but not lose patience with myself if it dissipates a little on bad days or sad days.

I'll share one little secret with you. Last night I had a sketchy dream which didn't last very long but featured, as is the case a lot recently, a man from my past, a man whom I cared a lot for. There was little to remember from the dream with this exception. I woke up with a feeling of comfort and sheer joy. He had been talking to me and others before I had to drive away before returning a few hours later (the wheres and whys are apparently irrelevant!). Within minutes of coming back, he was holding me close as we lay outdoors in the heat, sheltered from the elements under a leafy tree. He was strong and caring, big arms around my cold scared body. He was so happy and I never felt so close to someone and so loved and cherished. I was protected by him, in his big gentle arms. I never wanted it to end. Unfortunately, it did, because I woke up for breakfast. But I carried that warm protected feeling with me all day, keeping me smiling and happy, reassuring me that there is pure love in my real life. I have become quite negative and quite sad in general, feeling constantly on edge and anticipating bad news. I felt vulnerable and unsafe for so long that I have begun to mould into a complicated mess. I need to find 'me' inside all of this chaos – the real 'me' seems to have dissolved away into a container of mood fluid. I have a larger abdomen and I don't love the way I look right now. I focus on that so I remain sad and down. I see now that I MUST focus on the positives, the many wonderful positives! Dreams and nice plans help…

I've decided that, after a good day like today, hope is definitely my favourite emotion.

Chat again soon.

'Get busy living, or get busy dying'.
Stephen King, Rita Hayworth and the Shawshank Redemption

18th April 2018

Dear friend,

Today I decided to give you a timely update into what has been going on with me. It's not a bad day but I'll never cease to be amazed by the myriad emotions that hit me on any given day. They sway between sadness, fear and anxiety to, sometimes minutes later, elation and joy.

I am afraid to feel happy for long, conscious that it may 'jinx' my situation. If I am happy and optimistic, something will flip and I'll be forced to face the prospect of being unwell again – forced to hand back my independence, my freedom, exchange my life for a life. If I think too much on all that has happened, I am living in fear, never too confident about my current circumstances, never allowing myself to feel certain that, currently, things are actually okay. The pain of the past is still so raw, the emotions still so tender – I'm not ready to face anything like them yet – or for a very long time. Maybe I've a touch of PTSD? (Is it possible to have a 'dash' of PTSD or is that along the lines of being a 'bit' pregnant?) I'm not sure but I do feel that, right now, most of my waking thoughts are of livers, mutations, surgery, cannulas, ducts and dopplers and medication.

I know, from experience, that this will fade with more time. I just hope, dearly, that I have the adequate time to allow that to happen...

Another new quality of mine that I have observed is my accelerated / elevated impatience. I've never, ever been a patient woman but these days I want things to happen immediately. I think perhaps I lost 2017, spending most of the year being eternally patient; every day I had to wait to be attended to, waits for meals, wait for visits, wait to see a doctor, wait for scans, blood transfusions, IV antibiotics – wait for a much-needed liver.

Now, I can't wait to get going. All of my lists, my promises to myself, my plans for post-transplant, composed and promised to myself last year – must come to fruition sooner than later. I want to have my garden full of spring flowers and have the fence painted, I want to go on holidays, organise a family dinner at my house, swim regularly, have a spa treatment, buy new post-transplant-body-appropriate clothes, visit the zoo and bake muffins. I haven't done any of those things yet; too busy walking to get fit (and tone!) and attending appointments in St. Vincent's. I am quite anxious to fulfil those plans before it's too late, before I die or before I find myself back in hospital, not allowed to travel – and not allowed to leave. I must do these things before it's too late. I must seize the day, live my life fully, not take a single second for granted. Who knows when this time will run out? When I will be facing having 'no time' in the future? I cannot face the possibility of being back in hospital, reading my unfulfilled wishlist just because of, what; laziness, tiredness, lack of enthusiasm or drive?

I feel that I need help to get me through these feelings. Some of my 'wishes' are stuff that I <u>must</u> achieve, not things I really <u>want</u> to achieve. I notice that I am adding to my anxiety by focusing on my unticked list, only pushing myself to achieve, but not for the right reasons. I am putting pressure on myself to live in the future and still fretting about the past. I feel as though the present is being ignored. Maybe there's a way to train myself to live a different way; to take one step at a time and – just be. Right now, I find myself putting this on a list – train yourself to live in the now – what a vicious circle I have created for myself!

oOo

I am still sharing my time living in my own house and with my parents who, happily, have taken on a lot of responsibility in minding Scamper. Of course I'm still very much involved in his care – but have the reassurance of two very enthusiastic dog-sitters whenever I need a break. I feel guilty and dependent living with them, my own house lying idle at times, calling out for much-needed attention. The truth is, when I go to my own house, I feel incredibly lonely. I've had so many people occupy my life for so many months, on a constant basis last year (welcomed or not), that time spent alone, though welcome, is also daunting and vacuous. It's scary too, and so silent. The town I chose to live in over 20 years ago, too, seems unfriendly and just 'not me' anymore.

My Mum and Dad have become such an integral part of my life again – a support system – that I've come to rely on them as much as I did over 20 years ago. They have been there for me as my primary emotional support, advising, worrying, reassuring, smiling, completely taking onboard my health scares, the good days, the very bad, the nasty side effects – the reality. I hate having them worry; they've aged in recent years, not so youthful as my parents of my 12-years-ago brush with death.

They've had to experience, albeit from another perspective, my numerous encounters with dying and have literally placed me number one on their agendas, before themselves, so anxious to ensure that I'm happy and healthy, and as worry-free as possible. I hate putting them through this, not letting myself off the hook for giving them so much stress and worry. I've always tried to spare them from worrying and fretting about me, keeping them from fear, worry and disappointment in me, in my life and the decisions I've made. I hope that by making them proud, by sharing with them the good days, the happy days, that I can somehow undo the wrongs; hopefully letting them see more of the rights.

o0o

So, today, I am grateful. I still find it difficult and raw to think of you but I am so conscious that you're there and a part of me. I know that, in time, I will once again accept you as the life-saver that you are, the amazing miraculous friend that I have been granted, a true hero during my time of need. I promise to take good care and do everything in my power and control to keep part of you alive and well. I want to keep you as my friend for a very long time…

'There are no goodbyes for us. Wherever you are, you will always be in my heart'.

Mahatma Gandhi

18th October 2018

Dear friend,

So now, I feel compelled to bid you adieu and complete my meanderings. I've given you an insight into my life, which has been so influenced and shared by others. I wouldn't be here, wouldn't have a life, wouldn't have survived my personal quirks and health complications had I been a pygmy in Burundi or born in Outer Mongolia. I wouldn't have a life had I been born in the 19th century; or even 20 years before my 1974 arrival. I would have been snuffed out quietly; probably with a jaundiced body and distended abdomen – deemed merely unhealthy or cursed.

And I wouldn't have survived without you.

If this were a novel, I'd now create an appropriate ending – a happily-ever-after event so readers would feel inspired, saddened, warm – or alternatively nonplussed and unimpressed.

This is not a novel – this is my life and so my whimsical (or otherwise) chatterings can simply just stop as soon as I see fit. But I can't do that. I feel plagued by my own personal obsession to understand and define my own happily-ever-after. I've always liked things to be neatly tied up – in every aspect of my life – why not, then, should I not provide it for me, based on my own raison d'être. A typical happily-ever-after resonates around a goal achieved, a fulfilled love life, a marriage, a new adventure – or perfect health.

Let's face it, there's no such thing as a happily-ever-after – no life's desires that all come to pass, no life that wraps up into a perfect parcel, no perfection frozen in time – that's why novels are mostly fictitious. Was Elizabeth's Mr. Darcy a good kisser, a perfect husband, a nice father? Was Jo and Professor Bhaer's school hugely successful or was it closed down after one of the students fell out a window and sued? Did Jem and Scout continue to respect and admire Boo Radley, or did they, as sulky teenagers, give him the silent treatment?

So, today can be my Day Zero in which I'll describe where I am – now. I am well today. I have no pain but a mild ache in my bones and I am fatigued. I am pale and breathless so assume I am a little anaemic. I have nightmares most nights and tend to waken up tired, as though I've been racing all through the night. The dreams vary, never of hospitals or pain but of anxious waits, chasing trains, missed opportunities, samurai swords and the loss of old friends.

So here's my today. I'm just back from a walk with my beautiful, mischievous, intelligent and dog-intolerant little guy. We walk most days – Scamper and I. I'm making up for lost time. It's a pretty warm day and I'm wearing denims and a pretty flowing top, my legs tanned and normal-sized (fake tan and factor 50 sunscreen obviously). I'm wearing denims but they're tight around the middle, quite tight. My weight is more difficult to manage than pre-transplant II, despite my almost-weekly swimming and daily walks. My abdomen refuses to be flatter and I'm not happy about this, not really. They're the costs, I guess. A liver and a healthy prognosis - in exchange for some collateral damage. I was lucky to escape with little else though, I know that. I know how lucky, truly lucky and blessed I am.

For now, I'm free to use my time walking, reading or devouring books (*A little Life* by Hanya Yanagihara is my latest love), spending quality time with my family, close friends and Scamper. I will return to work eventually – I'm not ready yet, physically or emotionally. Work to me, right now, seems all too unimportant, too mundane and wasteful of my precious time. Also, it strikes me with an overwhelming sense of fear – that facing a number of people, some of whom I haven't met in over two years, will make me emotional and teary, that just seeing faces that I haven't seen since before my horrific days will certainly educe me to tears and uncontrollable shaking. I'm afraid, too, that returning to work will make me forget, might make me less grateful for the life that I have, might awaken in me the workaholic Karol that has been replaced by the more calm, life-appreciating and life-earning version. I'm just not ready yet.

I'm making a huge dedicated effort to be nicer and kinder to myself, to not push and push, and to try and accept less of myself than sheer perfection. I still feel quite levelled, battered and bruised by a crueler life than others seem to have, but that's what I've been dealt. On a bad day I'm a little jealous of people, including my working, getting-on-with-life friends. On good days, I recognise that everybody has problems and things are not always how they appear, and I HAVE A LIFE.

I've taken a trip to Amsterdam with Mum, my first overseas trip in three years. We went in June, just two weeks after I was hospitalised with a very low haemoglobin concentration. I got two units of blood and spent three nights in the new and improved St. Brigid's Ward – the original ward was eventually closed down as infection after infection broke out and spread to all of the patients – shared wards and toilets are now no more, thankfully.

Amsterdam, the flight, the trip, the walking and exploring was literally a huge step in retrieving my freedom and regaining that misplaced control over my own life. It was a fabulous break and the tiny regret was that we stayed for only three nights – 33 would have been a good start!

I try to be happy – sometimes that's like forcing myself to 'like' avocado, or to find an unentertaining comedian 'funny'. Where's the spontaneity in that? Happiness cannot be forced, surely? Especially now – when I cry more easily and subconsciously search for the dark and negative parts of life. It's become a habit ingrained over the last four years – the shadow of serious illness and the prospect of a death have changed me – hopefully not forever. I've become a worrier! I am much more anxious and jumpy than before. It's as though I'm not sure how to live without the fear of death and serious illness hanging around me. The bad health news, blocked artery, clot in abdomen, failing kidneys and pending transplant all became part of who I was, were what I concentrated on for such a long time, day and night. Now I feel lost without my constant companions - worry, fear and pain. Sure I've got my MPN – always, recently I've developed pancytopaenia (a drop in all my blood counts; red, white and platelets), anaemia and my kidneys are, once again, showing signs of struggling. The third bone marrow biopsy I had undertaken in August showed no signs of fibrosis and therefore no progression of my ET; hugely welcome and fantastic news - but that could be in the future. I'm also on the verge of osteoporosis from years of steroids and nasty medication. I'm always monitoring my INR with weekly blood tests, careful never to let a clot develop on my watch. But, without serious illness and worry, I feel lost. The burdens of being ill and becoming more ill were burdens I learned to bear, familiar parts of my life that became a part of me. Now, it's as though I've completely lost sight of who I was before they invaded me.

I have bad dreams - of horrors, of being trapped, of feeling frozen with anxiety and deep fear. I dream of being bitten, attacked and fought. I never have strength or energy to fight back.

The key thing – the secret to my happiness, even if sometimes short-lived – is to have plans and focuses in the future, treats and times to look forward to. It's vital to have things to look forward to. Now, though, I realise that my timeline has had to be altered. I look forward to things in the very near future, never planning for one year from now, not even months. I live in the present tense, as that little nagging voice in my head insists.

I'm trying to live a full life, striving to make my life count, to be deemed special, worth remembering and missing, but my fatigue and blood disorder-related fatigue symptoms leave me feeling guilty and frustrated that my full life is only half-full. Right now, it feels like I live a half-life; resting lots but still trying to get the very best from my years. Bed beckons more than I'd like it to, but I won't give in and accept this. I'll continue my uphill battle, my ploughing through thick mud.

I know I have changed – my personality, I mean. I feel considerably changed; like a woman on the verge of a meltdown. I am grumpy, quick-tempered and on the brink of tears a lot of the time. I am impatient, more intolerant, prejudiced and so quick to complain – about such simple things. I've always liked order and organisation. Now I love it! I cannot stand disorder or any form of chaos. Reserved seats on a train should only be used by reservers; weather forecasters should get the weather right all the time; restaurants should deliver exactly what they promise; Mum and Dad should be healthy and live as long as I do; hospital-acquired infections should not affect clean, hygienic people; liver function tests and full blood counts should behave when I put so much care, work, organisation and preparation into my own healthcare; I shouldn't need a ~~third~~ fourth liver – if I take good care, and having put in such a fight for the last two.

But life is random, chaotic, disorganised and can be upended.

Nowadays, I am constantly rushing, organising, re-organising, attempting to be always prepared, always one step ahead of myself; always hygienic, tidy, prepared. I find myself needing (not so much wanting) to see everything, do everything, visit everywhere – before I die. It's a life of furious balancing that I've created for myself. It's manic; my whirring brain, exhausting myself to prove that "I'm living every day". If I stop, if I pause, then I'm wasting my time. I lay in hospital for so long, waiting my turn, wasting my time, just waiting, waiting. I made lists of my wishes, dreams, hopes, aspirations, my practical chores and my obligations. Now, I must see every one of them through – and more and more every day. I'm constantly tidying my house, decluttering, clearing out wardrobes, mowing the lawn, planting new shrubs and flowers – is it a subconscious need to leave my house as hassle-free as I can, for when I'm gone? When did my thoughts and involuntary actions become so morbid?

I realise how unhealthy this life is that I've created for myself, how anxious, stressful and intense it is. This has to stop. I have to stop this toxic, addictive, dangerous behavior. I want to; I just don't know how.

So, my friend, this is me. Not exactly the calm, life-loving transplant recipient I am meant to be…more of a hyped-up, manic, duracell-bunny-type woman who can't stop. I'm not the slow, relaxed, stress-free person I once was – that's a lifetime ago.

I am an exhausted, busy, anxiety-ridden version of myself.

Welcome to my world!

oOo

So again, the grasping of nice things, the planning of holidays and weekends away, sunny walks, wintry showers, coffee and cake, clothes shopping and hair appointments…that is key. Recently, at clinic, I met a fellow transplantee. He asked, demanded even, that I become involved in the transplant games and strive to become part of Team Ireland. I laughed, telling him I walk for exercise, that I've never been competitive or part of any team but a quiz team. He insisted I meet with the team and find a sport I can compete at; badminton, athletics, bowling. I intended to join the team in 2008, even took a snow-boarding lesson for the winter games but chickened out before I submitted any applications. Chickened out and became uncomfortable. I was a transplant recipient then, but, once some time had passed post-transplant, didn't want to be part of that club anymore. I was a person with an MPN who developed a blood clot that destroyed my liver. I wanted to move on. Now, though, I've accepted a little more the cards I've been dealt and the community that I belong to. I'm going to give it a shot, going to focus more on my general fitness and find my athletics niche – it'll be an opportunity to travel with like-minded and like-living people; one bunch of solid organ acceptors with an aspiration to bring medals home to Ireland.

I'm also considering undertaking a counselling course; to learn a little more about myself, but also to tap into the inner workings of counselling and psychotherapy with a purpose to understand and support others in my life. That, with my aim to learn to play the ukulele and to, once again, pack my suitcase and travel, will be my reason for living, my carrots to look towards, my hobbies and life loves.

And so, I strive to be happy. I strive to be positive. For my family's sake, my Mum's, Dad's, sisters' and friends'. For you, my friend, for James – and for me.

Worrying and fretting won't allow me to be prepared for the future, whatever that may bring. I strive to live – every single day, to just be, to relax and be mindful…

But in another part of my brain, I am striving to travel, to see the world, to jump from a plane, to change jobs, move house, to make a difference to the world I've lived in for 44 years.

Carpe diem versus 'just be'.

I know that I must focus on the important things in life – the key to life – my people. Not money, house, possessions. My people, my family, friends, acquaintances and every day random strangers I meet on trains, in liver clinics, in coffee shops – people are the cornerstones of life…

So, am I enjoying my life? Huge portions of it, most certainly, but I still struggle to find enjoyment when there are a myriad past fears and horrific future worries and dreads. There's almost always a fear, a dark, nagging, haunting terror of the future. . .so my aim, my goal, is to learn to live in the now...that, and just living, just being. One step at a time, always.

Dear Reader,

I hope you enjoyed my first (and last) contribution to the literary world, or if you didn't enjoy it, that you learned something new – about medicine, human nature, life - or yourself. As I've read through my series of letters, I am, today, struck by a number of emotions. I feel somewhat saddened that this is the path my life took. I could never have anticipated anything like this for me. Serious illness hits other people; I was literally gobsmacked when it happened to me. The arrogance of my attitude! Illness hits people unexpectedly and becomes their story, be it an interval during their lifetime or the final chapter of their lives. Serious, life-threatening illness is devastating, horrific, infinitely scary and unimaginably chilling. It is also something everyone should experience. It is definitely the one experience that focusses attentions like no other. As I once stated in these pages, dying – or almost dying – taught me how to live. Yes, I struggle daily with anxiety and fatigue, experience daily and hourly fears, remain constantly vigilant of my body and its various functions – those I am aware of. But I am so, so very aware of the frailty of all of our lives and the miracle of being here to experience fresh air and the numerous banal extraordinary things that life has to offer – in the here and now!

In the preceding pages, I believe I demonstrated many occasions when my mental health was adversely impacted by illness and the many, many issues my blood cancer and subsequent transplants threw at me. I felt uncomfortable admitting to my anxieties, fears, worry and stress, not because mental health is something to hide but because, as a transplant recipient, I felt I was expected to feel happy about my 'gift of life'. I believe in honesty and openness and so I decided that while admitting to my discomfort with accepting a deceased person's organ may offend or even shock you, I felt it was an important admission, and maybe even one that others share? Additionally, I recognise that the anger, hurt, anxiety and 'urgent living' I experienced in the weeks and months following, particularly, my second transplant were normal responses of someone whose life was almost taken away and whose control was completely lost for a very long time. I had the monkey of a clotted artery on my back for almost three years and that, with the horrendous feeling of uncertainty or insecurity about recovery, had the potential to push a very sane individual into a severe depression. Now, I understand that it was very likely normal and expected and I don't criticise or disapprove of my personal feelings in any way. Now, I just accept them and embrace them as mine.

Something else that occurs to me when I read the pages is that, in general terms, I am now deemed a complete failure. Please read on before jumping to inaccurate conclusions. In life, in this 21st century, we all measure our success against 'typical' achievements and milestones. Career, car, house, clothes, gadgets, jewellery and spouse spring to mind. I am well educated but my career has been downgraded to a job, a means to feeding and clothing myself, and ensuring I have a roof over my head. My little house is unlikely to ever be upgraded to a bigger model. I am single and childless, another so-called measure of success, a target to denote 'achievement'. But I have learned, the VERY hard way, that we / I place these pressures on ourselves. I don't fit the typical success mould now, but when I view my life and measure it differently, truly, I have achieved great things. I have been very successful, possibly even more successful than the Tesla-driving, multi-property owning, trophy wife-owning millionaires of this world.

Finally, and I have repeated it enough throughout the pages, I see that living in the present, not planning for the future, not mulling over, regretting or yearning for the past, is the key, the answer to a happy, fulfilled life, whatever you perceive that to be. It is tough, practically impossible, and achieving this is a steep learning curve, but, on the occasions when I am mindful and living 'in the now', I can be content, joyful, appreciative and 'just me'. Certainly, I have recurring negative thoughts but in the welcome period of relative calm that I currently find myself in, I am content.

oOo

This is just one account of transplantation, living with a blood cancer or lifelong condition and an extended stay in hospital. It will not resonate with everybody, obviously, but I am certain that there are many, many of you who have experienced critical illness, consequential absence from work or a destruction of career and are, on a daily basis, struggling with aspects of what I've described in my memoir. If you struggle with this, physically or emotionally, seek help and support. For me the MPN Voice charity has been invaluable. Unfortunately, there is no liver transplant association or support in Ireland. How unfair and short-sighted is this? Maybe this will change in the future. It is certainly needed. In the intervening time, I encourage you to arrange for your organs to be donated upon your death. It is vital, selfless, brave, urgent and, as someone who promotes the three Rs, it is the ultimate act of recycling!

oOo

And so, my apologies for my somewhat fatigue-induced ramblings... I am still not an author so if you observe errors, incorrect punctuation or repetition, please forgive me! For the recurrent evidence of my lack of understanding of medicine, please forgive me! I tried to understand the intricacies of my treatment, surgeries and medication but, as a non-physician, I am definitely not qualified to offer advice other than from my own individual experiences. For any people I have offended, annoyed or angered by my story, I might not be sorry because this is a truthful account of my own life and experiences. I aimed to demonstrate, as realistically as possible, how illness and poor diagnoses can impact on many elements of one's life, have endeavoured to be as kind as I could have been so please do not sue me!

My thought of today is this; we live forward but we understand backward. Learn from me and my experience that life, when it is good, is for grabbing, enjoying and cherishing. It's not for putting off or waiting until the day when everything is in place and subsequently 'you achieve happiness'. Happiness, like other gifts and indeed nasty experiences, arrives unexpectedly and randomly. Recognise it and be greedy for it; it may not stay for long but it's quality over quantity, and we all deserve it!

Love,

Karol xoo

Sunday, 31st March 2019

Printed in Poland
by Amazon Fulfillment
Poland Sp. z o.o., Wrocław

51497631R00159